We then stumbled across a train chugging its way across an open field, heading west ahead of the retreating Germans. So the four of us lined up in single file to put the locomotive in our sights. As Frye went in, suddenly the sky darkened with puffs of flak and tracer bullets from gun positions on flatbed cars of the train, putting him in their sights. The antiaircraft fire missed him and he missed hitting the locomotive, but he took a last swipe at the cars being pulled, including the gun positions and a car possibly loaded with ammunition. I was next. My eyes were glued to that locomotive as it was centered in my gun sight. Ignoring the flak and bullets on all sides of me, I pulled the trigger and, lo and behold, the engine exploded, sending pieces skyward. Already our outfit had lost a pilot who had run into the remains of his target as they shot upward in his path. Would I clear this mess accompanied by a huge belch of steam?

DUMB
BUT
LUCKY!

CONFESSIONS OF A
P-51 FIGHTER PILOT IN
WORLD WAR II

RICHARD K. CURTIS

BALLANTINE BOOKS • NEW YORK

A Presidio Press Book
Published by The Random House Publishing Group

Insert photographs courtesy of Richard K. Curtis
Author photo © Indiana University

Presidio Press and colophon are trademarks of Random House, Inc.

www.presidiopress.com

ISBN 0-345-47636-0

Manufactured in the United States of America

OPM 9 8

First Edition: July 2005

To Emily, Brian, Virginia, and Gregory

That you and your children
will never have to suffer a century of war,
such as we did in the twentieth century

ACKNOWLEDGMENTS

I wish to thank Joseph Nye, dean of the John F. Kennedy School of Government at Harvard University, for his suggestion that I write of my World War II experiences for publication. I also want to thank Deirdre Lanning of Ballantine Books for "rescuing" my manuscript and sending it to Ron Doering, senior editor of Presidio Books. Above all, I must thank Myrt, my wife for sixty years, for her hours of typing my original manuscript back in 1944–45, and for her continued encouragement and suggestions.

"I don't understand what you were trying to prove by flying the way you did—screwing up and disobeying laws."

—Brig. Gen. "Chuck" Yeager (Ret.), fellow P-51 pilot

PREFACE

In recorded history or biography there are two factors vastly underrated in time of peace, and more so in time of war. One is stupidity, the other, luck.

This is a firsthand account, taken from daily diaries and letters, of the adventures—and misadventures—of a P-51 Mustang fighter pilot.

At eighteen, just five months out of high school, when everything seemed possible and no man—especially this man—was vulnerable, he enlisted in the Army Air Corps in November 1942. So impressed was his flight instructor after ten hours in a Piper Cub that he printed in this aviation student's logbook, "THIS MAN IS *NOT* PILOT MATERIAL!"

Other heads—wiser heads to be sure—prevailed, and this brash cadet managed to complete fifteen months of pilot training. But not before being confronted twice with impending court-martial for antics in the sky unbecoming a potential Army Air Corps officer. In the second instance this involved disobeying a direct order from a major general.

As luck would have it, this maverick escaped his day in court. At the same time he learned that his older brother, Bob, a navigator on a B-17 Flying Fortress, had been killed in action, hit by a German fighter plane, an FW 190. Bob's death was preceded by the death of his twin brother, Bert, at nine. An earlier brother, Philip, had died in infancy. And that was preceded by twin boys miscarried and aborted.

So it would seem that this new pilot, graduating with silver wings and gold bars, was next in line to be marked for death. Dana, a younger brother, was by this time training to be an aerial gunner in the Marine Air Corps—and was later killed in Korea. Betty, the kid sister and the last sibling of this pilot, would still later mourn the death of "Tim," her firstborn, in Vietnam.

Shipping out to Italy in May 1944, this second lieutenant came gradually to the realization that perhaps he was no longer invulnerable. The rumor circulated on board ship that this was the "hottest" shipment in the war to leave Newport News, Virginia. For aboard were thirty or more fighter pilots, green as grass, leaving without the one hundred or so hours of transition and combat training that was customary. Their last plane was an advanced trainer, the AT-6 Texan, with a top speed of just over 200 mph. They were about to step into a P-38 Lightning, a P-47 Thunderbolt, or a P-51 Mustang, all with top speeds more than twice the Texan's. In the case of the Mustang, the fastest of them, the 8th Air Force in England required two hundred hours of training in the P-51 itself before the pilot was ready for combat.

Why the rush to send these pilots into action without the requisite training? Because those pilots "in the pipeline" were not arriving at the 15th Air Force in Italy fast enough to replace those who were being shot down or returning home on furlough, their fifty-mission tour of duty completed. This was simply a stopgap measure to tide over the fighter squadrons that were by this time so shorthanded that there were fewer pilots than planes—when two pilots per plane was the official complement. This meant that these pilots were being scheduled almost every day for a mission, whether for escort or for strafing. Often lasting from five to six hours, these missions left the pilots exhausted, and more at risk than ever.

To the 52nd Fighter Group went twelve of this emergency contingent. Of the twelve, five were assigned to the 4th

Squadron, where twenty-seven Mustangs had but seventeen pilots to fly them. Just how green were these twelve was soon seen when several crashed, either in the minimal twenty hours of transition and combat training or in their first few missions. Learning of this, Nathan Twining, commanding general of the 15th, ordered that all further training be done in the P-40 Warhawk, of "Flying Tigers" fame. With some reluctance, this particular pilot, having checked out satisfactorily in the P-51, took to the air in the P-40. Slower, more sluggish, it seemed more warhorse than warhawk, and this "flyboy" promptly crashed on landing, leaving it good for nothing but parts. But he emerged unscathed and was assigned to ferry Mustangs across North Africa and up into Italy to complete his transition time.

Back to the 4th Squadron after two weeks, this pilot learned that half of the original twelve had been shot down, including both his tentmates. A few more hours of combat training, and he was hustled into combat. A month and two days after his first combat mission, he discovered that the only other pilot still flying Mustangs among the twelve had just been shot down over Yugoslavia in a strafing mission. This was the same mission in which this sole survivor of the twelve watched his flight leader, from a distance of less than ten yards, burn to death in his crashed plane, riddled with machine gun fire.

With more than forty missions still to fly, this Mustang pilot confessed to his diary that, for the first time in his twenty short years, he was "really scared." But it didn't last long. The dumb but lucky pilot persisted, his antics in the sky never ceasing—one court-martial threat after another being issued. If it wasn't for taking up a plane without permission, it was for leaving his jeep unattended, unlocked, and with the keys in the ignition. Finally, eight months later, having completed fifty-one missions in his P-51, he celebrated VE Day on May 8, 1945, by executing a "Victory Slow Roll" off the roof of none other than General Twining's 15th Air Force Headquarters in Bari. This time a court-martial appeared a certainty, and would have been had it not been that the unabashed pilot had just completed his tour of duty and earned a Distinguished Flying Cross. But his antics did prevent his earning a captaincy, which he'd been nominated for by his squadron.

In two weeks he was headed for home to walk the aisle with his bride, the same "Myrt" whose name had graced the side of his P-51D, the one with the big black *N* on the yellow tail. The war was over in Europe, but not in Japan, and this married pilot was being prepared for another tour of duty far across the Pacific. There to welcome him and any other invaders were nine thousand kamikaze pilots ready to die for the motherland. Suddenly August 15 came, and with it Japan's surrender, making at least a million of us GIs scheduled to invade the islands relieved that we would not be among the million or more that were predicted to be casualties in any invasion.

Assigned to the Air Transport Command, our "hero" was given the boring job of ferrying planes from across the country to their "final resting place" just outside Tucson, Arizona. So dull was the job that further shenanigans were inevitable. At last, after two more close calls, Myrt called a halt to it. In plain words, she'd "had it."

It was February 1946, with threats of court-martial still ringing in his ears, that this renegade quit the Army Air Corps for good. Not only did Myrt breathe a sigh of relief, so did the Air Corps. Dumb luck had trumped stupidity.

This is my story, gleaned when I blew the dust off diaries and letters I'd kept from 1941 to 1945. Ed Lahikainen, my brother-in-law, and Dick Newton, my cousin, both pilots in World War II, labeled me, when they heard my story, "the luckiest guy" they'd ever known. I guess I can't argue with that.

CONTENTS

I

BY THE NUMBERS

"This man is *not* pilot material!"
—Joe Webb, Flight Instructor, 52nd College Training Detachment

It was the last week in October 1942 when I heard on the radio that the president was to end enlistments and rely on the draft, where the military could dictate the branch I'd serve. So I decided, as my older brother Bob had done, to take a shot at becoming a pilot in the Marines. I got Dad's permission to enlist, but not in the Marines. It stuck in his craw that the Navy had rejected Bob for something Dad scornfully dismissed as a "heart murmur." It would be the *Army* Air Corps. After all, it was the Army Dad had served in during World War I. And even though he'd been grievously wounded in a mustard gas attack, affecting his lungs so he couldn't speak for three and a half months, he remained a true-blue patriot and still committed to the Army.

Like Dad, I was putting in sixty-hour workweeks at Norton's, the big grinding wheel company in Worcester, Massachusetts. It proudly floated the triangular blue flag emblazoned with a big *E* for excellence in the war effort. But now, with others in my high school class already enlisting since June, it was time to call a halt to civilian life. So the next day I picked up application forms at the Army Air Corps recruiting office and was filling them out even as I listened to the latest news of Capt. Eddie Rickenbacker, missing in the

South Pacific. The following Monday I submitted the application, together with two recommendations, and was told, after a check of the papers, to report with them the next morning at 0800 hours at Fort Devens.

It was only thirty-five miles to Ayer, but it took eighty minutes for the train to get there, long enough to introduce myself to five others from Worcester headed there. The six of us chipped in fifteen cents apiece for a taxi ride to the fort where, after producing our credentials at the gate, we were issued passes. I soon realized that it was a lot easier to get that pass than to pass the several exams that made up the Air Corps mental test. There were 150 questions on such subjects as English, geometry, algebra, physics, and current events. Of the seventeen of us in the room, only eight passed, getting at least 76 right. When I learned that I got 112 right, or 19 more than the next highest grade, I had good reason to thank the teachers I had at North High for thorough preparation despite, at best, my lackluster performance.

I may have been top man on the totem pole in the exam, but in the eyes of Charlie Rich, my boss and my ride to Norton's since I got a job there after graduation, I was still a dumb cluck. So dumb, in fact, that he offered ten dollars to my five that I'd never be chosen for pilot training. So confident was I that he was wrong that I refused the bet, even at two-to-one odds.

On Monday the 9th of November I was back at Devens for a thorough physical, riding the train with Al Barrios and George Arnberg, both in their twenties and Al with a year or more of college under his belt. The only reason the Air Corps was accepting the likes of George and me was that they'd run out of men with at least a couple years of college. The physical turned out to be just as comprehensive as the mental. Nine months earlier my brother Bob had taken his, where the Army also detected something wrong with his heart. Determined to fly, and with two years at Clark University sitting under such professors as Robert Goddard, the rocket pioneer, and with a private pilot's license as well as membership in the Civil Air Patrol, Bob was not about to take no for an answer. So he'd returned no less than six times to convince them he was fit enough to fly. At last he wore them down, and now he was training as a navigator.

When I returned to Devens for the results of my physical, I learned that two others had washed out for color blindness, critical for depth perception. That left five of us of the original seventeen, and two of these were in doubt. As I took the train back to Worcester I couldn't help but reflect on my good luck. For ten years earlier, as a result of an eye exam in grade school, Dad had taken me to Dr. Fairbanks, an optometrist. There he found my left eye so bad that he fitted me with glasses in which the right lens was fogged. Finally, after two to three years, my left eye had caught up with my right eye, and I could forgo the strange spectacles that had made me the butt of ribbing at school. Little enough price to pay, now that my eyes were 20/20.

It was almost a year since Pearl Harbor, and the war news was hot and heavy. What really caught my attention were the accounts of the fliers. Vividly I recalled the words of Winston Churchill on August 20, 1940, as he stood before the House of Commons but spoke to the world in praise of the RAF fighters who'd turned back Hermann Goering's Luftwaffe, which had been doing its dead level best to pound the British Isles into submission for an invasion. "Never," the prime minister proclaimed, "in the field of human conflict was so much owed by so many to so few."[1] That was the same time that our own Army Air Corps assembled all of its forty fighter planes as part of the largest war games since World War I. Of the forty, only three were airworthy enough to complete their mission. In scarcely more than eighteen months we were at war with Japan, Germany, and Italy, each with hundreds of fighter planes able to complete their missions.[2] Now, less than a year after Japanese dive bombers had laid waste to much of our Pacific Fleet at Pearl Harbor, I was learning from the radio that the Japs, as we nicknamed them, disgusted that they'd not been able to down a single B-17 Flying Fortress, had resorted to bombing them from above with their dive bombers—to no avail. Then came the news that in an air battle over Guadalcanal our fighters had destroyed twelve enemy bombers and five fighters, with the loss of but seven of our own. So it appeared that our pilots were giving a good account of themselves. The question was, if I became a fighter pilot, could I give as good an account of myself?

It was Friday the 13th of November, and far from running into bad luck, I learned that I'd enlisted none too soon. For teenage boys, it was announced, could now expect to be drafted, and some before Christmas. More good news, with search planes discovering one of Rickenbacker's crew floating on a raft in the South Pacific. The next day Eddie and two more of his crew were rescued, after an incredible forty days adrift on another raft in shark-infested waters. Now the question was, could I ever be so lucky?

The following day, the 14th of November, I was sworn into the Army Air Corps Reserve, awaiting orders to be called up. At the same time it was announced that there would be three registration periods in December when all males who'd turned eighteen after January 1 would sign up. That would have included me, so my luck was holding. On November 20 came the prediction that by the end of the year the United States would have a million men overseas. A letter from Bob in Fort Monroe, Louisiana, indicated that he'd be one of them by the spring of 1943. In between swatting "these damn flies!" he penned that he was "darn glad" I'd been accepted into the Air Corps. After all, he reasoned, it was here that I had "the most opportunity because it [was] the fastest expanding branch of the entire fighting service." It was obvious that, though he'd been disappointed in not being able to follow our cousin, Dick Newton, in becoming a Marine pilot, he was happy to be training as a navigator. Learning that I'd gotten 112 on my mental test, he confided he'd gotten 130, but was kind enough to write, "I think it has been made a little harder since I took it." On the contrary. If anything, by lowering their standards, it would appear they'd made it easier. Not only had he had his nose to the grindstone at North High, but he had gotten a good dose of math and science at Clark.

Bob then proceeded to give me some good advice. As for Devens, "Don't believe more than half the baloney they dish out to you, for they don't know a thing about what will happen to you." As for my pay, "Save all the money you can in War Bonds, or you'll have to chop out a big chunk for the income tax." And when it came to my return to Worcester, "Don't plan on getting home again until the war is over." As for his plans, "When I graduate I'll be headed to Egypt, Australia, or England within a week. But," he cautioned, "don't tell Margie Winslow, my fiancée, the bad news. Keep it a secret."

Then Bob got down to my choice of a place as a flier on a plane—thinking, of course, of a bomber, where he'd be serving. Would I opt for pilot, navigator, or bombardier? In any case I'd be a commissioned officer. Of the three, Bob counseled the first two, and of these, he confided, "I chose navigator, even though most guys pick pilot." Why navigator? "Because pilot training is the longest course, and the most dangerous," as well as "very monotonous." Furthermore, "It takes lots of practice and not as much brains as a navigator." And, he added, "It takes a certain amount of luck." The question that now hung before me was, if I was deficient in the brains category, could luck make up for it? Before closing his eight-pager, Bob made a point of adding, "Pilot training is chosen by most guys because there's sort of a 'romantic appeal'—a glory—to the pilot's job. But don't let it fool you—size it up according to your opportunities and abilities—and which ever one you think you'll do best in." Then he closed with "That's my advice—if you want it." I certainly did, even though I heeded only some of it.

By this time Uncle Sam was leaning on civilians to do their share of the war effort. Not only were there sixty-hour weeks in defense plants, but restrictions were multiplying. On November 30, Worcester, like other cities along the East Coast, was placed under a strict dimout. No lights were to be seen in stores or houses, streetlights were dimmed, and the upper half of headlights were blackened. Across the nation the speed limit was 35 mph, or 30 at night, unless otherwise posted, as it was in Worcester at 25. But at that, it was faster by far than the 8 mph restriction at intersections, as Dad had pointed out. Of course, that was written in the days of the horse and buggy, yet it was still on the books.

Now, even with gasoline rationing, the oil shortage in New England was critical, prompting the Office of Price Administration chief to announce that if it came to a choice, he'd rather have New Englanders catch pneumonia than our servicemen do without oil. By November 25, the selling of heavy cream was forbidden. Then I learned that the War Production Board had closed a local plumbing supply store for a year for operating a black market.

The next day was Thanksgiving, and I had plenty to be thankful for. To celebrate it after a sumptuous meal I invited Dana, my kid brother by sixteen months, to join me at the movies, along with old-time pal Malcolm "Specs" Midgley. It was in his house I'd filled out my enlistment papers, and it was his father, the city clerk, who'd provided one of my two recommendations. So it was only right that Specs should join us, as long as he didn't mind risking a ride in the '33 Ford Bob had bought for $50 and had willed me when he enlisted. Downtown we found a long line queued up at the Capitol

Theater, waiting to watch *The Flying Tigers*. Gen. Claire Chennault had his P-40 Warhawks painted to look like sharks, and they'd become a legend throughout the world as they supported the Chinese in the war against the Japs. I left the theater as pumped up as I was when I was sworn in at Devens. My question now was, how long would I have to wait before being called up?

As November moved into December and the first anniversary of Pearl Harbor, the home front was again called on to pull in its belt. Cans were to be collected, schools were to contribute one out of five typewriters, and the manufacture of ice cream was cut to save butter fat. By this time the oil crisis in New England was so bad that no oil would be sold to homes where the owners refused to convert to gas. Luckily, Dad had switched from coal to oil and, the previous spring, to gas, after braving the coldest winter in eight years. Now local stores were being closed for several days at a time to conserve fuel oil. Furthermore, if we didn't want to freeze to death, we were warned, we'd better consider doubling up with other families.

FDR, as commander in chief, had bigger problems. For here were railroad workers threatening to strike, all 350,000 of them, if they didn't get a 30 percent raise. And 1,500 workers at Bethlehem Steel Corporation went on strike, in violation of the no-strike pledge of all plants for the duration of the war. So the president cracked down and sent War Department production director William R. Knudsen out to tour the plants. When he got to Worcester he declared that "we must work like hell" if we intended to win this war.

Our home-front privations were little enough sacrifice as we learned of the continuing hits the Allies were taking in this, the start of our second year of war. On December 3 we were gripped with the news of the Allied invasion of North Africa. Despite German air supremacy there, the Allies claimed they sank eighteen Axis ships while losing sixteen.

According to Churchill, the war was now entering its "tensest phase." On the 5th we learned that the Allies were softening up "the soft under-belly" of Europe, Italy. Our bombers were pounding the docks and railroad facilities at Naples, hitting a battleship and two cruisers without so much as a challenge from Italian fighters in the air. It was fast becoming clear to Hitler that, if it were left to the Italians, Italy's boot would indeed represent a "soft under-belly." So he stripped the Russian front of fighter planes to counter any Allied invasion from the Mediterranean, even as he ordered his Wehrmacht down the boot to reinforce the toe.

On December 7, 1941, we all learned something of the power of air warfare at Pearl Harbor. With but 105 planes, the Japs had sunk a battleship and severely damaged four others, as well as three destroyers, a seaplane tender, and a repair ship. Worse, they had killed 2,343 Americans.[3] It appeared that Billy Mitchell had been vindicated in his insistence—leading to a court-martial for insubordination—that air power should be the top priority for the United States as, back in the 1930s, we faced the prospect of yet another war.[4]

To celebrate the anniversary of Pearl Harbor properly, the Army Air Corps teamed up with the RAF to pound "Fortress Europe" with 150 bombers, escorted by 400 fighters—the biggest daylight assault yet. As for the Japs, they made the same mistake the Germans made in failing to take advantage of their air superiority and invade England, turning instead to Russia. Had the Japs capitalized on their five-to-one advantage in the Western Pacific, they could easily have captured Hawaii. Instead, they gave the Allies the chance to catch their breath, roll up their sleeves, and gradually begin retaking the islands and mainland the enemy had captured, extending out in a 2,000-mile perimeter from Japan.

With the day of my call-up coming ever closer, I was taking a keener interest in the war than ever. On December 8 I learned that the French navy, anchored at Toulon, had scuttled seventy-five warships rather than have the Germans commandeer them, leaving only twenty afloat. By the 9th the Allies were girding for an all-out assault on Tunisia, the RAF was pounding Turin—the royal arsenal city in Italy—for the fifth time in a month, while in the Pacific our dive bombers and torpedo planes were raising havoc in the Solomons and Guadalcanal. Meanwhile, I was absorbed in Seversky's *Victory Through Air Power* and coming to believe it.

Apparently Hitler was also believing it.[5] Enraged at his heavy losses and retreating military on the eastern front, and determined that this would not happen in North Africa, he was rushing reinforcements there in huge transport planes and gliders. In Tunisia, British general Bernard Montgomery was engaged in a seesaw battle with German general Erwin Rommel, the "Desert Fox," while Allied planes, gaining air superiority, were making short work of the German Tiger tanks. Retreating on one front after another, Hitler summarily replaced his chief of staff as an obvious incompetent, even though it was the Führer himself who was micromanaging the war, snapping out outrageous orders to his increasingly restive general staff.[6] Impatient with his generals, he was more impatient with his Italian allies. When a German U-boat pack sank a British transport carrying 1,500 Italian prisoners and 500 other Axis troops, the captain exclaimed, "I'd have fired my torpedoes if half of Italy was aboard!"

In the Far East, Allied planes were just as successful. In Burma, U.S. fliers were knocking out twelve Jap planes from the sky for every one they lost, while in the Pacific our dive bombers were targeting the Munda air base in the Solomons and seizing the Buna airfield. And who were the men flying these planes that were threatening Hitler's dream of a thousand-year Reich and Tojo's dream of ruling the Pacific? The newspapers here at home revealed that it was the "happy-go-lucky" pilots, young enough to fear little if anything, confident that they were invincible.

If it took "happy-go-lucky" to help fashion a fighter pilot, here was a qualification I could lay claim to, possibly the only one. At two my curiosity lifted me out of my high chair and toppled me headfirst onto the kitchen floor, giving my nose its peculiar slant the rest of my days. At five my love of adventure put me in the driver's seat of our grand Haynes touring car, parked in front of our house on a steep hill on Beverly Road. Then, with Dana perched happily in the backseat, I released the brake and ended up a hundred yards away against a wayward utility pole. At fourteen, with a giant hurricane racing up the coast, mauling Providence and nearing Worcester, where did my mother find me in the howling wind but atop a poplar tree, exulting in the widest arc I'd ever experienced at treetop. A year later I threw caution to the winds and led the rest of our scout troop down a steep maple sugar trail and was soon laid out, my ski pole inserted squarely in my left knee, earning me yet another lacing by "Dutchy," our scoutmaster. "Curtis, haven't I told you—time and time again—never to ski out of control?" At seventeen, pathetically late for a prize date, I ran into a roadblock in the form of a string of cars on a two-lane road, facing a sharp curve under a railroad bridge just ahead. What to do but cross the yellow line in the middle of the road, zip past the laggards, and regain the 80 mph speed the new '41 Ford reached when the accelerator was floored? Pulled over at last by the state police, I got another dressing-down and a suspended license, but it was Marilyn's cold shoulder on the dance floor later that really hurt. Actually there were few ventures I wouldn't try on a dare, and fewer still on a double-dare.

EVERYTHING IS BASIC

But now I was eighteen and presumably responsible for my acts. Would I be? Could I be? About the time of my nineteenth birthday I at last got the call from the Air Corps and a week later was bound once again for Fort Devens.[7] My mind was a whirlwind even as I made small talk with Al and George and another Worcesterite, Joe Esper. Big olive-drab GI trucks met us at Ayer and delivered us to Devens for our first taste of Army chow. Hardly had we finished before we were hustled aboard another train, headed for Atlantic City, New Jersey. Formerly the East Coast playground for the rich, it was now the first stop in basic training for us lowly buck privates. Though only three hundred miles or so from Devens, it took over ten hours before we could brush the ashes and soot from our civvies and step from the smoke-filled cars to our destination. GI trucks soon deposited us at the Richfield Hotel, poor cousin to the Boardwalk's Ritz-Carlton. Instead of luxury suites and cushy mattresses, we were handed mattress bags to fill with straw and lay atop the springs of Army bunk beds. So tired were we at 0230 hours, that we could have slept on the floor.

There may have been mercy in my being assigned to the one nonsmoking room, together with Al and a new man, Johnny Baldor. But there was no mercy in the blare of reveille at 0530 hours, followed by a braying corporal warning us that we had exactly fifteen minutes to dress, wash, shave, and prepare our rooms for inspection, with blankets drawn tight enough for a quarter to bounce when dropped on them. Here, I soon discovered, was the hurry-up-and-wait routine that the Army had perfected to a fine art. For no sooner had the drill sergeant hustled us over to the Traymore Hotel than we were waiting—and waiting—in a long line for a breakfast that we didn't need nearly as much as a few more hours' sleep.

From there we were again "marched"—if that could describe what we did—to the huge cavern called Convention Hall, there to exchange our motley colors for the homogenous olive drab. Packaging the civvies to mail home, we were then lined up for as thorough a physical as I could imagine. Here was no quickie five-minutes-for-five-bucks that Dr. West used to give us scouts before we headed for summer camp at Treasure Valley. Here we were, naked as jaybirds, in an assembly line as one specialist after another poked and prodded, scrutinized and listened, leaving no nook or cranny overlooked. That completed and now dressed as inconspicuously as possible in olive drab, "Fall out!" reverberated throughout the hall, and we were headed back to the Traymore for the noon meal. We were coming to understand that in public we were never to be seen simply walking or ambling. It was always marching, sometimes double-time—meaning we were jogging—again presumably together, and sometimes to the beat of our singing which, in retrospect, was no better than our marching.

There was no question about it; everything was now by the numbers. My serial number, punched into my ever-present dog tags, was 110 578 74. I was now officially a number. I was, further, 73 inches tall and 170 pounds, with 20/20 vision, a 32-inch waist and a 34-inch inseam, marching the Boardwalk to the metronome of the rasping drill sergeant's "Hup—two—tree—whore!" as I made for Brigantine Field in 10-degree temperature and a 25 mph wind cutting through my greatcoat. There I was introduced to .30-caliber rifles and .50-caliber machine guns, to disassemble and assemble again in two minutes flat, in between taking aim at targets, some stable and some moving. By the time I returned my shivering body to the Richfield and had a moment to reflect on what was happening to me, I realized that the Army, intent on melding us into a big, anonymous blob, took special pains to obliterate any individual idiosyncrasies. Furthermore I was being taught that ours was "not to question why, but rather to do and die." Our obedience to command was being reduced to simple genuflection, as automatic as it was unquestioning. We were becoming a giant machine, our various parts lubricated by the singing of raucous tunes that substituted lust for harmony. A teetotaling hypocrite, I belted out with the rest, "Drunk last night/Drunk the night before/ Gonna get drunk tonight like I've never been drunk before. . . ."

There was decidedly less verve as I sounded off with the signature songs of the infantry and artillery, the Navy, and the Marines. But with the opening lines "Off we go, into the wild blue yonder," I doubled the decibels. Especially gripping were the words "we live in fame or go down in flames . . ." as I wondered if either of these would be my fate. In reality, the "flames" didn't sound all that bad to ears being nipped by frostbite. I was especially taken by the compassion of our men as they fell out of formation to assist one of our number who'd succumbed to the cold. I could usually count on three or four dropping out to help the unfortunate soldier to the nearest infirmary.

Brigantine Field was more than an introduction to the usual guns and bayonets. There were mortars and grenades to deal with, along with tear gas released inside a Quonset hut as I rushed to don my gas mask. For some reason I could never get it on fast enough to prevent my rushing from the building with tears streaming down my face. Perhaps it was for the same reason I was all thumbs with disassembling and assembling my weapons. It all came back to me that I'd never been able to turn off a faucet at home when Dad asked for it. Invariably, it seemed, he'd let out a yell as, catching a final drink on a hot August day from the end of the hose, he'd suddenly get a faceful.

By the end of three weeks I was sick and tired of Atlantic City. Shots and more shots, interviews and more interviews, drill and more drill, all interlaced with scorching reprimands from anybody who wore a stripe. Even the haircuts had become routine. Each civilian barber seemed to take a special pride in shaving our locks down to a bristling butch. In three minutes flat he'd stop the electric clippers, shake out the cover, and pocket another thirty-five cents, even as he'd call out "Next!" We had no way of knowing whether the fair sex would admire our new looks, for we were under strict quarantine. With no nights on the town there was no opportunity to seek the opinion of women, much less their ardor. To keep us safe rather than sorry, in any case, we were exposed to the most lurid black-and-white VD films.

In the couple hours of free time each evening the pay of fifty dollars a month had a way of multiplying—or disappearing—in games of blackjack or craps. But I'd been burned the previous fall at Norton's when I lost ten dollars on a "sure thing" in an office football pool. In addition, my red eyes and wheeze in the thick cigarette smoke rising from the klatches of addicts only spelled trouble. But even these guys forsook their games on the night a USO show brought the big, busty Kate Smith to Convention Hall to belt out "God Bless America" as only she could sing it. It was "The Jell-O Hour" being broadcast across the land, and it was an oasis in the desert of numbing sameness when virtually everything was by the numbers, scripted by the book.

Two other events broke the monotony of basic, neither of them pleasant. One of the men contracted spinal meningitis and died, so we all chipped in a collection for his folks. Then I got a letter from home, telling of Art Creamer, a member of my Pine Tree Patrol in Troop 6, killed in action. These two shockers summoned the ghosts of two other deaths, ghosts that lurked just beneath my consciousness. The first, when I was six, was being ushered into a corner bedroom at 48 Beverly Road by Dad, there to recoil at the sight of Bob's twin, Bert, ghostly gray and still as he lay dead of pneumonia. For some reason Dad had refused to take him to the hospital, and he'd died the night before. The second ghost was that of old Mr. Peterson, eight years later, frozen solid in a snow bank not more than twenty feet from our front door. He'd stumbled up the sidewalk the night before in a blinding blizzard. When he was declared missing by his distraught family, we scouts were summoned to make a search. Armed with long poles, we'd poked the drifts until the cry went out. We'd rushed to the lifeless corpse, there to glimpse with a certain grisly fascination the man who, just hours before, and so close to refuge in our house, had been alive.

Despite Bob's writing that he hoped the war would be over within a year, by the end of three weeks it had settled on me anew that this war was serious business. Just how serious, however, I could scarcely imagine as I packed my duffel bag and boarded another troop train, this one bound for Seymour-Johnson Field at Goldsboro, North Carolina. Here was a sharp contrast with Atlantic City. It was mercifully warmer. It was more relaxed. And in four days the tests and interviews were over. With a rousing rendition of the Air Corps song by the field's brass band, I joined the others as we stepped on the train headed for Indianapolis, Indiana.[8] Atlantic City, Goldsboro, Indianapolis—these were cities I'd only read about. I felt almost as naïve as did Dwight Moody, founder of the Northfield Schools, just fifty miles west of Worcester, when, a century earlier, he'd left school after the sixth grade, convinced that all the land west of the Mississippi was a vast desert.[9] My nose was glued to the train window as I took in the sight of knots of people in the hills of Appalachia standing by the tracks, waving as we passed. Finally we emerged on the flatlands of Indiana, and I paused to give thanks that I'd proven Charlie Rich wrong. For I'd been chosen for pilot training! Or so I thought.

AN INTRODUCTION TO HIGHER EDUCATION

It was one thing to be chosen for pilot training. But it was something else to complete that training—to avoid being washed out, or killed in training—and finally receive the coveted silver wings as well as the gold bars of a second lieutenant. Some fourteen months lay ahead of me, months in which I'd be declared unfit to fly, hopeless, a case of adolescence so reckless that it appeared I was trying to beard the Grim Reaper in his den. My sole flying trip had been a half hour in a Piper Cub a couple years earlier. My high school classes gave me little advance warning of the complexities of solid geometry, calculus, and trigonometry, nor of aeronautics and other subjects meant to introduce me to ten hours of learning to fly a Piper Cub. Bob was still egging me on to navigation, suggesting, "You get along pretty well with math and aren't exactly dumb, so you shouldn't find it difficult." Those were words more kind than accurate. By this time Bob was completing navigator training and would soon be heading overseas for combat. Dana had enlisted in the Marines earlier in the spring, and would soon be training as a gunner on a bomber. Would we—could we—return unscathed, marry, have families, and grow old to watch our children and their children grow to adulthood? It seemed too much to ask.

As painful as my ignorance was, I had a few things I did know. I knew I needed all the education I could squeeze into the next three months of college training. I knew I'd have to apply myself as I never had in high school. I knew I wanted to fly fighters. The previous December I'd seen two movies, *Flying Tigers* and *Flying Fortress*. I'd take a tiger to a fortress any day. But I also knew that my record as a reckless klutz could kill more than my chances.

There was another thing I knew, I told the lieutenant behind his desk when he put the question to me: "Soldier, have you had any experience drilling men in marching?" With that, I told him of my scouting experience. Of course I told him nothing of my impaling my ski pole in my leg because I was skiing out of control. But I did tell him that, as senior patrol leader and then as assistant scoutmaster, I had marched scouts in close order drill many times. Furthermore, I had been awarded the rank of Eagle Scout when I was fifteen. I was eager to tell him more, but he interrupted with, "Good! I'm putting you in charge of Platoon 3 of Squadron A." Just like that I'd been promoted to a lieutenant, with an A/S for "aviation student" insignia for my uniform.

I soon was to learn that I'd broken the very first rule of this man's Army: never, but *never* volunteer, for you can never anticipate the consequences. Best to lie low and let others take the heat—and the responsibility. If the Law of Unintended Consequences worked anywhere, it worked in the military. It wasn't long before I was bumping into some of those consequences. Now, as a lieutenant in charge of a platoon, I had to hit the deck at the first sound of 100-decibel music that constituted reveille as it was blasted over the speaker system of Hinkle Fieldhouse on the campus of Butler University, a small liberal arts college on the northwest side of Indianapolis. I was fortunate, Bob wrote, to be at Butler, for he'd learned from a buddy that "Butler used to be a classy joint," adding, "just cross your fingers that you stay there. Those of us who've been through these 'war camps' as cadets certainly envy you." I was fortunate, too, to be on the bottom bunk of a three-tiered bed and thus could make a dash to the nearest "head," as the Navy contingent there termed the washroom, there to wash and shave, then rush to dress and make my bed before rushing outside to take a head count of Platoon 3. What really caught the morning sun were my belt buckle and my shoes, so I had to take special pains to set an example for the rest of the men.

There were two complications in all of this rushing to and fro—just the beginning of my unintended consequences of volunteering. Our 350 aviation students were in addition to 700 sailors already in the fieldhouse, and all of us tucked into three tiers of beds, so the morning rush was something to behold. The second complication was the presence in my platoon of a short, carrot-topped guy with mischief forever on his breath as well as in his eye. It was Higginbotham who took a fierce pride in his independent streak that the Army was doing so much to eliminate. Now all I wanted, as did the Air Corps, was for Hig to conform and obey orders. Hig would have nothing of it. On the other hand, the A/S adjutant, Freeman, was even more impatient than was I as he accosted me. "*Loo*tenant Curtis, what the hell kind of outfit are you running here?! Get your men to shape up or we'll ship you out of your position!" More often than not, he had his eye on Hig, who was either out of step in marching, or out of line, or ogling the coeds we passed, or singing a different song from the one we were singing.

No doubt about it. Hig, like his looie, had been born on Independence Day. And it was always exciting—and sometimes even fun—being a maverick, as I'd discovered in my nineteen short years of tormenting various leaders. The trouble was that the shoe was now on the other foot. Even as I racked Hig back and forth, and gigged him left and right, forcing him to walk tours on the weekends when he could be out on the town, I still held a grudging respect for his nonconformity. Hig, it turned out, was incorrigible to the core.

If, for a moment, Hig forgot himself, there was Al Barrios, eager to carry the flag of independence even as he applied his innovative genius to one of our marching songs. Having felt repeatedly the lash of Lieutenant Cunningham's barbed tongue, Al concocted new words for the old song: "Around her leg she wore a purple garter / She wore it in the springtime and in the month of May / And if you asked her why the hell she wore it / She wore it for an airman who was far, far away." Now Al decided that the neighbors would hear different words as we marched at 0630 hours to mess. "Around our legs we wear our purple garters / We wear 'em in the springtime and at Butler U. / And if you ask us why the hell we wear 'em / Just ask ole Long John and he'll tell you."

Despite Al's creative juices at high tide, and despite his care in teaching us the new words so even Hig could sing with us, there was Cunningham, as purple as the garters we were supposedly wearing, storming into the CO's office, demanding that the whole platoon be gigged. But his raving left Capt. Samuel Gist, a reasonable and avuncular veteran of World War I, unmoved. Just as long as the platoon was not profane or vulgar, they could sing as they pleased. Of course, Cunningham complained, Gist missed the point. The song was both profane and vulgar by trashing him before the neighborhood! No surprise when Long John transferred to another outfit, with few of us mourning his passing.

While Bob was suggesting I try the newfangled Kleenex instead of handkerchiefs because in the long run they were less expensive, Mom was writing that the newspaper was predicting the war would soon be over, even though *Look* was warning, "It's a long way to Tokyo."

Having my plate overflowing already, it appeared that I didn't know when to quit volunteering. So when we were asked for someone to assume responsibility for a new section in the Butler *Collegian,* to give the latest news of our aircrew, my hand was up before my brain had begun to work. And just what were my credentials? Why, back in the eighth grade I was responsible for starting *Lincoln Highlights,* where my lasting contribution was the repeated use of Jonathan Swift's imaginative name for the oversized people he met, Brobdingnagians. I made certain that with each issue my editorial would feature, if nothing else, this humdinger that defied spelling as well as pronunciation. Graduating to high school, I became a contributing editor to the North High *Record,* where I'd managed to bring cackles to Bob and his buddy Bill Janes when they feasted on my first article. Graduating from North, I was soon using some of the nine hours of free time in a twelve-hour night shift at Norton's writing letters to the editor of the Worcester *Evening Gazette.* Needing filler, and having no idea who I was, he inserted one letter of mine after another. So that was the sum of my journalistic endeavors, hardly enough to qualify me for this new responsibility. But all I could figure was that they were as desperate as the *Gazette* editor, and gave me the job. Within days I was floundering in the cold waters of voluntarism, so to the rescue flew other Worcesterites, and soon I had a full staff. Of course it didn't hurt when I gave them a vivid description of some of the flouncing coeds also occupying the pressroom.

If there was some question of our column, "Prop Talk in the Air Crew," as ranking somewhat below the noblest monuments of English prose, there could be little question as to our resolve. Indeed, at its best, that section ascended to the rarefied heights of Al's musical innovation. With 350 more aviation students replacing a like number of graduating sailors, our readership doubled overnight, in addition to taking in even a few of the coeds who seemed to have nothing better to do. Just how avid our readers could be came home to me one day when an A/S, fists at the ready, stormed into the pressroom, eager to straighten out my crooked nose. It seemed he'd taken umbrage at a broadside I'd leveled at his platoon for some shenanigans they'd pulled at a recent dance hosted by the coeds. Sensing my nose was in for possibly another twist, I invited him to step outside. If blood were to flow, better it not splash any of the coeds. Once out the door, I made a beeline for the Coke machine, dropped in a nickel, and another nickel for potato chips—a peace offering— while I tried calming his vexatious spirit. Soon he was reasonable and I remained unbloodied, if cowardly.

Come March 16 and the *Collegian* announced that 169 coeds had signed up to attend the aircrew dance, featuring Butler's all-girl orchestra, "Belle's Sharps and Flats." The following Saturday everything was in order. The cafeteria was reserved, the refreshments were prepared, and soon the place was jumping. But, sad to say, this cadet was not among the aircrew jamming the place. I, who'd arranged the dance, was not dancing. Rather, I was marching on the ramp, back and forth in full dress uniform, down to the white gloves grasping a heavy rifle on my shoulder. I could picture my steady date, Margie, in the arms of another guy leading her on to the dance floor, and it was not a pretty sight. Who to blame? It seemed that Lieutenant Cunningham had, after all, gotten in his last licks. Had I not, in yet another weak moment, volunteered—this time to take responsibility for keeping the fieldhouse spotless? Had I not spent hours posting schedules so that each platoon had a certain section of the place to keep clean? Had I not gone each day throughout to see that all was shipshape for Cunningham's inspections? But that one day came when, due to leave for another post, he made one last inspection and from his lips fell the verdict, "Filthy!" Then came a nasty dressing-down, gigs, demerits, and now, marching.

Earlier, he'd decided that he'd had it with me. For one evening he caught some of our platoon engaged in an impromptu hokeypokey where we'd pushed back the three-decker beds. To the accompaniment of harmonicas, a flute, a Jew's harp, and drumsticks, the guys soon had a big and appreciative audience, singing, clapping, and dancing in the aisles. It was a moment we were all relishing when, suddenly, who should make his appearance but Long John, his pencil and paper at the ready. Bad enough that we'd moved the "furniture." Worse, we were supposed to be studying. And here we'd incited a near riot! The demerits were piling up, especially for the one supposedly in charge of this platoon.

All was not lost, however. Confident that such a display of

raw talent deserved a larger stage, I hit on Gist at our regular Monday morning meeting to permit an amateur night. I volunteered to be Major Bowes, the emcee of the program that had been such a hit in the 1930s. We opened it up to the last contingent of 350 sailors, provided they understood that they, too, would be gonged if the talent was more rancid than raw. All 1,000 of us, plus the brass and a few visitors, were on hand for the classic event. When all contestants had done their dead-level best, the winners were determined by the applause of the audience. Yet, with compassion approaching our passion, we awarded consolation prizes to the losers.

As much as the audience seemed to take to the event, however, it was nothing compared to Harry Rose's USO show when it hit the fieldhouse. Here was stand-up comedy straight out of Broadway burlesque, and the audience ate it up. Here was popular jazz with a seasoned orchestra knocking out toe-tapping tunes. When they struck up Glenn Miller's "In the Mood," the aisles were instantly crowded with guys doing the hokeypokey. But what really raised the roof were the gorgeous gals with their see-through dresses and come-hither songs. So, we in Platoon 3 conceded, who could compete with that?

One other USO show that hit the Hinkle Fieldhouse was billed as "All-colored." With nary a "Negro" among the thousand of us, it should have occurred to me how deep and insidious was the divide between black and white. Yes, we relished the spirituals, sung as only they could sing them. Yes, we set our own toes tapping in time with the tap dancers'. And yes, who could stifle a guffaw at the yarns spun in the style of Step'n Fetchit, the movie character who couldn't do enough to burlesque black subservience to whites.

Yet beneath the applause, just below the surface, I sensed a certain uneasiness. Prejudice based on skin color came as easily to me as the air I breathed. Of the eight grades in my elementary school there was not a single Negro enrolled. In my high school graduating class there were just two, both girls, and I never remember talking to either of them. But I do remember putting on blackface from burned cork for a minstrel show sponsored by Dad's Lincoln Men's Club. The only Negroes I ever saw in any number were those who occupied the top balcony in the movie theaters in Worcester, which we whites designated "Nigger Heaven."

So I was in for a shock when I read an article in the *Collegian,* quoting Robert Redfield, dean of social sciences at the University of Chicago. Race, he maintained, was "a singular human invention, devised by Whites to retain their supposed superiority." The few superficial differences, such as skin color and the shape of lips and nose, were of "no consequence in human behavior." Furthermore, he maintained, this fabricating of "race" was a "false science," a "modern mythology" that only served to interfere with the war effort. For here were "White men stopping work in the war industries because Negroes are employed to work beside them." And as for Jews, "The best man for a war-time position may be passed over because he is a Jew."

Here was a two-by-four right between the eyes. It not only caught my attention, but grabbed my prejudice by the neck. I thought of the thousands of Japanese on the West Coast, stripped of their property and shipped to "internment camps," solely on the basis of similar superficial differences. Had we done the same with Italian and German Americans, we'd have stirred up a hornet's nest. I thought too of other Japanese and African Americans forming their own fighting units. I was coming to realize just how naïve I was, making it obvious that I had a lot more to learn than my classroom subjects.

Much to learn, yet I couldn't seem to keep from volunteering, even as I was running out of gas. And when I didn't volunteer, our CO volunteered for me. He asked if I would serve as an agent—a secret agent no less—for G-2, Army Intelligence, reporting each week by code to an anonymous superior anything hinting of a subversive nature. So I added that. He asked if I would deliver a fitting—and short—tribute to the last contingent of sailors about to leave. And I did that, though just how fitting was open to question. Then, without asking me, he assigned me to sit on a review board of aviation students to hear cases of serious infractions of regulations, and impose punishment on those we found guilty. So conscientious was I in this that, discovering I'd rested my elbows on the table at mess, I promptly gigged myself.

Could this Gist, I wondered, be a descendant of another Samuel Gist, the colonial Virginian who, with our first president, formed a partnership in the notorious Dismal Swamp Company? Here was a pre-Revolutionary scam perpetrated by a dozen or more of our forefathers engaged in land speculation. It brought to mind the more recent buying of swampland, sight unseen, in the alligator country of the Florida Everglades. If this Gist scorned such money-grubbing, he certainly seemed to have his namesake's power of persuasion.

By the end of March I was paying dearly for my compulsive volunteering. At last the student adjutant faced me down on the drill field after my platoon performed even worse than usual. "*Loo*tenant Curtis, your platoon looks like hell—and so do you. You'd better check in at the infirmary." I not only checked in but kept on checking in every few days or so, just to get caught up on my sleep. It was there that I was in for another shock when I observed the genitalia of another guy, swollen to triple their normal size. He was wallowing in the misery of VD. Instantly the black-and-white horror movies at Atlantic City flashed before my eyes, and I doubled my resolve.

The difficulty lay in the fact that, just as we had tried proving our manhood by enlisting, so now, with our testosterone flowing at high tide, we were out to prove our manhood to the fair sex at Butler. Yet there in the *Collegian* was the dean of Swarthmore College, cautioning the military contingent on his campus to "remove all distractions of sex from the classrooms and labs." What was going on? We had no coeds in either place, nor at mess, nor in the fieldhouse. We had to content ourselves with marching past them on the streets, or rubbing shoulders with them in the hallways, in the library, and for some of us, in the pressroom—just enough to give us contact for dating on the weekends.

So fetching were these corn-fed beauties that when some of them sent photos of themselves to Bob Hope, legendary king of the USO shows, challenging him to select five "breath-taking beauties from Butler," he studied them ever so carefully. Then he dithered. At last he bit the bullet and back came his best judgment, closing with "In a dither-ingly, Bob Hope." Now, we concluded, if there was no hope for Hope—twice our age—how could we hope to mind the advice of the Swarthmore dean?

To compound the difficulty, there were the coeds, praising us in the school paper for "raising student morale with continuous singing and cheery hellos." One went so far as to insert, in the spirit of Elizabeth Barrett Browning, a poem to compete with Al's. Titled "Men—Men—Amen!", it served to reassure us that, far from being a distraction, these coeds were a powerful motivating force: "Men are troublemakers all / With mischief they abound / But life would be so very dull / If there were none around!"

I was determined that Margie would find life anything but dull with me around. So one lovely spring Saturday, when I should have been catching up on my sleep, I noted to Margie the stables near her house. Did I ride? Of course, I assured her. After all, I'd sat astride a pony at seven to have my picture taken. I'd ridden pigs at the "poor farm" and graduated to cows in a nearby field. With that less-than-illustrious equestrian experience, my only hope was that I'd be assigned an old swayback, a nag that was content to plod.

Alas, it was not to be. As we meandered along the trail, Margie suggested we canter, and off she went. My steed needed no urging, and broke into a canter to catch her. Then Margie's horse broke into a gallop and lo, mine did the same, with me bouncing ever more to the right, holding on for dear life. Suddenly I realized my left foot had lost its stirrup and, sure as Satan, I was slipping off that bronco. I hit the ground and found myself being dragged along at breakneck speed on the scruff of my neck, my right foot caught in its stirrup, my eyes set on the trail receding in the distance. Margie, hearing my shouts of distress, turned to witness my plight, reversed course, and returned to catch my reins, bringing me to a halt in a cloud of dusty humiliation.

So much for my riding. The question remained as April 1 approached and flight instruction was to start, would I fare any better in a Piper Cub? But before I could prove myself on All Fools' Day, there was an incident in the fieldhouse that bears telling. It so happened that on an especially chilly night the remaining contingent of sailors, issued but two wool blankets, clashed with us who'd been issued three. As usual, a couple of our guys walked along the top tier of bunks, opening the windows, only to be followed by sailors closing them. One thing led to another, from protestation to name-calling to cussing to shoving and finally to fistfights. Then each side poured in reinforcements, and soon mayhem ruled the roost. To complicate it, the lights suddenly went out.

Alarmed, the CQ put in a hasty call for the CO and in a trice there was Gist, flanked by two trusty lieutenants. He spoke firmly but nobody heard him. He shouted. He bellowed. Then, suddenly, down he went, a GI boot having found his head a tempting target. Slowly he struggled to his feet, reclaimed his glasses, and ordered his aides to find the culprit. It was a lost cause, so, concluding that sailors had not been issued GI boots, he ordered that we A/Ses would be confined to the campus that weekend.

OFF TO A FLYING START

Promptly at 0800 hours on April 1, knots of five of us were assembling with our flight instructors at the Hoosier Airport. Our instructor was Joe Webb, a weather-beaten veteran of thousands of hours in the air. Slowly walking around the Cub, he patiently explained the functions of the major moving parts. Then he demonstrated how to spin the prop, got in, and gave the thumbs-up sign to each of us as we took turns spinning and listening to the sputter of the engine as it caught. By this time we were chafing at the bit—none more impatient than I as I watched the others take their rides.

At last it was my turn. "Curtis, how many hours of flying have you had?" Recalling my stretching the truth with Margie and its consequences, I replied, "None, sir."

"You don't have to address me as 'Sir.' I'm just a civilian who happens to know something about flying. Now, Curtis, when you see my thumbs-up signal, you swing that prop. When the engine starts, you hustle into the backseat and strap yourself in."

My heart was thumping as I buckled my shoulder harness and listened to his command.

"Now, put your hand on the stick, gently, and your feet on the pedals, lightly, and follow my movements."

It was simplicity itself as I followed his movements in taxiing out and stopping, just perpendicular to the end of the runway. With his feet on the brakes, he gunned the engine to "check the mags." This was, as I'd learned in ground school when I happened to be awake, a check on the engine's manifold pressure to determine that the plane had full power for takeoff. He then looked to his left to make sure no plane was coming in for a landing. He looked to the right to see a green light flashing from the control tower. It was a go. So he pulled out on the runway, lined up the plane in the middle, and pushed the throttle as far forward as it would go. By this time my heart was a trip-hammer, my mouth and throat were cotton, and my head was throbbing with an electric tingle. As we sped down the runway, my hands and feet followed his every move. Suddenly there were no more bumps, and I knew we were airborne. Straight ahead we climbed to five hundred feet. Then he banked 90 degrees to the left and we climbed to five thousand feet. First the people, then the cars, then the houses blurred until the fields below formed patterns I'd never seen before. All the while I was swallowing to equalize the air pressure in my ears. This I knew to be critical, for Dr. West, back in Worcester, who examining me for an earache after a week at Treasure Valley, declared the canals connecting the three parts of my ears the smallest he'd ever seen. Had he poked farther, he might well have said the same thing about my brain.

At last Joe figured we were high enough that he'd have ample room to recover from any of my inevitable blunders. His first order he gave in a deceptively calm voice: "Take an easy turn to the left and try to keep the ball on the flight co-ordinator in the middle." That presumably would indicate I was coordinating stick and rudder, something I was bound to have as much trouble doing as I'd had trouble coordinating clutch and stick shift in Dad's '41 Ford two years earlier. But I moved the stick to the left and bore down on the left pedal, only to see the ball moving wildly to the left. Then, as I tried to correct, it flew to the right.

"I told you an *easy* turn. This is no Mack truck! Relax and give me a *smooth* turn to the right."

It sounded so easy. And it looked so easy—when he did it. Soon my heart was in my throat and I felt sweat oozing down my back. Was I simply a born klutz? At last I heard the welcome words, "OK. I'll take over." With that, he descended to the traffic pattern and landed, greasing 'er in with nary a bounce. Was it possible that this could be that easy?

By the third lesson and little improvement in my coordination, I was ordered to fly parallel to a road below, tough enough on a calm day. But—wouldn't you know—there was a strong wind and it was blowing 90 degrees across us. So it was the devil to fly a straight line, much less parallel to anything. By the fifth lesson I was taxiing and taking off, which I found a whole lot easier in the seventh lesson than landing. It was landing, I'd also learned in ground school, that was the most dangerous part of flying.

"Maintain your speed. Keep above the stalling speed. Set it down gently in a three-point touchdown." If only the flying were as easy as the words! By the eighth lesson I was either leveling off too high and dropping like a rock three feet or more, then bouncing as I tried to keep the plane on the runway, or I was hitting the runway at an angle and bouncing again and again as I desperately tried to keep from running off the runway. Or, again, I was trying to land too far down the runway and in danger of overshooting, so I'd hear the words, "Give 'er the gun and go around again!"

By this time I was hearing an underlying note of exasperation in Joe's voice. Then he turned me over to Hanks, the senior instructor who'd convinced the Air Corps to use his airport for ten hours of instruction during the quickie course in the college. My check ride with him was no better; I simply could not relax.

As hard as it was to please Joe, as often as I wished I could be alone in that plane to relax and enjoy myself, I was relieved when it was Joe at the controls on my ninth lesson. For suddenly we found ourselves in a blinding snowstorm. The visibility was zero. Dead reckoning was out of the question. With even this veteran at the controls, the little Cub was buffeted about like a cork in rough water. I thought I was going to lose my breakfast if not my life by the time we saw blue sky again. Never had my feet felt better than when I emerged unscathed from that cockpit to find solid ground beneath me.

By May 6 I'd completed ten hours of flight instruction and was facing graduation, but with two final responsibilities. The first was to march my platoon before Gen. Robert Harper, to the sound of a band from Fort Benjamin Harrison, while the other two classes, neighbors, and the curious watched and seemed to wish us well. I would need their good wishes, for there were Hig and Al. Would they—could they—conform in this high-octane situation?

It was a great honor, we were told, to have the assistant chief of staff to commanding general Henry "Hap" Arnold sit on the reviewing stand that morning. Why did we deserve such an honor? Because, we soon found out, Robert Harper Jr. was among us, unbeknownst to most of us. Did Squadron A, Platoon 3, win any award? Not a chance, even with Hig and Al on their best behavior. We just couldn't cut it. And neither could Squadron A. But we did tie with Squadron E for third place, for what it was worth. Still, the good general, his silver stars on his epaulettes glistening in the morning sun, seemed pleased as he returned our snappy salutes, so pleased, in fact, that he granted us our last open post, till 1200 hours that night.

My second responsibility took the form of my sitting behind a small table in the pay line. The coeds next to me were begging big bucks for war bonds and getting them, so I figured my plea for small change to put out a special photo edition of the *Collegian,* emphasizing the aircrew, would find them receptive. And it did, with my counting out $57.11 to pay for the souvenir edition.

That night the three contingents assembled in the fieldhouse for graduation ceremonies. There was music by our detachment band as well as from our glee club. Then Professor George Leonard, liaison between the college and the Air Corps, wished us well, as did our CO. Like the earlier parade, all was prim and proper, with Hig and Al doing all they could do to rein in their impulses. But with dismissal it was obvious that the steam in their boilers was about to explode. I became suspicious as I saw them eyeing me even as other guys were being shanghaied and passed overhead by hundreds of hands, all in the direction of the swimming pool.

"What's going on?" I asked a passerby.

"Oh, nothing. They're just dunking the student officers."

With that, I made a beeline for the door, only to be brought down in a flying tackle by Hig and Al.

"Gotcha!" they crowed, and thereupon passed me overhead to the pool. I emerged dripping wet to the smug satisfaction of these conspirators over whom I'd lorded, yea, these three months.

Far from being satisfied that they'd exhausted their creative juices, Hig and Al suddenly pulled down fire extinguishers from the walls, and what was bedlam became a full-blown riot. Of course, these two had a perfectly reasonable explanation: they were simply testing the devices to make sure they'd work OK in an emergency. Come midnight, only a fortunate few found a dry bed.

The next morning, looking worse for the wear, and with precious little sleep, we lined up to board the buses for Union Station. Suddenly a messenger from the printer rushed up with a big box, and we quickly distributed our souvenir edition. There on the front page was a letter I felt would quicken our pulses as we left Indiana for Texas.

April 21, 1943

To All Personnel of the Army Air Forces:

In violation of every rule of military procedure and of every concept of human decency, the Japanese have executed several of your brave comrades who took part in the *first* Tokyo raid. These men died as heroes. We must not rest—we must redouble our efforts—until the inhuman warlords who committed this crime have been utterly destroyed.

Remember those comrades when you get a Zero in your sights—have their sacrifice before you when you line up your bombsights on a Japanese base.

You have demonstrated that the Japanese cannot match you in aerial combat or in bombardment. Let your answer to their treatment of your comrades be the destruction of the Japanese Air Force, their lines of communication, and their production centers which offer them opportunity to continue such atrocities.

> H. H. Arnold
> Commanding General
> Army Air Forces

This was followed by the distribution of our flight log-books, tracking the details of our progress, and my heart sank. For there, in big, bold, and black letters, was Joe Webb's conclusion following his bout with me. He had gone so far as to underline the key word: "This man is *not* pilot material!"

INTRODUCTION TO THE LONE STAR STATE

"Sack," technically SAACC, the San Antonio Aviation Classification Center, was our destination as we boarded the troop train for Texas. Here was the state that prided itself on one's being able to fly in a straight line half the distance of the two thousand miles to our destination, and still be within the state. My own state of confusion progressed from despair, then, with encouragement from some of my pals, to a wan hope. Was Charlie Rich right, after all? Would I actually be picked for pilot training? For it dawned on me that it was in San Antonio that the final decision would be made. After all, we were headed to the Classification Center. Everything up to now was simply preview. If Uncle Sam was going to spend $80,000 over nine months or so, until we got our wings, he was going to be sure he was selecting those with the "right stuff"—whatever that meant.

There was slim chance for anything but fitful sleep in the overstuffed, big, and dirty green seats, with the incessant clackety-clack of the rails, the stopping and starting for water, the shrieking whistle as we entered towns and roads that crossed the tracks, the cigarette smoke, and the shouts of glee and roars of anger floating up from the craps and blackjack games—all this in addition to the smoke and thick ashes drifting in from the steam engine pulling us. At last the "Red Eye Express" ground to a halt in San Antone. As we stumbled from the train with our duffel bags and boarded trucks for our new base, I doubt there was anybody looking more like a sad sack than I. Was it possible that the Air Corps was so desperate for pilots that they'd take the likes of this A/S who couldn't manage even a mediocre grade on his first ten hours of instruction? If I couldn't handle a simple Piper Cub, how on earth could I be expected to fly the big trainers, much less a combat plane? And if, by some miracle, I was chosen to fly fighters, surely there was not a prayer that *I'd* be chosen to fly the hottest of the hot planes coming off the assembly line: the P-51 Mustang. For here was the holy grail of pilots, even those chosen to fly bombers and transports.

As it was, the P-51, in the short time it had been in combat, had made possible the escorting of our big bombers out of England and far up into Germany, even past Berlin. In fact, it was helping in a big way to turn the tide of the war in Europe. For if air power was essential to victory, then the bombers would suffer without proper escort. Until less than a year earlier, American bombers in their daylight raids out of England were easy prey for German fighters, once the shorter-range P-38s and P-47s had to turn back for lack of fuel. But the Mustangs, with two wing tanks of 108 gallons each, in addition to the 265-gallon tank in the fuselage, could now accompany the bombers as far as they could go. Beyond that, the German fighters, primarily the Messerschmidt ME-109 and the Focke-Wulf 190, were no match for the speedy, maneuverable 51. So if the German fighter pilots were avoiding combat with the Mustang pilots, and 80 percent or more of the bomber pilots would rather have been flying fighters, and 100 percent of those would rather be flying the P-51, then it stood to reason that it was the Mustang that had become the queen of the fighters, among the Allies as well as the Axis.

Winston Churchill had paid eloquent homage in 1940 to the vastly outnumbered fighter pilots of the Royal Air Force, who'd scored so heavily against the best of the Luftwaffe.[10] Now, three years later, he was paying tribute to the RAF as well as Montgomery's 8th Army, for driving the Germans and Italians out of Africa. "All this shows," Churchill exulted, "how much luck there is in human affairs and how little we should worry about except doing our best." Here, I figured, was the nub of my problem. Could I count on Lady Luck if I wasn't doing my very best?

Bob and Dana were undoubtedly doing their very best. Bob was already on his way to the 8th Air Force in England. Contrary to what he'd written the previous fall, he'd been given a brief leave in the States, so he and Margie Winslow were married on April 10. No surprise that he declared his honeymoon "the happiest week of my life." Dana, having enlisted in the Marines in March, was now in basic training at Parris Island, South Carolina. Soon he would start training as a gunner on a bomber. With a navigator and a gunner, both scheduled for bombers, I hoped against hope that I'd be a pilot, and not necessarily on bombers. So I could picture Dad, dutifully and proudly replacing one blue star with two and now with three, to hang in the window of the front door, there to notify the neighbors that Al and Vena Curtis were doing their best for the war effort.

One thing for sure, I had no desire to fight this war on the ground, as Art Creamer and most of my buddies back in Worcester were doing. Dean Gordon, another member of our Pine Tree Patrol, was headed for the ski patrol, to fight—and die—in the mountains of Italy. It was a chilling account of life on the battlefield that Phil Ault, United Press correspondent, had reported from Tunisia in April:

Blood spilled on Tunisian battlefields has turned American soldiers into crafty, hating, killing, fighting men. Gone is their egotism, their aimless joking, their foolish bravado about the enemy being a pushover. War is a personal thing now. They've seen men die trying to surrender. They've had enemy soldiers, who walked up with hands upraised, chuck grenades at them. They've seen the enemy's ingenious booby traps turn men into smashed pulps. When they first encountered the enemy on November 8th, they thought the war was a mere nuisance and the enemy a vague body of men waiting to be chased away. But no more. One private standing in a slit trench said, "Hell, I probably won't live through the war anyway, but before I get mine I'm going to kill a lot of those Jerries."

This the *Collegian* had recorded just a few days before my arriving in San Antonio. Now I wondered if I had any more chance than that private of returning alive. But at least I'd be flying—above the grit and the grime, above the mud and the snow, above the blood and the gore of the battlefield. That is, if I could only convince the Air Corps that I did have the makings of a pilot. If not, then I'd opt for navigator. After all, Bob had written the previous November, "*Anybody* can be a pilot. It takes *brains* to be a navigator." But had Bob so soon forgotten what a dumb klutz his kid brother was? If he had, it was certain that when I took the battery of tests—physical, mental, and emotional—at "Sack," the brass there would know.

What were my preferences? they asked. To be on the safe side—a side I was usually unfamiliar with—I listed navigator first, then pilot. After all, Joe Webb had done his best with me, with a patience I could only marvel at. A physical checked me out at six feet, 172 pounds, with a thirty-nine-inch chest and a thirty-two-inch waist. The eye test confirmed the 20/20 I'd shown earlier, with no sign of color blindness. Then came the coordination test for this world-class klutz and—wonder of wonders—I passed! They then thrust me into a Quonset hut that served as a high-altitude chamber and took me "up" to thirty thousand feet and back to earth. Where some were doubled over with the bends, grasping their knees in agony, I emerged unscathed. That left the mental test, and here, I was certain, this Napoleon would meet his Waterloo. As luck would have it, I scanned the bulletin board the next day and there, classified for pilot training, was "Curtis, Richard K." I read it again and again, scarcely able to believe my eyes or restrain my relief. I'd been given another chance!

It was this sweet prospect that buoyed my spirits during the following weeks of demeaning hazing and mind-numbing repetition. I may have had Charlie Rich and Joe Webb eating their words, but I was eating something else again—sand and dust in a wind that never stopped blowing this mixture, along with tumbleweeds, across the grounds and against the barracks. They could stop the weeds, but not the sand and dust, which in an hour could sift through the tightest of windows and coat everything, including the inside of our lockers. This suffocating mixture, I soon found out, under the boiling summer sun, made our daily hour of calisthenics an exercise in sheer survival. Add to this daily regimen our obstacle courses, gas mask drills, KP, guard duty, and policing the grounds—all of this under the watchful eye of lieutenants armed with notebooks and pencils to keep track of our gigs—and "Sack" was no ball.

Apart from the occasional open post, when we could make the rounds of the city, and a USO show, featuring Pat O'Brien, what made the stifling monotony bearable was my prospect for flight training. Something else served to break the monotony, and that came in the form of a telegram from Dad: "BOB IS MISSING IN ACTION. DETAILS FOLLOW." I couldn't believe it. He'd just arrived in England. Less than two months earlier he'd been married. He was a great guy. And smart. And here he was, making plans to enter the ministry when released from the service. Where on earth, or in heaven, was the justice of it all?

One emotion after another gripped me. Surprise was followed by denial, and denial by dismay. Then followed anger, and guilt. If a Curtis was to be sacrificed on the altar of Mars, god of war, why Bob? Why not me? Unschooled, unsophisticated, uncoordinated, and unattached, I was under no illusion that I could match the contribution that Bob could make to this sick world.

Only gradually did the details dribble in. One of a crew of ten on a B-17 Flying Fortress, Bob had spent a few weeks in May and June on training missions. On June 11 he flew his first combat mission. He wasn't scheduled for the 13th, but the scheduled navigator called in sick, so Bob volunteered to take his place. It wasn't until August 21 that I got anything like a clear idea of what transpired on Bob's third mission. That emerged with the publication in *The Boston Globe* of a dispatch from a former reporter, Lt. Clark S. Nichols, the twenty-six-year-old son of a former Boston mayor from 1926 to 1929, Malcolm E. Nichols.

A bombardier on the B-17 *Kathy Jane,* Nichols on that fateful day was at thirty-five thousand feet, where the temperature, even in June, was 35 degrees below zero. He was on his way, with two hundred other 17s, to Kiel, home base for the deadly U-boats that had raised such havoc with Allied shipping in the North Atlantic. This target was known as "the hottest corridor in Germany," and one that the Allies were determined to put out of commission. The mission of the 13th constituted the largest American mission against Fortress Europe. The *Kathy Jane* flew directly behind the flight being led by the mission's leader, Brig. Gen. Nathan B. Forrest. Soon Nichols and his navigator were clearing ice from the Plexiglas nose, feeling that they were riding in "an overgrown electric lightbulb."

They didn't have long to muse, for no sooner had they crossed the Channel and into Germany than they were peppered with antiaircraft fire. So thick was the flak that it appeared they were hitting "solid walls of black, ugly puffs," forcing the formation to take strong evasive action. Yet this was only a prelude to the attack by enemy fighters, swarming in "like angry bees." The gunners were letting loose from their turrets and a Jerry, caught in a fatal cross fire, started to spin, fire and smoke from his engine trailing him downward. The sky, continued Nichols, "was streaked and criss-crossed with tracers, constituting every tenth bullet, leaving a white trail to permit gunners to correct their aim. Mixed with the tracers were the black puffs of exploding flak. Weaving, diving, then climbing, the bombers managed to stick together."

The nearer the 17s got to their target, the thicker the flak and the more desperate the pilots became as two hundred or more FW 190s attacked them out of the sun. As he stopped to reload his gun, Nichols saw the general's plane smoking. Soon his own plane started smoking as "an enemy slug chewed its way into one of our oil lines." Then the navigator tapped Nichols on the shoulder. "Four minutes to Kiel." So Nichols turned to his bombsight. Over the interphone he reported, "Bomb bay doors opening." Now, oblivious to the flak and fighters besieging him, he concentrated on his single task. "Wait! Steady! On course! Hold it!" Then, hitting the bomb release, he yelled, "Bombs away!" The general's plane, though still smoking, had also released its bombs. Within minutes Kiel was ablaze.

Now the problem for Nichols and his crew was to make it back across the frigid North Sea to England. Bad enough that one engine was out and still smoking, as they faced into a 50 mph headwind. The flak was still filling the sky even as the "yellow-nosed FW 190s were diving and looping through our formation." Their guns were picking one, then another Fortress and sending them earthward, trailing smoke and frequent parachutes. Rothschild, the pilot, was doing his best to stay in formation as he "skidded about the sky, dived, then plowed on through flak and fighters," all the while the 17s' guns blazing. As difficult as it was, they had to stay in formation for mutual protection.

At last the enemy fighters broke away "like frightened buzzards," and the crew relaxed somewhat, only to be alerted on the interphone by the top turret gunner. The Jerries were again after them. By this time the 17s were more vulnerable than ever, flying only three hundred feet above the sea and lagging behind the formation. Nichols watched as a 17 staggered, then crashed into the waters below. "Fortunately the crew was rescued later after floating about two hours in their dinghies."

When at last they landed back at their base, "somewhere in England," they took a hard look at the *Kathy Jane*. It was "punctured and battered from flak and bullets." Yet, miraculously, no one was hurt. "We were just tired, cold, dirty, and hungry." Nichols paused to reflect on his good fortune. "We had seen some of our friends go down and it wasn't a pleasant memory to have." The crew could only conclude, "We were lucky, plenty lucky."

Like many of the other B-17s on that mission, Bob's wasn't so lucky. An FW 190 hit his plane after it cleared the coast and was out over the sea. Ablaze, it fell into a spin, yet most of the crew managed to bail out. They had their Mae West life vests, but no dinghies. In that icy water a body went limp in less than ten minutes and slipped beneath the waves. One of the crew was rescued by an alert U-boat crew, but the captain refused to search for other possible survivors. It wasn't till after the war, when the rescued seaman was released from a POW camp, that we learned these further details. By this time my folks had received—and framed—a bereavement card from the War Department: "General Marshall extends his deep sympathy in your bereavement. Your son fought valiantly in a supreme hour of his country's need. His memory will live in the grateful heart of our nation."[11]

Nice sentiments. A beautiful card, neatly inscribed with a red and white flag and a single gold star at the top. Still, it was only a card. And when the $10,000 automatic life insurance was sent to the folks rather than to Margie, because she hadn't been married at least six months, it helped. Still, it was only paper. How much, I asked, was a life worth? Especially a life holding such promise, cut off in its prime? Yes, Bob had lived thirteen years longer than his twin brother, Bert. And, yes, he'd lived twenty-two years longer than Philip, the firstborn in the family. Yet Bob had another forty or fifty years ahead of him, time to watch his children and their children grow into adults. How much he would miss!

Again the flag on the front door at 48 Beverly Road would change. By January of 1944, with months passing since Bob was declared MIA, he was declared KIA. Now there were two dark blue stars and a gold star set against a white background. And the question continued to linger. Would there be another gold star on that flag before the war ended? Being next in line to Bob, the thought crossed my mind more than once.

The hours were being swallowed up in days, and the days in weeks. Soon I'd cross the street to Preflight. Apart from

Bob's MIA status, I had more than enough to make life miserable. If it wasn't exposing myself to the merciless sun, resulting in immediate itching skin as the sunburn healed, and long-term cancer, it was gorging myself on food and drink, mixing blocks of ice cream with quarts of milk, pimples and whiteheads the immediate result. If it wasn't shin splints from running on the hard, hot roads, it was athlete's foot keeping me awake at night. To top it off, I was hacking and spitting, the result of God knows what. The flight surgeon took X-rays to see if I might be suffering from "latent TB." For I'd told him I'd tested positive on the Mantoux test back in the eighth grade. Yet now there was no sign of it. What continued to buoy my spirits was the sweet prospect of pilot training.

The last night of classification was a replay of the last night at Indianapolis. Again all the repressed instincts of testosterone-driven adolescents vented themselves in fire hoses being played, barracks against barracks. Through the windows the water flooded the top floor and seeped through the floorboards and down the stairs to the beds and lockers below. And when that filthy water reached the sacred waters of the barracks sergeant, we exploded in laughter. It may not have been clean fun, but it was good fun. Especially so when we spirited his bed out where no mortal eye could find it, not even the practiced eye of the man who'd lorded over us for these two months.

PREFLIGHT

As we wrestled our gear into the barracks across the street, the significance of that thin separating line was not lost on us. We were now officially classified for pilot training and the brass had done their best to make sure the $80,000 they were investing in the training of each of us—almost the $85,000 cost of a new P-51—was not wasted. They were determined to get their money's worth. There was a new game plan, with more ground school to capitalize on our introduction at Butler University. There was physics as it informed aeronautics. There was identification of ships and planes, with a tachistoscope flashing fleeting images at 1/100th of a second. There was Morse code to master at sufficient speed. There were lectures on everything else, from VD to engine carburetors. And always, in the back of the room, there was the beady-eyed Sergeant Johnson, ready and eager to jab bobbing heads awake on steamy afternoons.

Like common sense, sleep had never been my long suit. Instead of catching up on weekends, I'd invariably head into the city for canoe rides down its famous river, or fourteen-course meals for $1.58. If I couldn't catnap in class, then I'd try it on guard duty—or when I was posted as guard on the road leading to the rifle range. Given a red flag to wave down everything approaching this danger zone, I'd warn the stopped driver, "Go like hell the next mile, if you don't want a bullet in your tires—or worse!" But the traffic was sparse, the sun was hot and the humidity high, so I found the shade of a nearby tree too tempting. I hung the flag on a road sign and retired to the shade of the tree, where I conked out until I was relieved in an hour. Rather than rat on me, the new sentry took my advice and did as I did. Imitation, I'd been taught, was the sincerest form of flattery.

It was obvious I had to beat the rules to beat the heat. So I took a look at the crowded cadet pool, then at the officer pool, and concluded I could do laps far easier there, and still escape detection. I figured it was hard to tell the difference when cadets and officers both sported white shorts. I took note in the mirror of my GI shorts, flirting with my knees, and decided I could do better. So I took scissors and off went five inches, only to find an intrusive looie out to get the facts as he grasped his pencil and notebook: "5 permanent demerits—1 for each inch!" From then on he kept a jaundiced eye in my direction, so when I passed him as I emerged from the mess hall and failed to salute, he racked me back. "Soldier, don't you salute an officer when you pass him?!" So I accommodated him, only to find my cap come loose as an apple, an orange, and a banana tumbled out. It wouldn't have been so bad except that this was the same looie who'd inspected our barracks and found assorted fruits in my boots and locker. Then and there he'd ordered me to scrub the entire first floor so I could witness for myself the scampering legions of cockroaches, drawn to food such as I had secreted there. Now there were more demerits, more tours of duty, more marching in full dress uniform, shouldering a rifle that grew heavier with each passing hour.

If it wasn't the looie harassing me, it was another cadet, Roenche by name. One night after I'd hit the hay on the bottom bunk, I was suddenly awakened by cold water drenching my sheet and my face. My bunkmate, in collusion with Roenche, had waited till I was fast sleep, then had taken a leap onto his bed, where a couple of rubbers (condoms) had been thoughtfully placed between his mattress and his spring. Another night I flipped back the sheet to catch some shut-eye and crawled in—but leaped out, hitting my head on the bunk above me. For there in my sack Roenche had hidden a swarm of big red ants to keep me company. The roar of laughter throughout the barracks added insult to near-injury, and I had to restrain the urge to punch Roenche's lights out. The only thing that saved him—and me—was a letter I'd just gotten from Dana, telling of a bar fight he'd had with another Marine. Dana had suffered two broken fingers as he broke the nose of his assailant, and both were threatened with "deck-court punishment."

Just to make sure I'd be able to take on Roenche, I took to the gym and vented my anger on the small punching bag, then saw his face on the big bag and let him have it—until I strained my wrist. So sore was it the next morning that I checked into the infirmary, only to find the flight surgeon prescribing heat treatment. So he put my wrist under a heat lamp—and promptly forgot it. A half hour later he re-appeared, rushed over and withdrew a wrist covered with blisters—probably wondering why I'd not had sense enough to remove my wrist when it was being burned. No longer did the strain bother me, so intense was the pain of the burn. There was precious little sleep that night. Next morning the doc applied an antiseptic solution that burned off whatever skin was left, and applied a dressing that fell off after a few more minutes with the big bag.

Well, I figured, if I couldn't wallop Roenche, I'd learn to run fast enough to escape him. So I took to the cross-country course, improving my time each day until my watch told me I'd beaten the course record. So when a race of presumably the best runners among the ten thousand of us in Preflight was scheduled, I figured I had it made. With the crack of the pistol I was off, determined to take an early lead and hold it among the hundred runners. For all of 2 miles in the 3.5-mile course I kept that lead. But as I approached the 3-mile mark, I glanced back over my shoulder to see a runt of a cadet gaining on me. Ahead of me was "Cardiac Hill," the killer on the course. As I stumbled up that hill the runt passed me, his short legs beating methodically, like a trip-hammer. Then, to my amazement and disgust, three others passed me in a final dash, and I crossed the finish line not first but fifth. How, I asked, could that runt have trounced us all? "Don't you know," was the reply, "he was the AAU champion in the cross-country last year." So much for my "record."

In addition to the news that I was heading for pilot train-ing, I received a great boost when at mail call I found a letter from a certain Myrtle Fisher, back in Worcester. I'd dated my share of girls there and in surrounding towns, but Myrtle re-mained a standout I'd tried to date, with no luck. I had my eyes on her instead of the tennis ball as it whizzed past me for an ace. Rather than argue that I wasn't ready for the serve, I asked my opponent who this striking beauty was, walking down the sidewalk on the other side of Burncoat Street. Determined to get to know her, I phoned her for an interview after learning she was the editor in chief of the *Mercury,* the student newspaper at Commerce High. Perhaps she would be willing to share some tips as to how she'd won a regional award for her paper. She was gracious to a fault, and I found myself asking her questions having nothing to do with the paper. But I failed to ask her for a date, so I phoned back, only to find her out and her kid sister on the phone. What did I want? A date to play tennis? Sorry, but she was already tied up with a steady boyfriend. And that was that.

Then, just a week or two before being called up by the Air Corps in January, I saw her again at a newfangled skating rink the city had built at Green Hill Park. The problem was that I was with another girl, Leah, a colleague from Norton's, who just happened to be wearing an engagement ring. She was tied to a guy in the service but had agreed to a skating date. And there in the warming house, as I was putting on her skates, I happened to look over, and there she was! Not only that, but she was looking directly at me, wondering what this eighteen-year-old was doing, already engaged to be married. Of course, I didn't know till later what she was thinking. I only knew she was the most gorgeous creature I'd ever seen, and each time I passed her on the rink only confirmed this conviction.

With my call-up I forgot Leah and almost forgot Myrtle. Now here was a letter from her. And she took pains to spell out that she was not pursuing me. It seemed that she'd boarded a bus downtown for Beverly Road, where the terminal was at the top of the hill, and walking distance to her house. The bus was crowded, but she found a seat next to a middle-aged woman with a small Boston terrier tucked under her arm. They struck up a conversation and the older woman pointed out the church she attended and asked Myrtle if she attended church. Why yes, and nearby. Did she happen to know her son, Dicky Curtis? Yes, she'd met me and recognized this as the mother of the navigator that had been reported in the paper as MIA. Then in a bold but providential stroke, the older woman, whom Myrtle now recognized as my mother, asked her if she'd write to me. For, she was sure, I must be lonely down there in that big state of Texas. Myrtle was taken aback by the request, but nonetheless agreed. So Mom tore off the back of an envelope with my address, and Myrtle promptly put it in her coat pocket and forgot it. But with September approaching, she decided to send her coat to the cleaner and emptied the pockets, there to discover the forgotten note. Now her conscience bothered her, so she sat down and wrote me. I tore open the envelope on Friday, August 27, 1943, the very day I learned I'd be heading for Brady, Texas, for Primary Flight Training.

August 23, 1943

Dear Dick,
In all probability your mother has told you how we met on the bus. . . . I hope you don't mind my writing to you this way. Until your mother told me where you were, I didn't even know you were in the service. Keep 'em flying and best of luck to you. As ever—as before. Myrt.

What a lucky dog! Here I was, one of 204 of us aboard seven buses and headed for "the heart o' Texas," with my own heart singing and her letter next to it. As we made our way 130 miles to the north of San Antonio, never had the time passed so quickly, nor so beautifully.

2

THE WILD BLUE BECKONS

"Kuykendall, why don't you take Curtis. I can't do anything with him."

—B. H. RODDIE to TOM KUYKENDALL, civilian instructors

PRIMARY FLIGHT TRAINING

There was no doubt about it. Curtis Field, surely rightly named, was a major improvement over the blistering heat, the blowing sand, and the sweltering humidity of San Antonio. In place of the nondescript, two-story barracks were several long lines of neat, flower-lined, white, single-story barracks, set down in green grass and concrete walks. Other amenities included platter-sized steaks, more than a cut above the horse meat that many civilians, including Myrt's family, had been reduced to. Polishing off meals fit for kings, we had no KP to worry about. This, as well as the serving, was done by Negroes—who were also known by other names that quickly made it plain that Texas was part of the South. A casual informality made for an ambiance that stood in stark contrast with the gig-happy looies hiding around every corner at "Sack." If the purgatory there was meant to purge us of our waywardness, then Curtis Field looked like a giant step toward the heaven of combat flying.

What set my heart thumping was the sight of 160 P-19A primary trainers, all neatly lined up in rows on the concrete ramp. At orientation we were told that, after sixty-five hours of successful flying, we would move on to Basic Flight Training. As much as any cadet, I could appreciate just how iffy that completion would be. Though I was definitely "*not* pilot material*,*" Webb had insisted, here I was, being given a second chance. To top it off, I was given a temporary assignment as squadron adjutant. I would be tested for leadership, to help determine my rank upon receiving my wings. I would either be a flight officer—corresponding to a warrant officer in the regular Army—or a 2nd lieutenant.

In the two months of Primary Training I was confronted with two major obstacles, even more formidable than the obstacle courses the brass had bedeviled me with at "Sack." The first was the loss of other cadets in flying accidents. It was just four days after arriving that I learned that an upperclassman, a 44B cadet—meaning he was scheduled to get his wings in February 1944—a man with twenty hours of flight time, fell into a spin, failed to recover, and was killed on impact. I soon learned of another who also panicked in a spin, freezing at the controls. Fortunately, his instructor in the rear seat had the presence of mind to unlatch his control stick, lean forward, and crack the cadet over the head, whereupon he released his grasp of his stick so the instructor, reattaching his own stick, could recover. Fortunate, too, was the fact that they had enough altitude to accomplish all of this. As if these accidents were not enough to sober me, I also learned of a cadet who, washing out, hanged himself. Suicide seemed the only option when confronted with what he—and many of us—considered the ultimate humiliation. Which of the two obstacles would I oblige? Clobbering myself or washing out?

Here were the two realities that served to tether my balloon of hopeful exhilaration to earth. These took momentary flight when I was issued flight togs, helmet, and goggles. All decked out, I headed for the nearest photographer to order a dozen eight-by-ten oil-tinted photos for two dollars each. And who were the lucky recipients? There were Marilyn and Margie, Gladys and Babs back East. Then, right there in Brady there were Cora Belle and Marie, Helen and Marvel, each of whom I'd meet in the coming weeks. But above all there was Myrtle. Back came pictures, to be pasted on the inside of my footlocker cover, but none more fetching than Myrtle's.

All too soon I learned that it was one thing to look like a budding fighter pilot, but something else to fly like one. By the end of my first week I'd been introduced to my civilian instructor, B. H. Roddie, a weather-beaten veteran of the skies who must have been more than twice my nineteen years. Assigned alphabetically, the five of us, Crowder, Crull, Cummings, Curry, and Curtis, took turns cranking the prop and listening to the Texas drawl of an instructor we hoped would be as long on patience as he was on flying hours.

As it turned out, Roddie needed that much—and then some. Cummings let loose his breakfast all over the cockpit during maneuvers, forcing us who followed to switch to another plane. Roddie simply sighed, figuring that cadet would have to get over his queasiness or wash. It was when the last of the five climbed into the cockpit, however, that Roddie had a true test of his patience.

If I wasn't flubbing my recovery from simple stalls high in the sky, I was stalling out, dropping, and bouncing off the runway when I leveled off too high in landing. I soon found I got the same bumpy result when I yanked back full flaps over the runway. Ordered to fly a rectangle, using the road below to guide me, I flew as though I'd never studied geometry. Then, exasperated by my continuing blunders, Roddie ordered me to head for home. Trouble was, the string that tied my helmet to my head had come loose, so the invading rush of wind deafened me to his order, repeated again and again. At last I gathered from his frantic gestures that I should head for Curtis Field and obliged him. That evening, as I recorded his blistering of my hide on landing, I chanced to be in the latrine, after taps. And along came our CO, Captain Jackson, catching me scrunched over my diary. That was good for five demerits, enough to award me a tour of marching.

It got so bad that by September 21, with eight hours of dual time, I was still trying to recover from simple stalls, and still trying to stabilize the pesky instrument ball in the middle, even during the most elementary maneuvers. Meanwhile my classmates, including Al Barrios, were soloing and proving their success by being baptized in the shower, clothes and all. I sized up the increasingly desperate situation in my little green book: "Am getting worse every day—tensing at the controls involuntarily—if I could only relax I wouldn't have any trouble."

The trouble was that I was not only a klutz but an intimidated klutz. True, unlike others, I wasn't plowing into cattle, grinding hamburger on the spot. And true, I wasn't overshooting the runway, making a beeline for the control tower, sending the tower operator flying down the stairs for his life. But it became all too evident that Roddie was at the end of his long tether when, learning that fellow instructor Tom Kuykendall had washed out one of his charges, Roddie pleaded with him, "Kuykendall, why don't you take Curtis. I can't do anything with him." Shades of Joe Webb!

It wasn't long before I came to appreciate just how patient, just how tender Roddie had been. It wasn't only the tongue-lashings, convincing me anew that I was the stupidest klutz in the 44C class. But Kuykendall had a habit of accentuating each cussword with a lashing of his stick back and forth. Since his stick was connected to mine, it not only gave me black and blue knees but killed any chance that I'd ever relax.

Would I ever solo? Had my ground school been stellar, it might have redeemed my flying. On edge from such a lack of sleep that I actually dozed off during a barnstorming movie,

Target for Tonight, what chance was there for one droning lecture after another? Before long I'd fallen victim to paranoia. My instructors on the ground and in the air had it in for me. Paranoia, it is said, detects a villain behind every tree. I scrounged up another reason: flying in an open cockpit at seven thousand feet or more, with only summer flying togs, and fall coming on, left me shivering and unable to coordinate. Back on earth and in a warm classroom, thawing out left me sleepy. I was desperate enough to seize these and other excuses by the neck, for all the good it did me.

If only my flying and ground school matched my extracurricular life! At the welcoming dance the second day at Brady, I found Marie to be an ideal representative of the Lone Star State. Further dances and chance meetings added others: Helen, Marvel, and—of course—Captain Jackson's secretary, Cora Belle. Who could tell how soon it would be before I would need a good word put in for me with the CO? Soon I was convinced that Texas fillies were on a par with those from Indiana and Massachusetts—with, of course, the exception of Myrtle, whose pictures and letters were warmer with each passing day.

October 25, 1943

Dear Dick,

So you want to know when my birthday is. Well, my mother tells me that I was born during an ice storm on Feb. 4, 1925. That makes me 18 now. Your picture sure looks swell. I have it in a frame on a table next to my bed. Well, it's almost 9 o'clock and time for Lux Radio Theater, so if you'll excuse me I'll join the rest of the family around the radio.

When weekends should have found me catching up on my sleep, I was invariably elsewhere. If the rec hall wasn't inviting me with Hollywood's latest hits, then it was the endless games of Ping-Pong. Sunday mornings it was the parishioners at the local Baptist church inviting me to dinner—once I'd awakened to the sound of the organ introducing the closing hymn. But it was Saturday nights at the local dance hall/bar/social club that proved the highlight. For there, when the orchestra took its break between dances, I stepped onstage to host another "Truth or Consequences," with the latter resulting, for example, in a cadet's date administering him an egg shampoo. Or it might involve the lining up of two chairs, two "cockpits," with the cadet in the rear chewing out his date for screwing up her performance. Among those who appeared to be enjoying it all was our CO. He went so far as to have Cora Belle help mimeograph and distribute flyers to the field, advertising the game. As the weeks extended into months, I found I would need every shred of his goodwill I could scrounge.

A word about Brady. Three times a week, if I had no tours to march, I took advantage of open post to acquaint myself with some of its five thousand citizens. In the center square the "cowboys" gathered: wizened men whose skin resembled leather, whose hats, boots, and spurs—once shining and expensive—were, like their other clothing, now dirty and tattered as they leaned against the stores to take in these newcomers.

In the eight months that had passed since my call-up in January, I'd added seventeen pounds to my scrawny 170-pound frame. Yet my persistent lack of sleep and lousing up my diet on snacks had me drawing blood every time I shaved. So covered with pimples was I that the flight surgeon recommended I visit a local hospital each week for six weeks to undergo X-ray treatments for my face. These lasted, perhaps, fifteen to twenty minutes, with nothing disappearing except the $18 from my $75 monthly stipend. Little did they seem to know of the link between radiation and cancer.

It was on September 23 that Roddie had dumped me on

Kuykendall. I had fifteen landings under my belt, with ten to go before I could solo. On my sixteenth I was determined to show my new instructor that I had what it took. My diary that evening revealed the sad story. "I screwed up royally on the landing pattern, then bounced on landing, and climaxed it by turning into the wrong parking space." By this time it must have been obvious to "Kirk" that old B. H. had outsmarted him.

With each passing day I seemed to be singing the same miserable dirge in my diary. "Chewed out by Kuykendall— who I dislike more intensely every day!" Though I had little doubt that the feeling was mutual, I was struck by his persistence in trying, day after blundering day. Here was an obvious masochist-turned-sadist, intent on screwing my head on straight after all the grief I was giving him. Did he see potential in me that Roddie had failed to see? His language didn't show it, turning as foul as the weather that was turning the field to mud.

Finally a miracle occurred. I soloed. Where the other eight in the two groups I'd joined had soloed in eight to ten hours, I'd managed with thirteen. Still, I'd done it, and no shower— clothes and all—ever felt better. Partly it was due to the fact that six others on that day had washed out, all the result of accidents. Even Dick Beane, a buddy, got lost on his solo trip, went in for a forced landing, and broke his prop.

I had completed one giant step toward getting my wings and commission and entering combat. And it looked like, far from the war being over by the end of the year, as Adm. "Bull" Halsey had predicted, we had a way—a long way—to go. But the war had definitely turned in our favor, due to many factors, not the least of which was sheer luck. What made the difference as much as anything else was our gaining supremacy in the air. By this time the Axis had lost no less than 519 planes in the air and another 1,000 or more on the ground. The Allies, meanwhile, claimed to have lost only

175, a ratio of almost ten to one.[1] Operation Husky, the invasion of Sicily, the first attack against what Churchill termed "the soft under-belly of the Axis," had begun. Though 160,000 Allied troops were pitted against 250,000 of the enemy, our bombers had been devastating strategic strongholds on the island. It seems that Army Intelligence, G-2, had gleaned valuable information from the Sicilian Mafia, in exchange for turning a blind eye to its operations in the United States.[2]

In just thirty-eight days Sicily fell, in large part due to Allied supremacy in the air, preventing German bombers from breaking up the fleet of ships in the invading force, and providing cover for further Allied advances. With Sicily's airfields in their hands, the Allies concentrated on softening up Italy for their next invasion. Of special interest were the dozen or so airfields around Foggia, just south of Italy's spur on its boot. Already Hitler had met with Mussolini in the north, demanding that Il Duce defend Italy to the last man, so that "Sicily may become for the enemy what Stalingrad was for us." However, as it turned out, Mussolini had to flee Rome, leaving 167,000 Axis troops lost in Sicily, compared to 25,000 Allied losses.[3] On September 8, 1943, while the Germans were surrounding Rome and the Italian fleet was steaming to Malta to surrender, the Allies invaded the beaches at Salerno. Overhead, bombers and fighters were engaged in a royal battle for supremacy of the air. The Germans tried four times to throw the Allies back into the sea, and failed largely due to the cooperation of the Army, the Navy, and the Air Force working as a single unit. By September 14, planes of the Allies had flown two thousand sorties, forcing the Germans to retreat toward Naples, and forcing Nazi propaganda chief Joseph Goebbels to change his tune: he'd been trumpeting that the Germans had smashed the beachhead and won the Battle of Salerno.[4]

By October 1, 1943, Naples had fallen, and so had Foggia, with its chain of airfields. From there our bombers would have within their range not only Italy and the Mediterranean, but Africa, southern France and Germany, and Austria and the Balkans. "The land of the Caesars," as historian Francis S. Miller put it, "was now to become one of the bloodiest battlegrounds in all history." It would take twenty months to conquer, and cost Gen. Mark Clark's 5th Army alone 110,000 casualties, with the Germans losing almost half a million men.[5] And it was here that I would be heading in another eight months.

My soloing on October 4 could hardly presage such an eventuality. Given the time, the start of fall 1943, the place, a little cowtown in the middle of Texas, and the circumstances, with seven more months of training to get my wings, then another six to nine months of transition and combat training before being eligible for overseas combat, the possibility looked slim indeed.

Alone in the P-19 open cockpit trainer at last, I was exhilarated by the thought that I was no longer under the heavy thumb of Webb or Roddie or Kuykendall. There were periodic checks and further dual time for advanced maneuvers, including cross-country flights, but I'd be on my own most of the time. Kirk's first check wasn't exactly a stirring commendation. "Curtis, you've still got your head up your ass." He was probably right, but of one thing I was certain. Both parts of that anatomy were getting chilled to the bone, making a hot shower on landing a welcome thaw. Not until October 8 were we finally issued heavy, fleece-lined leather jackets and gloves, as well as long johns.

On the 7th we were told that the last half of our Basic Flight Training would be in AT-6s, the advanced trainers, while the last of our Advanced Flight Training would be in P-40s. The brass was tightening our schedule to get us overseas sooner, since there was a definite shortage of pilots in the European theater.

Alone in the plane at last, I was relaxed and enjoying my

flying as much as I had come to dread it under an instructor. There was a heady time when, flitting in and around the clouds, I'd play follow-the-leader with Barrios and Arnberg. Before I knew it, I had a check ride with the chief check pilot, something I thought sure would give me the shakes. Yet I was more relaxed than I'd been with Kirk—and warmer. I passed—just barely—but I had done it!

Kuykendall had much else to teach me and—glory be—I was beginning to relax even under the barrage of criticism he had in store for me upon landing. And it was the landings—the toughest part of flying—coming in smoothly, or "greasing 'er in"—that eluded me. Trying a series of spot landings, touching down, then giving 'er the gun and going around again, I found myself up to my old tricks. I'd either land too far down the runway, or I'd level off too high and drop like a brick, bouncing up several feet on the first bounce, and gradually less on successive bounces until all three wheels were on the runway. When the landing gear refused to collapse, I figured it was as tough as Kirk himself.

But as tough as it was to land at Curtis Field, it was tougher at auxiliary White Field. For there I had to cut power in the traffic pattern, then land with my wheels touching an orange line marking the start of the supposed runway—a grassy field. Furthermore, I had to perform this feat without either "slipping" to lose altitude, or "gunning" to gain altitude. Eventually I got the hang of it and Kirk was teaching me my first aerobatics, including snap rolls, barrel rolls, and loops. Clumsy as I was, I gradually developed a repertoire of aerobatics that sent my blood racing. It was fortunate that when I tried a five-spin maneuver, and went for seven and a half turns before I could recover, I had started at 6,500 feet.

Learning I was due for a forty-hour check on the 19th, I figured I'd better perform my own check by checking into the hospital on the 16th. I was suffering, I told the doc, from "a cold, a headache, and a general feeling of depressing mental fatigue." That was enough to admit me. As I contemplated my test ride with Lieutenant Martin, I confided to my diary that it would be curtains if I didn't do better than I had the last two days. I'd wash out for sure. And my ground school grades, on fifteen separate subjects, wouldn't begin to help, even after attending deficiency classes for boneheads and sleepyheads. For sleeping in class I was collecting demerits as though they were crown jewels, and marching tours as though I needed the exercise.

With the echo of Kirk's put-downs joined by stinging reprimands from my ground school instructors ringing in my ears, I had no basis for optimism as I climbed into the front seat of the trainer on the 19th. The winds were heavy and my heart was pushing at my throat. But, incredibly, Martin was satisfied. Breathing a huge sigh of relief, I made my way to my quarters, only to find that Harry Davidson, my upper bed bunkmate, had just washed out.

By the 21st I was trying to perfect my aerobatic routine, moving without pausing from one maneuver to the next. My practice was confined to the plains between the low mountains on one side and the Colorado River on the other. I began with a snap roll to the left, then to the right. This was a quick 360-degree roll of the plane, keeping the nose fixed on the horizon. From this I went into a slow roll, the same maneuver but executed more slowly. In the next maneuver, the barrel roll, I took a much larger swath of the sky to roll, with no attention to the horizon. After completing both of these to left and right, I performed a split-S, turning the plane over quickly and heading into a dive. When I reached sufficient speed, I'd pull 'er out and climb back up to complete a loop. That done, I'd split-S again and climb back up as in a loop, except that I'd turn the plane upright at the top of the loop in an Immelman. At this point I'd fall off into a spin, heading for the ground like a seed from a maple tree. I'd recover after a few turns and head for home and the familiar traffic pattern, positioning myself a set distance behind the plane in front of me as I prepared to land. All of this, of course, was supposed to be done smoothly, with the ball on the instrument panel hugging the center—except in the spin, when the plane was no longer under my control, until I recovered. Gradually, ever so gradually, I got the ball to stay closer to the center.

Here was an exhilaration such as I'd never before experienced. I was actually learning to fly that beautiful ship! Even in the frigid temperatures above five thousand feet, and in an open cockpit, I was in seventh heaven as I zipped through and around the white fluff of clouds, mock dogfighting with other pals. And when, in follow-the-leader, it was my turn to lead, I put them through their paces, I figured, with my aerobatic regimen. Before I knew it, I'd racked up fifty of the sixty-five hours I'd need to graduate to Basic.

Then came the weekend of the 23rd and 24th. I awoke Saturday morning with a vise shrinking my head. I had no appetite; only the runs. Checking into the infirmary, I found a dozen others suffering from what the doc diagnosed as ptomaine poisoning. Soon every bed was occupied, requiring others to remain in their barracks. Having eaten my share—and then some—the previous evening, I now had a temperature of 104.5 degrees. Still the chills shook my body, despite my fatigues and a thick wool sweater, So they piled on three wool blankets and turned up the heat. At last the fever broke. By Sunday morning I was feeling better so I headed for the latrine. I bent over a basin to wash my face and almost toppled over in a faint. As I held on to the basin for support, the spots gradually cleared from my eyes. Try as he might, the doc never did find the source of the poisoning, but fortunately we all pulled through.

Later that Sunday I returned to quarters to learn that Ken Doolittle, another Worcesterite, had won honors as the best all-around cadet in 44C. Even more of a coincidence, I dis-

covered that he was the younger brother of my grammar
school principal! I was as certain that I deserved no honors
as I was that Ken was behaving himself both on the ground
and in the air. Neither Ken nor I had any idea that in another
couple months he could well wish he'd never met me.

There could be little doubt that I was not following in
Ken's footsteps when, soloing on a cross-country jaunt, I
found it boring flying straight and level, as was prescribed,
keeping my eyes fixed on the compass to make sure I hit my
destination. So I dropped down, flying closer and closer to
Mother Earth until I was zipping in between the trees, jumping over the bushes, sending cattle running in all directions
as I skimmed over their heads. After all, they ought to have
something better to do than simply stand there, chewing their
cud! This was called hedge-hopping, strictly prohibited. In
fact, flying below five hundred feet, except when taking off
or landing, was not to be done. Yet it was an irresistible high!
My pulse climbed, the roots of my hair tingled, and sweat
oozed down my back. Was it a high because it was forbidden? Partly. But it was also due to the fact that, when I was
skimming the ground and its obstacles, the 110 mph seemed
double that!

In all the excitement I lost track of time or direction, so
when I regained altitude I looked around to find a field and—
sure enough—there it was, but it was auxiliary Snead Field,
a long way from home. I pushed the throttle to the wall and
was soon hitting the top speed of 120 mph. Then off to the
right I spotted Shep Cummings. Back to Brady we raced, and
I beat him only because I dove down to enter the traffic pattern about 25 mph faster than allowed. In all, it had been a
great day! During the remaining fifteen hours Kirk introduced me to "falling leaves," which, as the name implies,
meant the plane moved from side to side as it dropped, but
always under control lest it fall into a spin. But it was when
he turned the plane upside down and kept it there for what

seemed hours that I came in danger of wetting my pants or heaving my breakfast as I hung, suspended, held only by my shoulder harness from falling out of the plane. Yet this too I gradually added to my aerobatic repertoire.

Before I knew it October 28 had arrived and with it an inspection by Major General Brant. I volunteered to be part of an honor guard to greet him officially when he climbed from his Lockheed Lodestar, a big two-engine job, and headed for us. Acknowledging our salutes, he stopped to talk with each of the eight of us. "Cadet," he addressed me, "how many hours of flying time?" I fairly spit it out, "Sixty-one hours, SIR!" The two stars glistening on his shoulder meant this man was to be listened to—and obeyed.

The next day I got in my final four hours and on Saturday, the 30th, we formed by platoons to execute close order drill before our honored guest. He seemed pleased, but learned—even as I did—that of 204 of us who entered Primary Training, only 150 were graduating, a washout rate of over 25 percent. I could only conclude that I may have been dumb, and I may have been a klutz—albeit an intimidated klutz—but for sure I was lucky! Now the question remained, would my luck hold through Basic?

BASIC FLIGHT TRAINING

> "If that damn fool gets out of that plane alive,
> court-martial him!"
>
> —MAJOR GENERAL BRANT to Captain Jackson, CO, Curtis Field

If for a moment I thought my last two months had brought its measure of bonehead mistakes and intimidation, gigs and tours—enough to put me within a shudder of washing out—I soon found I hadn't seen anything yet. Here, amid new resolutions, I joined with the rest of the class in celebrating graduation from Primary, with a grand party at the local country club. Returning to the field, we took turns ringing the bells all night long to wake up the lower class. When they tore out after us, a riot was in the making until the junior officer of the day arrived to broker a peace.

With the cold of fall settling in, and altitudes of ten thousand feet or more, I was grateful we were out of the open cockpits of the PT-19 and into the enclosed cockpits of the BT-13 and the BT-15. The canopied cockpits not only were warm with heaters coming direct from the engine, but also permitted something like rational discourse in place of shouts and hand gestures.

Ken Doolittle now joined our trio of cadets under the continuing tutelage of Tom Kuykendall. Deliberate, steady, responsible, a cadet who knew the rules and obeyed them, Ken was the ideal student to become, as he did, a bomber pilot. As it turned out, neither Fay Clark, Adolph Downing, nor Doolittle would try Kirk's sanity as much as the cadet he'd made the mistake of taking off Roddie's hands. Who could know, Kirk must have figured, maybe this dumb klutz, Curtis, could learn a thing or two from Doolittle.

It all started off so very well. On the first day of Basic, what should arrive from Myrtle but a fine wristwatch. I'd sent her twenty dollars to replace the GI-issued Elgin I'd lost at "Sack." My pulse quickened as I slipped the new "Ready" over my wrist. I was hoping it would make the time fly until, graduating, I'd have time with her during a furlough. After all, her letters had graduated from closing with "As ever" to "Love."

November 12, 1943

Dear Dick,

Gee, would I ever love to visit a flying field like where you're stationed. It must be a beautiful sight to see all those planes in the air. I just love planes, but for now I guess I'll have to be satisfied with what I see in the movies.

Meanwhile, from Bob's wife, Margie, I heard that she'd consulted with a Ouija board at a party, asking it to tell her Bob's whereabouts. He was, said the board, in Denmark as a POW. But, never fear, for she would hear from him in a couple of months, on New Year's Eve, and would see him in four months. To the others at the party Margie promised to throw another party on New Year's Eve to celebrate.

Coming back down to earth, here were two more months ahead, with another sixty-five hours of flying time until I could move to Advanced. Of the two trainers, I liked the BT-13. Equipped with a Pratt-Whitney "Wasp" engine, it had developed a reputation as a "climbing fool." To test this, I took to keeping just above the deck to the end of the runway, then shooting up in a steep climb before making my turn. That is, until the rasping voice of Andy, the tower operator, crackled over the radio. "Curtis, what the hell do you think you're doing! Make your takeoffs as you were instructed or I'll have your ass!" I'd already rattled his nerves by fairly flying on the ground as I taxied to the runway for takeoff. As often as not, there was Kirk standing next to Andy in the control tower, reinforcing his threats.

Now that we were down to basics in our flying, we could remove the grommets from our caps and look more like the raunchy fighter pilots we were pretending to be. But it would take more than removing our grommets to show that we were "HPs"—Hot Pilots. Here, I decided, was the next goal in my fledgling career.

Soon Kirk was teaching me how to "shoot a station." If I got lost, I was to drop down low enough to read the print on a railroad station, in case the name of the town was not there in big, bold print on the local water tower. He also taught me to "drag a field." Again I was to drop down to take a close look in the event I had to make a forced landing. Were there livestock in danger of being butchered by my prop? Were there ditches, hillocks, rocks, or puddles big enough to flip me over, tail over prop, or at least to take out my prop? The key words in both sets of instructions were "drop down." Here was my golden opportunity to buzz the deck.

With this and more under my belt, Andy and Kirk must have thought I had a strange—and dangerous—way of celebrating Armistice Day, November 11. I stopped perpendicular to the runway and checked my "mags" to assure I had full power for takeoff. Then, without looking to my left, I pulled out on the runway just as another plane was coming in to land. It missed me, but by inches. I shuddered to think of another cadet who'd done the same thing and was decapitated by the incoming plane. Andy must have thought I'd lost *my* head. "Curtis, what the hell are you trying to do? Kill yourself? And others?" There was never any beating around the bush with Andy. He knew our lives depended on our following explicit instructions. Next to Andy I made out Kirk, waving his arms in disgust.

By November 16 it should have been as plain as the pimples blossoming on my face that I still had my head, but it was "up and locked." I forgot to set my altimeter to the elevation of the field so that I landed 150 feet below sea level! Then, performing a slow roll, I heard the distressing crash of my mike falling off its hook and hitting the floor. To top it off, I came within a whisker of the 230 mph red line on my airspeed indicator, meaning that the plane's manufacturer would take no responsibility if the plane's wings came off in a dive exceeding 230 mph. I was not alone in my problems. Another cadet was in the middle of a spin when his joystick pulled out of its socket. Quickly he lifted it up to show his instructor in the rear seat. He then recovered. Had the cadet been alone, his only hope would have been to "hit the silk."

Thanksgiving came and with it my thanks for continuing good luck. The following Sunday it was obvious Kirk was not giving thanks for this klutz of a cadet. Bad enough he had to fly on the day he planned to spend with his family.

So he was in no mood to tolerate my clumsy attempts at aerobatics. "Well, Curtis, you managed to screw up your lazy-eights and chandelles to beat all hell!" His put-downs reminded me of nobody as much as Charlie Rich, who'd come to master that dubious art in my presence. Rich had been wrong about my being chosen for pilot training. Would Kirk be wrong about my ever becoming a fighter pilot? I began to wonder if I'd make it out of training, much less combat, alive and in one piece.

I scrounged what comfort I could from the screwups of my classmates. One cadet, hedge-hopping, hit a treetop, puncturing his wing and severing the strut anchoring his landing gear. But he kept mum about it, so the next flier found the plane vibrating so violently that he thought it would disintegrate before he could land it safely. Five other cadets managed to get lost on a cross-country trip to Wichita Falls. When only four returned, they explained that one had bailed out, leaving us another plane short. Then, just before Christmas, Jim Coan, a buddy, crashed on takeoff when his engine sputtered and died. Luckily, neither he nor his instructor was hurt. Their shoulder harnesses saved them. Then I learned that every previous class had one of their number killed when they attempted a cross-country on Sunday. And here we were scheduled for a cross-country the next day—Sunday. Would we break the jinx? There was a collective sigh of relief when all returned at the end of the day.

There were other records some of us were achieving. Within two weeks of starting Basic I'd managed to rack up fifty-five demerits, worth eleven hours of tours. If I wasn't late for mess formation, I was late from—or sleeping in—from calisthenics. If I wasn't being racked back for sleeping in class, I was getting it for playing my harmonica during study hours. Everywhere I turned, there was Lieutenant Plehal, pen at the ready with his gig sheet, even when I was marching tours. One night three of us decided that catching up on our sleep was more important than simply marching back and forth endlessly. So while two of us slept, the third kept watch, only to find Plehal had outsmarted us. He seemed to take sadistic delight in adding even more tours to our collections.

December 6, 1943

Dear Dick,
Be good now and keep 'em flying! Love and Lollypops,
Myrt.

It was obvious by now that Myrt had little idea of how hard it was for me to "be good." To maintain my reputation as an equal-opportunity screwup, I also collected demerits in the air. Was there a rule against spinning solo? I tried it—repeatedly. Was there a rule against lowering flaps above 140 mph? I did it, forgetting the flaps were down after dragging an auxiliary field. Was there a rule against landing on the left runway from the right-hand traffic pattern? I tried that too, leaving Andy and Kirk sputtering. The clouds were darkening even as Christmas approached. So desperate had I become that I asked my three flight-mates to chip in for a silver crash bracelet for Kirk. They did, and come the day we presented him with it, engraved with his name, to fanfare. Did it mellow irascible Kirk? For a day or so.

Christmas came, with all its festivities, turkey and the fixin's, a dance, and letters and gifts from home—especially from Myrtle.

By this time I'd learned that of forty men in our flight only six had applied for single-engine in their advanced training. Maybe one reason for that was the close calls we were having. One fellow in my flight, performing maneuvers for his instructor, forgot to switch gas tanks until the engine began to sputter. Quickly he turned the switch, without realizing his instructor had already done it, in effect turning the gas off again, so the engine again was sputtering, threatening to quit completely. What to do? Instantly the cadet jumped on his wobble pump, an emergency pump to be used by hand when the other failed. He was pumping, as I recounted it to Myrt, "like a madman, not knowing—in the dark—that it was registering 'off.' " Finally, as he saw the earth rushing toward him, he decided to hit the silk. In a panic, he yelled on the interphone to his instructor, "I'm getting the hell out of here! You comin' with me?!" Thereupon his instructor calmed him down and remedied the situation.

The following Sunday, Kirk decided to give me a gift in the form of an introduction to his family—as only Kirk could do it. Some distance from the field was a white farmhouse. But rather than simply point or tell me this was his home, he did a split-S from five thousand feet and dove down directly at his farmhouse. At the very last moment he straightened 'er out and slipped beneath the utility lines along the road fronting his house. Then, roaring back up, he executed as beautiful a chandelle as I'd seen. This brought the family rushing from the house to wave. In case I missed it the first time, he did it again. The blood rushed to my head as I gasped at this daring maneuver. A couple feet higher or lower and it would have been curtains.

Here was a new adrenaline high! This was more like it! The boredom of hours in a Link Trainer, the tedium of flying by the book on cross-country runs, the repetitive spot landings and takeoffs—all of this was nothing, now that I'd reached this new level of excitement.

That afternoon couldn't come soon enough. I was out on a solo flight, and Kirk unwittingly had flung down the gauntlet. Could I do less than follow this intrepid leader? To warm up I dropped to the deck for some hedge-hopping, dodging the trees and skimming the fields. Then, spotting utility lines along a country road, I climbed to five thousand feet, turned over in a split-S and dove down, slipping just beneath those wires and roaring back up, then straightening out in a chandelle. It was far from Kirk's deft maneuver, but it sent the blood surging! Then who should I see but the plane of a pal, "Coon Dog" Collier. Soon we were rat-racing and mock dogfighting as each of us tried to put the other in his gunsights. We landed in high spirits, convinced that it was fighters, not bombers, that were our Holy Grail.

Two days later I decided my maneuvers deserved another try. As I hopped the hedges I suddenly spied a flock of sheep grazing peacefully—too peacefully. Certainly they would thank me for sharing my excitement! So I climbed, then roared down on them and chuckled as they scattered in all directions. That was enough fun to warrant a second try. Except that this time the sheep farmer was at the door with a shotgun, determined to rid his sheep of this nuisance. The sheep scattered, the shotgun fired, and I decided it was time to take my leave and look for other "targets of opportunity."

Within minutes I'd crossed the lazy San Saba River, meandering through the countryside, flanked by poplars on either side. What better test of my piloting skills than to drop down and skim the water, flying between the rows of trees with each twist and turn of the river? And when the trees almost touched each other where the river narrowed, I flew beneath their outstretched branches, picking up a few leaves in the bargain. There was no doubt about it—flying was becoming a part of my bloodstream!

Then it happened. The sound of a pistol shot close to my ears shocked me. Something had hit the plane—and hard! In an instant I was up and retracing my path to make out what was lurking there to do me in. Nothing. So, calling to mind the cadet who'd damaged his plane and said nothing of it, I climbed to five thousand feet and put the BT-13 through its paces in my aerobatic regimen. No sign of a problem, so I made for the field with a sigh of relief. As I climbed from the cockpit something unusual on my right wing caught my eye.

A hasty examination uncovered what looked like telephone wire extending from the leading edge to the trailing edge of the wing. So that was what I'd hit! But my aerobatics showed it hadn't hurt the plane. I quickly removed the quarter-inch wire, rolled it up, and shoved it into the big knee pocket of my flying togs.

As I headed for my quarters, I began to shake. Supposing I'd flown just inches above where my prop had clipped that wire? Would it have flipped me over when it hit my landing gear? The thought was so unnerving that, unheard of for me, I couldn't eat my supper. As the possibilities weighed in on me, I slept only fitfully. Would I be found out? Would I be court-martialed and drummed out of pilot training? Would I end up killing myself as others had done in training?

In the next day or so Kirk introduced me to instrument flying and formation flying. In the first I'd pull a black hood down over my head so I couldn't see out. Dead reckoning was out of the question, even as it was when flying in an overcast, or sometimes at night. I was learning to rely 100 percent on my instruments. When it came to formation flying it was a challenge to snuggle inside each other's wings, so close as to be able—almost—to detect the color of the other pilot's eyes. When Kirk parceled out a compliment I was luxuriating. I was beginning to think I had it made.

Far from it. Reality set in when Delmer Miller, civilian director of flying, ordered all 150 cadets of 44C to meet in the rec hall. He was not a happy man. Who, he demanded to know, was doing all this hedge-hopping? I looked around. No other hands were going up. None were standing. I dared not look at him, thinking he was drawing a bead on me. At last, seeing that not one of the others was going to purge his guilt through confession, I slowly unwound myself from my chair and stood. Would others follow suit? No such luck.

Miller's voice was a rasp on my ears. "Yes, Curtis, we knew it was you."

How on earth, I asked myself, could they have known? I'd not even shown the coil of wire to my closest buddies.

As if sensing my bewilderment, Miller explained, for all to hear. "You see, Curtis, a sheep farmer copied down the number of your plane, 305, and phoned it in. All we had to do was find out who was scheduled to fly that plane at that time."

Was that the end of it? Fat chance! As other cadets were heaving sighs of relief, Miller continued. "We have reason to believe that not only did you mess with those sheep, but you cut through four telephone wires, knocking out service in the county on both sides of the San Saba River. Is that true?"

I nodded my head as I bleated out a faint "Yes, sir."

With this culprit hanging his head and pale from considering the consequences of breaking virtually every rule in the book, Miller dismissed the rest of the cadets, who were only too eager to vacate the confessional. He then led me to a small room, handed me a pad of yellow paper and a pencil. "Write. I want to know everything you did and just why you did it."

I was a dishrag, with the sweat being wrung from me, as I took my seat and racked my feverish brain. I was so desperate that I actually bowed my head in a pleading prayer of intercession. If there was indeed a God, this was the time for him to come to my rescue. In fact, I would be a Ken Doolittle the rest of my time there, the straight and narrow my determined course. Then I began to write. I had little problem describing *what* I'd done. It was all too fresh in my memory. But when it came to *why,* I drew a blank. What could possibly justify my antics? Slowly the words appeared on paper. I had no excuse. I knew the rules and had deliberately violated them. But I was desperate to fly, especially now that I was convinced Bob had been killed in action. I had a score to settle with those Germans. If I couldn't get the pilot of that FW 190 in my sights, I'd take out as many of the other Luftwaffe pilots as I could. I couldn't get overseas fast enough. Then I concluded my mea culpa, "With utmost regret," handed the pad to Miller and disappeared into the anonymous night to ponder my fate before returning, at last, to my barracks.

Soon the word was leaking out. I was being put on strict probation. Any more funny business and a court-martial was a certainty. Now, under those circumstances, it would appear that the prudent man would guard his steps scrupulously. Alack and alas, prudence had rarely slept at my door. So, with this sword of Damocles hanging over my head, I found myself on the last day of 1943, about to celebrate the new year the only way I could find fitting.

It seemed that Mr. Prudence himself, Ken Doolittle, was joining me on an instrument cross-country jaunt. I'd be under the hood on the way to Harpersville, and Ken on the way back. All was going well as we pulled within view of Curtis Field. I notified Ken he could release his hood, and I'd take 'er in. But first I wanted to familiarize him with my aerobatic routine. A snap roll became a slow roll became a barrel roll became a loop became a chandelle. With that I did a split-S and threw 'er into a three-turn spin, recovering just in time to enter the traffic pattern. But my speed was such that I passed a few laggards preparing to land. I landed, taxied, and as I pulled into my parking space, the airwaves were split by the sound of Andy's voice.

"Curtis, get your ass up here—immediately! On the double!"

What, I asked myself and Ken, could be the trouble now? Slowly, painstakingly, I climbed the steps to the tower operator, passing instructors on the steps looking at me in astonishment. Something was amiss. Then I was face to face with a red-faced Andy, flanked by Miller and Kuykendall—all in a high dudgeon.

"Curtis, you dumb son of a bitch, do you have any idea what you've done?!"

Andy was never reticent when it came to screwups. I shook my lowered head, fearing the worst.

"Well, for starters, you were doing aerobatics not only below five thousand feet but directly over the field!"

I gulped. "Oh, was I?"

"You know damn well you were. And how many others did you pass in the traffic pattern?"

I glanced up to see Andy's mustache twitching dangerously below his blazing eyes. He was just winding up.

"By the way, did you notice that Lockheed Lodestar waiting to take off when you were landing?"

I hadn't. Should I have?

"Do you know who was in that Lodestar, watching you spin down over the field?"

I didn't know for sure, but I had a hunch. Still, I shook my lowered head.

"It was Major General Brant, just leaving after inspecting the field. And what do you suppose was his order as he looked up and saw you spinning down above him, then passing plane after plane in the traffic pattern?"

I hated to think.

"Now, Curtis, listen closely." Andy's nose was almost touching my slunken head. "These are his exact words. 'If that damn fool gets out of that plane alive, court-martial him!'"

The general's rage was infectious. First Andy, then Miller, and finally Kuykendall got in their licks. My instructor made no bones about it. "Curtis, you dumb ass, you've screwed up for the last time. It's curtains for you."

That was it. There was no getting around it now. Even a two-star general's *wish* was a command for his underlings. As I descended the tower steps, one by one, on each step was an instructor hurling invective in my wake. Each apparently found it incredible that I would violate my strict probation by bearding nothing less than the inspecting general in his lair.

Here it was the last day of 1943, and bound to be the last

day of my training as a pilot. There was no doubt about it. A court-martial was inevitable. I'd be washed out for sure. Maybe I'd be transferred to the infantry. How could I break it to my family? To my friends? Especially, to Myrt?

That night at the New Year's dance I might as well have been dancing with myself, rather than another standout from the Lone Star State, but my thoughts were elsewhere. As I circulated my graduation book the next day, other cadets were jotting down, next to my picture, "To the H.P. of 44C" or some such, helping to boost my spirits. I'd apparently reached my goal of being a "Hot Pilot" in the eyes of some, but as far as the brass was concerned, those letters seemed to mean "Hopeless Pilot."

Every day, on the hour it seemed, I was scanning the bulletin board to learn my fate. Finally I saw my name. My heart almost stopped as my eyes raced to my punishment. I was to walk twenty-five tours for "the incidents of the past week." I couldn't believe my eyes. I read it again. And again. Could this be the sum and substance of my punishment?

Never did I walk tours more conscientiously, more sprightly. I'd have walked 250 tours if necessary. Even Plehal must have been surprised to see me, eager and alert, shoulders back and eyes glistening, as this former goldbrick marched as though his life depended on it. Marching hour after hour gave me time to contemplate not only my astounding good luck but to double my resolve to out-prudence Mr. Prudence himself. The improbability of my good luck marched with me. How on earth could it have happened, when the order for my court-martial had come straight from the lips of an enraged inspecting general?

Come to find out, the truth lay mostly in my having some real pals. For Harlan "Red" Crowder and Tom Crull, my flying buddies with Roddie, learning of my predicament, circulated a petition, signed by every cadet in both 44C and 44D, asking for leniency. Furthermore, the petition explained, not a single cadet from 44C had washed out in Basic. Why ruin such a record? Whatever their reasons for signing, I was grateful beyond words. One of the reasons may well have been that, the same evening the petition was circulating, other cadets, undoubtedly taking a hint from me, were buzzing Brady at rooftop level as well as the highway leading to the POW camp nearby. This they also buzzed, prompting the guards to turn the searchlights on them. When General Brant learned of this he immediately called Captain Jackson and read the riot act to him.

Now, however, with Miller's backing, as well as the CO's, I'd escaped that sword of Damocles—a court-martial "with prejudice," meaning I would never fly again—by scarcely a hair on my empty head. Then came more good news to lift me from what so recently had been Pilgrim's "slough of despond." Jackson called a meeting of the 44C class to announce we'd be heading for Advanced Flight Training within a week. My diary told it all. "What a swell day! Man, I could kiss a pig!" And that wasn't the end of the good news. In addition to a "lovingly" letter from Myrt, I was asked by Jackson to give a report, on January 4, on the progress of the war to the rest of the class. And why did the CO pick me? Was it because I'd been discussing the war with his secretary, Cora Belle? Ever since Bob's MIA status, I'd paid close attention to the war's progress, if not to my studies.

So I made my report, taking special pains to highlight the place of pilots and their crews. The eyes of the audience glistened as I told them of the P-39 Airacobra and the P-40 Warhawk being replaced by the new, hot P-51 Mustang, extending the range our bombers could count on with fighter escort far up into Germany. Navy pilots were also scoring well. In the South Pacific eight hundred carrier planes had gained mastery of the air in the amphibious landings on Makin and Tarawa, providing cover for the landing forces that waded ashore on November 20. In just four days the

Gilbert Islands had been retaken, and on December 1 MacArthur's land-based planes of the Army Air Corps started to prepare for similar landings on New Britain's western shore.[6]

In Italy, the main part of the "soft under-belly" of Europe, P-51s were being equipped with bomb racks beneath their wings as well as braking flaps and rechristened A-36s, attack dive bombers. They would provide air support for ground troops slugging it out with the Germans entrenched in the Appenines. On December 27 our commander of all Allied troops in Europe, Gen. Dwight "Ike" Eisenhower, delivered his farewell address to Allied troops in the Mediterranean. He pledged, "United we shall meet again in the heart of the enemy's continental stronghold." Then he closed with, "God-speed and good luck to each of you along with the assurance of my lasting gratitude and admiration." It appeared that Ike also knew something of the place of luck in war.

Whether at Anzio, as the Allies moved east and north toward Cassino, or at Naples, as they moved north, the Army Air Corps was playing a vital part. No longer was Goering's Luftwaffe holding supremacy of the air. This was bound to make the difference between victory and defeat in Italy. And this was the gist of the report to my fellow cadets. Jackson seemed to be satisfied. Was he wondering why I couldn't be just as knowledgeable about the simple rules of Curtis Field? It wasn't that I didn't know them. Knowing them so very well, my knowledge seemed to breed contempt, for it seemed I was always pushing out the envelope, stretching just how far those rules might bend.

As 1944 arrived I concluded that things were looking up for this nation at war as well as for this cadet who seemed ever at war with certain rules. Things looked even brighter when I passed my instrument check with Lieutenant Wyss. I had ten more hours of tours to march when I found I'd be leaving for Advanced Training at Victoria, Texas, on January 7. With but a day to pack and prepare to load the buses, I wondered if I'd be marching all night to fill my quota of tours. Again a delightful surprise. The remaining tours had been canceled!

I could scarcely take in my good fortune. For all the turmoil I'd caused. For all the blood pressure I'd raised. For all the lives I'd put at risk, including my own. For all the reprimands I'd brought down on my head, including the major general's explicit command that I be court-martialed. For all this and more I'd scraped by with but fifteen tours!

As I left the bus at the station I was breathing sweet air indeed. Behind me lay Curtis Field, now fully baptized by this prize klutz of a maverick of the same name. Ahead lay Aloe Field and the last of my stateside training. And it was to be in single-engine fighters! Where Ken, Al, and George and so many others were headed for bomber training, I was on my way—I dared hope—to flying not only fighters but the queen of them all, the P-51 Mustang.

If there was anything by this time obvious to the brass, it must have been that this flier had better be alone in his plane. No crew would want to be dependent on me for their lives in battle. Had I been a German cadet, I later discovered, and screwed up as I had, I'd have been court-martialed and, if found guilty, executed on the spot! I could thank my lucky stars I'd been an American cadet.[7]

3

GOLD BARS AND
SILVER WINGS

"Lieutenant, you're just the man we've been looking for!"
—COLONEL CONARD, Commanding Officer, Aloe Field, Victoria, Texas

ADVANCED FLIGHT TRAINING

It was Friday, January 7, 1944, and the train was an hour late pulling into Brady. There were four of us, just hanging around the station, when who should happen by but a gal we recognized from a dance on base. Hop in, she suggested, and with two of her female friends we were soon feeding the nickelodeon at the local country club, jitterbugging to Glenn Miller's "In the Mood" and other timely tunes. Back to the station and we were soon headed for Brownwood, arriving too late for our connection to Temple.

Bedraggled and exhausted by 0400 hours, we finally boarded the next train and a few winks in a Pullman car. A heavy sleeper, I didn't awaken until the others were off to the city. Awake and alone, I moseyed off to find breakfast and was just finishing it when I heard the train whistle. I plopped down some money, bolted for the door, and hightailed it down the street to the station, arriving just in time to see the caboose receding in the distance. Gone, too, was my cap, in which I'd stored directions and introductions.

What a pickle! I checked into the bus station, borrowed three bucks from the smiling Red Cross lady who could be anybody's mother, and finally pulled into Victoria at 2000 hours. I was still five miles from Aloe Field with just thirty cents for a cab. To my rescue came Fay Clark, a buddy from Brady, driving a GI truck to pick up some other Brady buddies who'd gotten soused en route.

I awoke the next morning to a truly beautiful sight, row upon row of AT-6 Texans and P-40 Warhawks glistening in the sun. I was heading for the big time! For it had been the P-40 that had been the mainstay of Claire Chennault's famous "Flying Tigers" of southeast Asia. My checking in twelve hours late was no problem because a blizzard in the Panhandle had held up cadets from other fields. When everybody arrived, there was no shortage of cadets, but such a shortage of officer-instructors that ten of us were assigned to Lieutenant Reichle. After an introductory walk around the Texan, he emphasized the new features of this advanced trainer and explained the starting procedure. We then lined up for flight togs, heavy sweaters, helmets and goggles, along with chutes, E6B computers, and slide scales. And, of course, an armful of books for ground school.

Closer than Brady to the Gulf of Mexico by several hundred miles, in Victoria there would be no blizzards, only a rainy season of endless, low-flying scud clouds carrying their moisture inland to thwart our getting in our sixty-five hours of flying time. While at Basic we had gloated that Curtis Field was one of only three such civilian flight schools in the country. Not only were our instructors civilians, but we had better chow, no KP, and janitors to clean the barracks. Furthermore, the discipline was more lax and open posts more frequent. Now, at Advanced, it would be more rigorous. After graduation, we were told, 40 percent of the class would be selected to go to Matagorda Island in the Gulf for four weeks of actual gunnery training. The synthetic training we would have would provide the competition that would lead to the selection. Those not selected would be transferred to a bomber pilot operational unit, or to cargo or reconnaissance units, or to towing targets or serving as instructors. But first there would be a ten-day leave.

There was much to occupy our time: lectures and homework, skeet shooting and simulated instrument time in Link Trainers. I'd come to Advanced armed with a dozen New Year's resolutions, all intended to make me the very model of deportment. But when it came to technical lectures, there I was, dozing off. Treated, however, to "Officer Transition," I was all ears, scurrying over to the PX and ordering my officer's uniform. Again there was that fateful gap between the persona I dared to project and the private person my record was exposing. By January 15 I'd checked into the infirmary, where I promptly fell asleep with the thermometer in my mouth.

Scheduled at last to fly on the 18th, I was expected to wait at the flight line for my turn. But waiting has never been my strong suit. Soon I was at the gym, working out on a punching bag, confident I'd be back in time. I got there twenty minutes early, just to be on the safe side, only to find Reichle steaming. One of the cadets didn't show, so here my instructor had been waiting three quarters of an hour for me. He was still muttering after he'd racked me back and we were airborne. One maneuver after another I executed, the ball dancing from one side to the other on the instrument panel. By the time I tried landing with this new retractable landing gear, I'd screwed up enough to earn ten demerits. I was off to a fine start!

To add to my consternation, I got letters from home on January 21 but none from Myrt. In fact, three weeks had passed and nothing from her. Worse, the letters from the folks bore the news that Bob's status had changed from MIA to KIA. Margie was now officially a widow. That evening I took to my diary to vent my grief and a cry for vengeance. "I just live for the day I can get some Nazis lined up in my

sights in a P-51. They kill off swell guys like Bob and leave
4Fs back home to raise hell!" This, of course, was unfair on
three counts. Few in the German armed forces were members of the Nazi party—the main reason that the SS had in-
filtrated the ranks, to weed out any hint of subversion. In
addition, it was unfair to many who'd been rejected when
they tried enlisting, like some of my friends back in Worcester. Finally, it presumed that those who were rejected were
raising hell, when most of them were at work in college or
in the defense industry. In any case, this was not the kind
of news to help me celebrate my twentieth birthday the next
day.

I may have been a year older, but apparently not much
wiser. My resolutions were evaporating like the morning fog
with the rise of the sun. If the g's in my 300 mph loop re-
coveries weren't blacking me out, then Captain Paas was
chewing me out for hedge-hopping. My perfectly reasonable
explanation that, being uncertain as to my location, I'd simply dropped down to "shoot a station," fell on deaf ears. Did
he think for a moment that, bored by straight and level cross-
country runs, I'd dropped down for some excitement? As it
was, I had to fly at five hundred feet to stay below the scud
clouds and return at seventeen thousand feet, requiring oxygen. Back at the field, to top it off, I'd not filled out my cross-
country grade slip properly, probably because I was either
talking or sleeping when I should have been listening. So
Paas added three more demerits to my growing collection.

By the end of the month it was painfully evident that
neither my ground school nor my flying was anything to
write home about. And when I did venture it, it had to be the
product of a very selective memory. Still leveling off and
dropping to bounce on the concrete runway, I added to my
problems by ground looping—running off the runway and
turning in a circle. I did scavenge some comfort—cold comfort—from the screwups of others. On February 18 several

of us were taking off in formation and, in the lingering ground fog, lost sight of our leader, Lieutenant Shipley, and just missed colliding with another formation taking off. Another formation landed at Ellington Field instead of the municipal airport and returned to the wrath of the brass. One cadet, three planes behind me in the traffic pattern, crashed on landing, shearing off his wings as well as his undercarriage and prop. Luckily the fuselage remained intact, with him safely buckled up inside.

Not so lucky were the two cadets who, flying dual among twelve of us headed for gunnery practice on Matagorda Island in the Gulf, suddenly disappeared. For some unknown reason they'd fallen into a spin, were unable to recover, and crashed and burned. One of them, "Monk" Wieneke, slept in the bed next to mine. I'd tried to paint his gal once from a photo he'd lent me. Fortunately I was not the one who had to notify her or his parents that he'd been killed on a training mission.

There were the good times, too, when it appeared I was shedding my reputation as the crown klutz of the outfit. It helped when a fighter pilot was flown in from North Africa. An ace with five or more kills to his credit, he sported a chestful of ribbons, including the Distinguished Flying Cross, the highest award given to fliers only. As he related his exploits he raised our hopes as well as our eyebrows. Then there was the day Lieutenant Reichle led two of us, one on each wing in tight formation, through a series of aerobatics, then dropping to the deck for some hairy hedge-hopping.

Reichle reminded me of Kuykendall, who'd introduced me to hedge-hopping back at Brady. Thinking he'd written me off as a bad apple if not an incorrigible klutz, I was tickled to get a letter from him, actually wishing me well! Then there was the moment I savored when my instructor went so far as to commend me for a successful rendezvous with him after a cross-country run, hitting time and place "right on the nose."

Such commendation was a precious rarity as well as a counterweight to the demerits I seemed bent on collecting. If it wasn't for dozing off in class, it was for not wearing my dog tags at inspection. If it wasn't for being late for chow, it was for trying to sneak past the tactical officer. Not content to rack up demerits, I found myself more forgetful than ever, locking my keys inside my locker, then borrowing a hacksaw to retrieve them, or losing my canvas bag with my ground school supplies.

It was obvious that my mind was on something other than the business at hand. No less than five weeks had gone by without a word from Myrt. What had I done? What had I written? Had she taken a cue from my instructors and written me off as a chronic loser? At last, on February 9, I got a four-pager from her, telling of the sudden death of her father, just fifty-three. This left her the sole support of her mother and two sisters at a time when Social Security was a pittance.

February 5, 1944

Dear Dick,

I'm thinking of you, your family, and Marjorie. Your hours of anxiety during these months have not been easy. Your mother has been an inspiration—always a smile and never a complaint. Boy, my heart jumped in my throat when I read of your narrow escape during your last few days at Curtis Field.

As sorry as I was about Myrt's family tragedy, I was relieved to know she hadn't ditched me. I answered her letter by asking her to keep her days as free as possible, "so I can get to know my favorite correspondent better—much better. Can do?"

On March 3, I witnessed a spectacular crash. The cadet lost control on landing and made a sharp ground loop to the left. He skidded on one wing at a 60-degree angle over the field, becoming airborne before stalling and flopping back. He managed to knock out his undercarriage, prop, and part of a wing, yet emerged unscathed.

Had I been collecting flying hours as diligently as I'd been collecting demerits and tours, I'd have had no worries about graduating with my class. Had I been catching up on my sleep over the weekends rather than checking into the infirmary during the week, I'd have accumulated at least forty hours of flying time by March 5. But on that sorry day, just ten days before graduation, nine of us were notified by Major Gerrard that, with less than forty hours, we'd be held over to graduate with 44D, the middle of April. This was the same major that I'd groused about to Myrt ten days earlier: "He is the most ornery cuss you could ever lay eyes on—in fact, we'd like to lay more than our eyes on him!"

What took some of the edge off was the news that I'd be graduating as a second lieutenant rather than as a flight officer. Corresponding to a warrant officer in the regular Army, the latter rank was given, ironically enough, to both Crowder and Crull, the two buddies who'd saved my neck at Brady.

The next day I joined four others in protesting this delay to the major. He blamed it on the weather and expressed his "deepest sorrow" that we'd have to wait another month. Here I'd already bought my fancy uniforms, plus gold bars and silver wings to give to Myrt. Now, I fumed, they'd be getting tarnished while I cooled my heels. But, in all truth, I was the least of the nine with anything to complain about. Apart from my frequent trips to the infirmary, just a glance at my demerit sheet should have offset any gripe I nursed. I should have thanked my lucky stars that I'd even made it, skin intact, to Advanced. Furthermore, none of the other eight cadets were in my leaky boat, with but thirty-four of the sixty-five hours required. Worse, nine of the thirty-four I'd gotten in on the last day of February.

For the next ten days, while 44C graduates concentrated

on getting their sixty-five, we nine found some consolation in being excused from reveille, formations, and inspections. At long last, too, I was able to catch up on my sleep. Could it be that the reason I ate more than the others was the same reason I required more sleep than they? Finally, on March 16, I was back in the air, enjoying gunnery practice, formation flying, and especially polishing my aerobatic regimen, always making certain I was far from the field lest General Brant visit here and see me again descending on him in a spin. And, as tough as it was, I resisted the temptation to hedge-hop. Miraculously, I even found myself on the receiving end of several commendations!

What made me toe the line as much as anything else was the sobering experience I had toward the end of March. In the midst of reading Wendell Willkie's *One World,* I was startled by the sound of a plane crashing nearby. Racing outside, I saw a plume of black smoke rising from the end of a runway. I jumped into a passing jeep and was soon helping to extract the instructor from the rear seat, onto a stretcher, and to a waiting ambulance. As blood streamed from him I thought he'd broken every bone in his body. As it was, his skull was fractured, as were his ribs and an arm, apart from massive internal injuries. The attending flight surgeon didn't hold out much hope for him. The cadet in the front seat was killed on impact. What had happened? The cadet had climbed too steeply on takeoff—shades of Andy back at Curtis Field, racking me back for doing just this! The AT-6 had stalled, then fallen off on a wing into the beginning of a spin when it hit the ground. That evening I checked to find the instructor still holding on. But the next morning, almost twenty-four hours after the crash, he died, leaving a widow two months' pregnant. If that didn't sober me up, nothing would.

By April 14, I had my sixty-five hours and had received a letter from Ken Doolittle, now piloting a twin-engine bomber. Though I envied him graduating with 44C, I was tickled that I'd be in fighters and not bombers—or worse, the Air Transport Command. But the next day I wondered if I'd be flying anything.

It started out so well. For almost an hour our class stood at ramrod attention while three P-40s took off in formation, skimming the runway to the end, then banking up sharply to the left. Gaining altitude, they suddenly executed a split-S and came screaming down toward us, passing just twenty feet above the runway. The hair on my head bristled and my back tingled. Then our CO, Colonel Conard, swore us in as commissioned officers and presented each of us with bars and wings. He may not have seen Lady Luck as he pinned my wings above my jacket pocket, but I was certain she was perched on my shoulder.

Dismissed, I made for the bulletin board to learn of my assignment, only to be stopped by an enlisted man saluting me with one hand, and holding out the other for the customary dollar that tradition dictated I award the first man to salute me on receiving my commission. I was happy to fork over my buck, but increasingly unhappy as I scanned the lists, in vain. At last, down in a remote corner of a page, I made out my name among a half-dozen others. We were being assigned to the field "pending further assignment."

I was discouraged but curious, so sought out the CO. "Sir," I said as I saluted, "I see that I've been assigned to this field pending further assignment. I don't know what you have in mind for me, but since my brother was killed in action as a navigator on a B-17 I've been itching to get overseas and pay back those Jerries."

"Lieutenant," replied the good colonel as he fixed his eyes on this volunteer, "you're *just* the man we've been looking for. We will send you overseas immediately. Come back Monday morning and pick up your orders."

I couldn't believe my ears. Though it looked as if there'd

be no furlough and I'd miss seeing the folks and Myrt, this was a lucky break! As I shared my good news with the other eight holdovers, I wondered what was to happen to the other five who'd been assigned to the field. Monday I reported bright and early to Major Gasseway at headquarters to learn that I'd be joining four others who'd be heading overseas without so much as a leave, much less the further six to nine months of transitional and combat training the rest of the class had in store for them. George Isaac and Roy Smith were brand-new officers like myself. The other two had already been commissioned and been transferred to the Air Corps. Joe Hawk was a first lieutenant and Bill Pleasant a second. Both were older than the three others of us by three or four years, and married, with families.

As we introduced ourselves, I liked to think we were a select group. This was April 17, and our orders had us reporting on the 25th to Greensboro, North Carolina, for preparation to embark overseas. Here we were getting a jump—a big jump—on the rest of 44D as well as 44C. I was tickled with my good fortune in drawing the best of the assignments, but couldn't help a stray thought that this might not turn out for the best. After all, the Air Corps was shortcutting the lengthy training it had long regarded as necessary for combat. Would this, in turn, cut short our lives?

I POP THE QUESTION

The next day the five of us headed out to the shooting range to practice on the rifle, the machine gun, and the Colt .45s we'd be issued, along with sleeping bags, steel helmets, and tents. That evening I wrote the folks and Myrt, telling them a furlough was out—bad news especially for the folks, still grieving over the loss of Bob. Yet even with this lingering tragedy, I was sensing that Dame Fortune was on my side. To celebrate our luck, we bachelors took off for Houston by bus and shared an $8.50 room at the Rice Hotel. With no furlough in the offing, we just had to kick up our heels. And there, as if waiting for us, were three Texas lovelies to help us celebrate in style. Though I didn't imbibe, I did cough up my share for the champagne, at $16 the bottle. We danced away the evening, took the gals home in a taxi, and hit the hay at 0300 hours, satisfied that we'd celebrated, if only for a single day.

Returning to Victoria, we found our celebration premature. Officially we were AWOL, a court-martial offense. What a way for newly minted officers to start off! But the assistant adjutant took a look at our orders and let us off with a reprimand. It was only then that we discovered that we'd forfeited a day of leave. For the brass had a change of heart and decided we should have a brief leave before arriving at Greensboro. Twice in my cadet days I'd courted a court-martial. And now as an officer the threat was pursuing me. Had we not been heading directly overseas, it might well have ended my commissioned career aborning. Here I'd squandered a day's leave, with the folks and Myrt a couple thousand miles to the northeast. Had I sought permission to leave for Houston, I'd undoubtedly have been told of the change in plans. It appeared I was still a member in good standing of that fraternity whose motto was, "Better to ask forgiveness than permission."

I mailed my gear to Greensboro, borrowed $100 from the Red Cross, and took the bus back to Houston to meet George. Soon we were bound via Braniff for St. Louis, where we spent the night because heavy thunderstorms prevented the next leg of our journey, to Chicago. The weather was no better the next day, so we boarded the club car train, "Buttermilk Falls," for Cleveland and points east. They called them sleepers, but having to share a bottom bunk with George netted neither of us much sleep. Still, he was such a good sport that he lent me $10 to make sure I'd make it to Worcester.

At last the train pulled into Union Station and I was sitting beside Mom at worship, surprised, with tears, that I should be there. Before Sunday dinner, always a big deal in the Curtis household, I rang up Myrt to tell her I'd be seeing her within the hour. Big mistake, for we were soon neck-deep in heavy conversation centering on Bob, since Margie had joined us. At last I broke away and was climbing the steps at 97 Calumet Avenue, my heart thumping at the prospect of taking Myrt in my arms. And there she was, descending the walk, wreathed in as fetching a smile as I'd ever seen, punctuated at each end with a lovely dimple. I was smitten! Even though I was late by an hour, she showed no hesitancy as I took her in my arms—the culmination of a courtship correspondence course. I vowed that in the thirty hours I'd have at home I'd not let her out of my sight for at least twelve. I returned with Myrt to 48 Beverly Road to find my sister Betty had rounded up a number of my friends to wish me well. As I took in a few of the girls I'd dated, and recalled some others in Indiana and Texas, I could only conclude that Myrt was heaven's gift to my universe.

That evening, alone at last with Myrt, I came to realize that surely I could find no better as a wife. Beautiful, smart, kind and thoughtful, she was a natural leader—everything, in short, that I wasn't. In a high school four times the size of mine, she'd graduated third in her class of one thousand while I'd squeaked by into the upper third of my class. And while I was just one contributing editor to my school paper, she was editor in chief of her paper and won a regional award for it. While I was a hanger-on in my school stamp club, she took the starring role in three plays at Commerce High. While I pitched hay and milked cows by hand during the summer for fifteen cents an hour, she was serving as secretary to an attorney for nearly twice that. And while I was bragging that I was doing homework to the tune of fifteen minutes a day, she was not only taking a college course like mine but a commercial course as well. But it was her gregarious, outgoing concern for others, and now as the sole support of her family, that made her tower over me. Just how much I needed her calm, reasonable advice I was just beginning to realize. If there was anybody who could take the crooks out of this dumb klutz, it had to be Myrt.

But was it possible, even remotely so, that this wondrous creature would have the likes of me as a husband? Now there was a thought! She was a year younger than my twenty years, trying her dead-level best to take the place of her father who'd died just four months earlier. Time was short, and I simply had to know if she would entertain the idea of walking down the aisle with me. So I popped the question. Could she, would she marry me? To my everlasting good fortune, she agreed. But there was a condition. We would have to wait till the war was over. She was determined to maintain responsibility for her family. Furthermore, she didn't relish the idea of becoming another war widow, like Margie. I was overjoyed, and eagerly agreed to wait. But would she announce our engagement and let me buy her a ring? She would need time to think it over.

The next afternoon Dad drove us to Union Station. Margie lent me $200 and we were soon greeting Myrt's former boss in New York City. He took us to a floor show where Myrt and I danced. Then over to Central Park where, on a park bench, we talked of everything in the moonlight. Amid wedding plans and the honeymoon, we pledged to be faithful to each other and remain virgins till our wedding night. This was no easy call, given a fighter pilot's swashbuckling reputation to uphold. But if there was anybody worth waiting for, it was Myrt.

The next day we parted at the train station, not knowing when—or even if—we'd see each other again. There were tears as I pinned a set of my wings on her. Bob had done the same thing with Margie less than a year before. Would we avoid their fate? Unspoken, this was uppermost in our thoughts as we kissed and I promised to be back to reclaim my bride.

April 27, 1944

My darling, Myrt,

My highest expectations were surmounted by that wonderful leave! It is astounding as I think of it. An hour after we'd been together alone on our first date, there I was, asking you to marry me. You might know I'd be in the Air Corps! I wish I'd left a ring on your finger. At any time you'd like to announce it, just whistle and I'll send a diamond for that fourth left finger.

Again Lady Luck was with me. For on May 6, now in Camp Patrick Henry in Virginia, I found I'd have a weekend free, so I phoned Myrt and the next day met her in the lobby of the Shelton Hotel. No rooms available, so we took one at the Commodore, which catered to officers and their families. It was Sunday morning, and we took in a church service where, true to form, I fell to snoring during the sermon until Myrt elbowed me. There was the collection plate, which promptly took from me five bucks of conscience money.

As it turned out, I needed that money, as well as a lot more, for that afternoon Myrt agreed to a ring and an engagement notice in the Worcester *Evening Gazette*. She picked out a lovely half-carat ring in the jewelry store of the hotel lobby. But it was $75, and I had but $40, so I gave it to the jeweler, who promised to mail the ring to Myrt when I'd paid the difference. Again we parted in tears. But the engagement was now official. I could scarcely wait to return to her. I'd forgotten my GI-issued sunglasses at the Automat where we'd lunched. But I'd never forget her lovely face as we again took leave of each other. My diary that evening had only room for a hint of the superlatives I contemplated as I made it back to Camp Patrick Henry.

Paid the next day, the remaining $35 soon had Myrt sporting the diamond and the local paper sporting a picture of the loveliest of prospective brides. No doubt about it—life was turning up roses. Luck was still trumping stupidity.

DESTINATION NAPLES

In between my two meetings with Myrt I had the further good fortune of meeting my brother Dana, in training as a Marine at Cherry Point, North Carolina. So behind was I in my sleep, just forty hours in fourteen days, that I fell asleep standing on the bus, almost falling to the floor twice. Arriving, I found him overdue on his liberty, so took the bus back to town, sorry I'd missed him. But as I pulled into the bus station, who should I see walking toward it but the kid brother! I couldn't believe my good luck. Back to the base after lunch, we took turns knocking flies out to each other, a favorite sport over the years. Then I tried entering the officers' club with this enlisted man on my arm. No dice. So we took to the enlisted men's club, where I broke the good news of my engagement and my heading overseas. Back to town, I stopped to take in a sidewalk service by the Salvation Army. So impressed was I by their sincerity and sacrifice that I sacrificed a ten spot for the collection plate, little enough repayment to the powers that be for my fantastic good fortune.

Back at Camp Patrick Henry, I was assigned fifty enlisted men, with three sergeants to assist me, and we were soon aboard a troop train for Hampton Roads, Virginia. Leaving the sergeants in charge, I quickly took refuge in the toilet stateroom, where I promptly fell asleep until we pulled into the station. As the men fell out for roll call, I found one missing. Worried that I'd stumbled across a goldbrick like myself, I was relieved to find a private who, like me, looked as if he'd slept in his clothes for a week. I then turned in, not to awaken until fourteen hours later, just in time to be issued a Colt .45, trench knife, sunglasses, a seven-jewel Elgin wristwatch, mosquito netting, and a bright yellow Mae West life jacket.

It was Tuesday, May 9, just two days after my engagement, that I marched the fifty men over to the baseball diamond to watch the St. Louis Browns whip our home team (men permanently assigned to base). The next day I proved to be no better in the boxing ring than I'd been at the piano in the officers' club. I stopped to watch enlisted men having a go at it, figured it looked easy, doffed my shirt and put on the gloves, only to emerge amid loud cheers—for my opponent. Humiliated, I beat a hasty retreat with a cut lip, a horrific headache, and a sure knowledge that my opponent—unlike me—knew how to box.

May 12, 1944

My darling,

I love you very, very much. I didn't know that a person could ever be as happy as I've been. The whole world seems so bright—so new—and so wonderful. We have so much to look forward to—a lifetime of happiness together. I told my family we were engaged. To tell you how pleased they were would be impossible. At the big party we had for my mother's birthday with 40 people here, she announced our engagement. I never was so thrilled or so proud in my life. No girl could be prouder of her ring or of the man she's going to marry than I.

On May 15 we were introduced to our ship CO, Lieutenant Colonel Ayres, a former classmate of Gen. George Marshall at West Point. Two days later the Liberty ship, *Frederick Lykes* slipped from her berth at Hampton Roads, Virginia, bound for "parts unknown." Having been issued mosquito netting and repellent, we soon heard a rumor that we were headed for India. Four of us pilots were put in charge of 505 enlisted men on the deck below us, so we divided the twenty-four-hour watch into three-hour shifts. It wasn't long before the air below was polluted with cheers and curses over games of craps and blackjack as well as the stifling stench of five hundred human sardines cramped into a space fit for one hundred. It looked and smelled, as I recorded in my diary, "like a pigpen."

Fortunately, rank had its privileges, and we four discovered an unbelievable contrast in our quarters in the infirmary. Not only was the room ample but it was spotless, with clean sheets and toilet. Here was my introduction to the difference between the treatment of officers by Army and Navy. And it climaxed that evening as we sat down before a linen tablecloth and were served roast duckling with all the fixings, topped off with apple pie à la mode. My mind wandered to Dick Newton, my cousin, now flying carrier planes as a Marine pilot in the South Pacific. Was he also enjoying this good life?

By the next day I'd heard another rumor from the gristmill, to the effect that this was the "hottest shipment" to depart Newport News since the start of the war. Did this have something to do with a mere reprimand at the three of us going AWOL back in Texas? I sized up the 2,500 enlisted men aboard, together with at least thirty of us pilots and several warrant officers—all listed on the manifest/work orders—and wondered just what made us so hot. Before another month passed I would know.

Soon our ship was joined by five other transports and six destroyers, the latter forming a perimeter around us to escort our convoy. Clipping the North Atlantic at 16 knots, we realized that not only was there safety in numbers, but especially so when there were an equal number of warships. Alone, or unescorted by the destroyers, we'd have been sitting ducks for Hitler's U-boats still prowling the routes between the United States and Europe.

With the cool of the evening several of us pilots found a haven just inside the bow, where we tried harmonizing on some of the golden oldies, such as "The Old Mill Stream," and some of the new war songs such as "Bluebirds over the White Cliffs of Dover." Joining us were the seagulls, singing in the wind above us, amid the crash of waves against the bow below us.

We sang and we talked. Where were we going? What would we be flying? How soon before the war in Europe would be over? Would we make it back in one piece? Some ventured that "if we get it we get it." We were simply pawns in this barbaric chess game called war. Others figured that it all depended on "how the cards were dealt." As we talked we discovered all of us were in the same card game, having been dealt what others might well consider a losing hand. For each of us had just been given our wings on graduation and here we were, heading for overseas combat without the eighty to one hundred or more hours of transition and combat training that, over the years, the Air Corps had figured was necessary for entering combat. Here Uncle Sam was cutting corners, spending little of the additional $45,000 beyond graduation to train us for combat. Why the rush? Ours, of course, was "not to question why." And all of us were certain that ours was to do, but not to die. Others did that. We were invulnerable. It might not be the *Frederick Lykes* we'd board to return stateside, but return we would. We shared just who we'd be returning to. A few, like Joe Hawk, had a wife and children waiting. A few others, like me, had fiancées. But most were not seriously attached.

Here I was, just twenty, and an officer if not a gentleman, a pilot with prospects so bright that I succumbed to bravado. Overlooking my coming out second best in the ring with the enlisted man, I accepted the general challenge thrown out by another as he stood in a ring of canvas thrown over a steel hatch with ropes improvised to keep the contestants from flying into the crowd that had assembled. The challenger had just polished off another enlisted man and was delighted—as was the crowd—to see an officer enter the ring. When the news reached the quarters below, many more men joined the crowd, all eager to see how one of their own could dispatch one of the looies who lorded over them. Within minutes there was bloodshed, and it was mine. Not knowing when to quit, I persuaded another officer to join me against two of our subordinates. Only this time we were all blindfolded. Haymakers were the order of the day, with some bound to make contact. It wasn't long before my nose was bleeding again and a fierce headache was splitting the difference between my ears. So we officers quit the ring, reluctantly acknowledging we'd been had, to the boisterous cheers of the audience that had climbed on anything it could find to get a good view of the mayhem. Only later, nursing my wounds, did I realize that, had a wild punch made contact with one of my eyes, I might have kissed my flying career good-bye.

By this time I realized also that boxing was not my forte. But how about wrestling? Recalling my teen years when I fared better in this sport, I entered the ring the next day with another enlisted man and soon had him pinned. Then another. I then tossed out the challenge to the noisy crowd. Who would be next? And into the ring stepped a little guy, a fellow officer. Emboldened, I figured this would be short work. And it was. In a minute I was pinned. Try that again, I challenged him. And he obliged. The crowd was delirious. Out of the ring, I asked him just who he was and how he managed to pin me, given my height and weight advantage. Far from my superior weight helping me, he ventured, he was using it against me. But how? Come to find out, he was a former instructor of the martial art jujitsu. Would he teach me? He again obliged. Was I any smarter? That may have been questionable, but there was no question but that I smarted when salt water flushed out my bruises and abrasions in a shower.

By May 22, I became convinced that my toll in the ring was longer term than I'd bargained for. I awoke to find my right eye almost completely shut. The flight surgeon had no clue. An allergy? I'd have to watch and wait. It was worse the next day, so he had me apply hot cloths for an hour. It was no use. By the next evening I had all I could do to distinguish Stanley from Livingstone in the evening movie. Maybe what I needed was sunning. So I took to the deck, sprawled beneath a hot sun, and returned to my quarters beet-red. The swelling did leave my eye, only to reappear on my lower lip. I was getting worried. How on earth could I fit an oxygen mask on tight enough to fly without suffering from anoxia?

By this time we learned that our destination was not India but Italy, the "soft under-belly of the Axis," as Churchill described it. It was the first issue of the ship's paper, *Heave-Ho,* that informed us, along with giving a rundown of the behavior and the diseases of the natives. *Stars and Stripes* had carried the news the preceding fall that Mussolini had been replaced, the country had surrendered, and the pope had pleaded with Badoglio, the new leader, to declare Rome an "open city." International law held that this neutralizing of a city meant that it had been stripped of fortifications and weapons and lay at the mercy of the invaders. Monitoring this was an impartial commission. Yet Eisenhower had good reason not to believe either Badoglio or Hitler, and refused. Not till the country surrendered on September 3, 1943, did Ike relent.

What I didn't know at the time was Churchill's strategy for invasion.

We "invade" all countries with whom we are at war. We "enter" all subjugated lands we wish to "liberate." With regard to a country like Italy, with whose government we have signed an armistice, we "invaded" in the first instance, but, in view of the Italian cooperation, we must consider all further advances by us in Italy to be in the nature of "liberation."[1]

So we were headed to Italy to "liberate" it from the occupying Germans and those Italian troops still in league with them. On May 27, even as the 8th Army of Britain's General Alexander was racing toward Rome, a lookout on our ship spotted a German plane, itself a lookout for Allied convoys approaching Gibraltar and the Mediterranean. Hitler had diverted his troops from western as well as eastern Europe to bolster his southern front, now that Italy had thrown in the towel. And he was determined that Allied reinforcements not reach the boot of land that had figured so much in ancient history. As soon as the warning of an enemy plane was sounded, our escorting destroyers threw down a smoke screen so thick that we had all we could do to keep from running into each other. Then we heard the deep-throated thump of explosions beneath the water and knew that the destroyers were releasing depth charges in hopes of destroying the denizens, lurking in the deep, that had wrought such havoc on Allied shipping. When the smoke cleared and the plane had disappeared, we all breathed a bit easier.

Soon the rock of Gibraltar appeared on the left while on the right in the distance there arose the mountains of North Africa. Ironically enough, it was as we entered the Mediterranean that we encountered the worst storm on our voyage, with thirty-foot waves tossing us about like corks. Seasickness was rampant, but none so serious as to remove us pilots from the infirmary. We passed Algiers and Tunis, then Pantelleria as the mountains of Sicily rose out of the sea. With the port of Naples appearing before us, we formed a single file and threaded our way between the burned and rusted hulks of ships, sunken and resting on the bottom of the harbor, their visible parts marking a graveyard for many. It appeared to be the Bermuda Triangle of the Mediterranean.

Before disembarking, we officers were again fêted with a last supper of turkey, chicken, and apple pie. We'd not see the likes of this again until Thanksgiving, and then in nowhere near the style and ambiance we'd become accustomed to. Duly appreciative, the four of us in the infirmary dug down and came up with a $20 tip for the waiter and $10 for the busboy, both Negroes.

It was the last day of May before we finally descended the gangplank and marched through the streets of Naples to the central train station. Along the way we could only sympathize with Italian soldiers, dressed in the remains of tattered uniforms, scrounging through the rubble that was all that remained of most of the buildings. There was precious little of any value in the rubble and, having sorted it, they carted it away. It was obvious that this major port had taken a terrific pounding, first from the German bombers, then from ours. As I scrutinized the faces of these men, our former enemies, I perceived, at turns, grief and resignation, resentment and envy, but above all, relief. Relief that they were no longer on the firing line in North Africa where their commanding general had been reduced to living in a tent in the backyard of the German general. Relief that the bombing of this city had now halted. Relief that the German oppressors had at last left the city, even though it was in ruins. And relief that now they could go about the task of trying to rebuild, enough to make it livable.

The Allies had "liberated" the city, but only after bombing what was left of it, and now the only ones who seemed elated at our appearance were the innumerable and ever-present *bambini* lining the streets, hands outstretched for anything we could spare. Their bodies little more than sticks held together by willpower, many were reduced to hobbling along on improvised crutches, others were missing arms or hands, and still others were blinded or deafened. Their pleading eyes were saucers beneath black, matted hair. So desperate were they and their families that they were pimping for their mothers and older sisters. Again and again they accosted us. "Hey, Mr. GI, you want some hot sex?" The one thing they all had in common was hunger. As we marched through the rubble-strewn streets we tossed them candy and watched them scramble for it, fistfights sometimes breaking out. When we lined up for chow, we invariably took more than we needed so we could share with the kids hovering over the garbage barrels with cans, bowls, or buckets to intercept what we were tossing out. Bill Mauldin saw it in the infantry there in Italy: "It'd take a pretty tough guy not to feel his heart go out to a shivering, little six-year-old squeaker who stands barefoot in the mud, holding a big tin bucket so a dog-face can empty his mess kit into it."[2]

Ernie Pyle, another war correspondent, described well the parents of these heartbreak kids: "Our soldiers were slightly contemptuous of the Italians and didn't fully trust them; yet with typical American tenderheartedness they felt sorry for them, and little by little they became sort of fond of them. They seemed to be pathetic people, not very strong in character but fundamentally kind and friendly."[3]

But when it came to the Italian Partisans, those who chose to throw in with the Allies against the Germans, we had not only sympathy but admiration and gratitude. For of eighty thousand Allied military taken prisoner in Italy, ten thousand escaped, due in large part to the help of the Partisans, who often risked their lives in doing so. The previous September Hitler had ordered Field Marshal Kesselring to "throw the enemy back into the sea" at Salerno, and it was then that the Partisans began to organize. When the British 8th Army encircled the German airfields surrounding Foggia, just below the spur of the boot, the Partisans offered their support. By the time Naples fell on October 1, Italy was caught in the throes of a civil war, the Partisans fighting those who'd stuck with the Germans in the north. And when the Allies waded ashore at Anzio on January 22, 1944, most of the Italians defending the shore were only too eager to rid themselves of their German oppressors and quickly surrendered.

If the Germans had been willing to surrender as the Italians, we'd have made short work of Italy. Tough, disciplined, seasoned veterans loyal to Hitler, they invariably put up stubborn resistance, dragging the war on for many more months. By February 16, four of Kesselring's crack divisions, armed with 450 big guns, tried to obey Hitler's new order to rid the Anzio beachhead of this "abscess." They almost succeeded by driving a deep wedge through the Allied line, prompting Churchill to write that we were in a "life or death" struggle for Italy. Into the breach the Allies poured reinforcements in the form of two divisions.[4] But it was not enough. What finally made the difference were the P-51s that had been fitted as dive-bombers and reclassified as A-36 "Invaders."

Though the British dismissed the dive-bomber as overrated, Pyle, attached to one of their units, found "several hundred pilots and mechanics who believed with fanatical enthusiasm that the dive-bomber was the most wonderful machine produced in this war." The P-51, Pyle acknowledged, "was a wonderful fighter. But when it was transformed into an A-36 by the addition of diving brakes [and bomb racks] it became a grand dive-bomber as well." Just how vital were the dive brakes he emphasized:

Those boys dived about 8,000 feet before dropping their bombs. Without brakes their speed in such a dive would ordinarily build up to around 700 mph, but the brakes held them to about 390.[5]

What Pyle didn't note was that the Mustang was redlined at 550 mph, meaning that to reach 700 mph would, in all likelihood, have buckled the wings in any recovery from the dive. With the accuracy as well as stability gained by slowing their speed, the pilots were able to provide support for the ground troops, the "dogfaces," as Mauldin called them. They were as appreciative of the dive-bomber pilots as any, for they could target gun positions, heavy weapons, trucks, or bridges less than a half mile ahead of the front. The only enemy fire came from the ground, for the Luftwaffe was so weak in central Italy that the Allies quickly gained control of the air. In addition, those few fighters the Germans did have had all they could do to intercept the B-17s and B-24s taking off from the newly captured Foggia airfields.

Not only were the P-51s needed on the Italian front but on the northern European front, where they could escort the big bombers of the 8th Air Force to Berlin and beyond. Hermann Goering, head of the Luftwaffe, had promised Hitler that Berlin would never be bombed. But on March 4, 1944, Flying Fortresses appeared over the city, escorted by Mustangs. Goering's response: "When they came with their fighter escort over Berlin, I knew the jig was up." Two days later no less than one thousand B-17s and B-24s darkened the skies fifteen miles across as they converged on heavy industry far up in northern Germany. In two more days a similar effort included none other than "Hap" Arnold himself. By the end of the month German pilots were refusing to meet American fighter pilots head-on, forcing them to drop to the deck to hunt them out—and there become targets for ground fire. All of this was to soften resistance to Operation Overlord, the invasion of Normandy on June 6.[6]

By May 1944, the month I landed in Italy, American casualties were higher there than on any front of the war, and nowhere higher than in the 15th Air Force, newly formed from the 8th. P-51s were escorting the heavy bombers flying out of the Foggia airfields and pounding, among other targets, the strategic oil fields of Ploesti, Romania. In addition the Mustangs were engaged in the far more dangerous strafing of supply lines, ports, and marshaling yards in northern Italy. By May 18, supply lines by rail and road had been cut in ninety-two places, with bridges and tunnels especially vulnerable. The following week fighters and fighter-bombers destroyed a thousand German vehicles and damaged an equal number. So wary did the Germans become that they forced Italian civilians to dig trenches and foxholes alongside the roads for troops and truck drivers to use when targeted.[7]

Now, this first week in June, GI trucks carried us out of Naples north to the 19th Replacement Depot—more commonly known as the "Repple Depple." I marveled at how our motorcycle escort avoided hitting the swarms of children pressing in from the roadside, calling for candy. One cycle did hit a woman trudging along beneath a heavy basket balanced on her head. Yet the few casualties the Italians suffered from ours and other convoys were nothing compared to the casualties the Germans had inflicted on the children. For one of the German ruses was to drop candy suspended from small parachutes, mined to explode on contact, killing many innocent kids and injuring many times that.

Further evidence of just how desperate the Italians had become I found at the depot. For there, behind a high fence, were dozens of young women, many of them girls in their teens, some as young as twelve or thirteen, selling themselves to the GIs. Forming long lines, the men climbed, one after the other, the high fence to be "serviced" on the other side for a couple bucks in the new currency we'd been issued. One girl accommodated so many guys that she fainted and was carried off. How many of these GIs, I wondered, would soon be coming down with VD?

The contrasting views from the depot were stark as I

turned from the open-air bordello to take in the utter devastation of the city below to the south, then turned my eyes northward to the majesty of the mountain ranges. And at night I could make out the distant streaks of molten lava flowing from the smoking Mount Vesuvius.

I had other sights to fascinate and inspire, none more spine-tingling than the mock dogfights between the British Mosquitoes and Beaufighters and the P-40s and P-51s high overhead. And I wondered, would I be so lucky as to fly one of those Mustangs? Just a few more days would tell.

4

FROM AN AT-6 TO A P-51

"Mustang pilots usually have 200 hours of practice in them
before entering combat."

—MAJ. GEN. WILLIAM KEPNER, Commanding General, 8th Air Force Fighter
Command, to Col. Don Blakeslee, CO, 4th Fighter Group, England

INTRODUCTION TO THE 52ND
FIGHTER GROUP

It was June 5, 1944, that I learned I'd be leaving the next
day for the 82nd Fighter Group just outside Foggia. I'd
emerged from an enormous swimming pool on the king's
castle grounds at Caserta the day before, almost as filthy as
the frigid water itself. To thaw out I rounded up other pilots
at the "Repple Depple" and took on the enlisted men in softball. Of course, they promptly trounced us. Learning of my
new assignment, I penned letters to the folks and to Myrt on
the new V-mail forms.

I wrote of the Germans retreating from Naples, taking
with them everything of value they could find, including—
especially including—"eligible females," to be exploited as
the Germans saw fit. This they had already done when occupying Naples. When and if the Germans were finished with a
particular female and returned her to her home, they could
count on a warm welcome, care of the rifles and ammunition
the Italians had cached underground. Shooting the Germans

in the back was none too severe for them. Enraged, the Germans would round up all the boys old enough to fire a rifle and select a few of them as an example to the rest—by chopping off their hands at the wrist.

The ride in the open GI truck the next day was as long as it was memorable. Approaching Cassino, we slowed to a snail's pace to take in the sights, the smells, and the awful silence of a town the Allies had taken just three weeks earlier. Behind the town, atop a mountain in the distance, lay the rubble of the monastery, matching the rubble that was all that remained of a town that had suffered repeated attacks. Few mountains had been fought over more desperately than Monte Cassino. Dug in, the Germans had the vantage point from which their big guns could pick off Allied troops below. Not until they could clear the mountain of the entrenched Germans would the Allies have a clear path to Rome. In a series of battles, American, British, Indian, Polish, and French forces clawed their way up the flinty slopes of the 1,700-foot mountain, only to be thrown back each time. There was no respite until Gen. Bernard Freyberg called in the heavy bombers to pave the way for his New Zealand troops. It wasn't until May 18 that Polish troops at last raised their red and white standard over the ruins of the monastery.[1]

My senses were assaulted as I tried to take in a town spread out like a vast graveyard, recalling the harbor at Naples. Hundreds, perhaps thousands of men, women, and children lay buried beneath the ruins, their flesh rotting on their bones. There was no movement, not even a stray cat. There was no sound, save the breathing of us GIs, transfixed by the ghastly scene. There was only the dreadful silence, made all the more penetrating by the thought of the bombs and cannon fire, the grenades and mines that had blown all to smithereens. Yet overpowering these sights and silence was the nauseating stench of the dead, mixed with the odor of fetid water that now filled the bomb craters. As we moved beyond the ruins, I looked back at the jagged splinters that had once been merciful shade trees in the hot sun, now pointed skyward toward a Providence that seemed to have forgotten these people. Only when the mountain receded in the distance did we resume normal conversation.

The truck ride was long and rough as we wound up and down a series of hairpin curves, our horn blaring to clear the way through carts piled high with produce for the local markets. Drawn in each case by a single mule no bigger than an oversized St. Bernard, each proved a challenge as it pulled ever so slowly to the roadside. Competing with the carts were the native women, plodding along with enormous loads atop their heads. Then there were bicycles pulling small trailers, piled high. And every so often we confronted miniature autos, horns blaring and trailing blue smoke in their wake. Off to the side of the road were horses and cattle, oxen and mules, often lying on their backs, their legs pointed up in rigor mortis.

This sensual assault did nothing to ease my general physical condition. The racket did nothing for my throbbing headache. My sunburn, now healing, found me scratching the persistent itching. My swollen ankle and infected elbow were painful memories of our softball games. My ear was now aching, the result of swimming in the king's pool. In short, I was in less than perfect shape to step into a P-51 as we entered the grounds of the 82nd Fighter Group. Yet there they were, lined up in rows alongside the runway. And they were not Mustangs. These were twin-engine, twin-fuselage P-38s, which had performed famously in the initial assaults on Italy.

Hitler had been confident that his airfields surrounding Foggia would withstand any assault from the sea. The Allies knew that no invasion was possible without supremacy over the skies. So they decided on a massive, low-level strafing attack by the 38s, flying in from North Africa over the

Mediterranean. Maintaining a line abreast, one hundred feet apart and twenty feet above the deck to evade the radar, 157 of them attacked. So low did they fly, reported a pilot, that "our prop wash shook the trees and flattened the grass in the fields." Around the church towers they flew, catching the Germans completely by surprise, encountering little ground fire and no enemy fighters. Doolittle had flown over Tokyo eighteen months earlier for just thirty seconds. These Lightnings, living up to their name, were over their target for just ten seconds. Yet in that time they destroyed sixty-five aircraft on the ground and damaged another twenty-seven, while losing only twelve of their own.[2]

There was no doubt about it; the P-38 was a hot ship. But it was not for me, said the brass. So the next day I was on the road again, winding north along the Adriatic coast to the spur of Italy's boot. There, as we rounded a curve on a slope, lay a beautiful sight. Row upon row of aluminum-sheathed Mustangs glistened as they reflected the afternoon sun. How lucky could we be, the twelve of us asked, as we drove up to the white stucco farmhouse that now served as the headquarters of the 52nd Fighter Group. I'd trained in the 52nd Air Corps College Training Detachment at Butler University, five thousand miles away. And there, after ten hours of flight training, I'd been declared unfit to fly. Now I was being given the chance to enter the cockpit of the newest and hottest of the Allied fighters. What a turn of events Lady Luck had provided! Yet the big question remained. Would I leave this outfit alive and well, my tour of duty completed?

At headquarters we met our group operations officer, who assigned three to the 2nd Fighter Squadron, four to the 5th, and five of us to the 4th. It wasn't long before we five understood why the 4th needed five—there were but seventeen pilots for twenty-seven planes. The appearance of "Swede" Larson, squadron operations officer, told it all. Set above his broad, handlebar mustache were bloodshot eyes, and beneath the eyes were heavy dark circles. He'd just returned from another mission, and had been flying every day, as had most of the men in the outfit. They were exhausted, and greeted us like long-lost brothers. With their grinding schedules they became increasingly vulnerable to enemy opposition, whether flak, ground fire, or fighters. They escorted the big bombers on missions that sometimes lasted almost six hours, alone and cramped in a tiny cockpit. But it was the strafing missions that were increasingly taking their toll.

As I was soon to learn, strafing, while taking perhaps half the time of escort missions, required maximum attention over enemy territory. The pilot had to watch his instruments and in particular his fuel gauge, for switching from the 265-gallon main tank to either of his 108-gallon wing tanks invariably took precious seconds before he would drop below stalling speed. In addition, the pilot had to be on watch for the rest of his flight, especially his leader, lest they collide in tight formation. Then there were trees, utility lines, and towers to avoid. Above all, the pilot had to be on the watch for enemy fighters and gun positions. If he chanced to hit a locomotive or an ammunition car on a train, he had the further risk of running into the flying debris from the explosion. Finally, he had to be alert to his flight leader's instructions over the radio. To take in all of this demanded a super-consciousness, such as few other jobs in life demanded. In the Mustang the pilot was especially vulnerable to ground fire for, unlike the big radial, air-cooled engine on the P-47, the P-51 was cooled by glycol. Just a single enemy bullet piercing that line, and the pilot had, at most, ten minutes to fly before the engine heated up and the plane went down. It was, in fact, the strafing missions—accounting for less than half our total missions—that took the greatest toll on our pilots.

As the five of us made the rounds of the rest of the squadron's pilots, we came to understand more clearly why we'd been singled out for shipment overseas as soon as we'd gotten our wings, and why the rumor circulated on the *Frederick Lykes* that it was carrying the "hottest" of cargoes. Here we were, as wet behind the ears as pilots could be. It was as though infantrymen were entering combat right out of basic training, with but a rudimentary understanding of their weapons and no training in combat. On top of that, it was almost two months since we'd graduated, and we were rusty.

But undoubtedly the biggest difference was that we were stepping from an AT-6 Texan, with a top speed of 210 mph, into the fastest of the Allied fighters. At 430 mph, the P-51B was not only more than twice as fast as the AT-6, but so sensitive to the pilot's touch that, trimmed properly, the plane could fly in tight formation with the control stick operated by a single pinky finger. This also made it highly maneuverable in a dogfight.

While others in 44D were back in the States undertaking one hundred hours or so of transitional flying, moving from the AT-6 to the P-40, and thence to the P-38 or P-47, we were about to be tossed into combat waters with but twenty hours or so of transition/combat training. We were to sink or swim; it was that simple. To contrast our situation with that of most P-51 pilots, it is instructive to learn of Maj. Gen. William Kepner's answer to Col. Don Blakeslee, asking that his group have their P-47s replaced with the new, hot P-51s. "Mustang pilots," reminded Kepner, head of Fighter Command of the 8th Air Force, "usually have 200 hours in them before entering combat."[3] This meant that a new pilot from the States, in addition to his eighty or more hours of transition/combat training, would have to undergo another 200 hours in the Mustang to be ready for combat. And here we were, the twelve of us assigned to the 52nd, getting less than a tenth of that training.

But why the rush to use us as a Band-Aid to stop the hemorrhaging in the fighters of the 15th Air Force? It is of some moment that the day we twelve arrived at the 52nd, June 6, was the very day of the Normandy invasion in Operation Overlord. General Eisenhower, Supreme Commander of the Allied Expeditionary Force, had printed a letter sent to all units, stating in part, "Our air offensive has seriously reduced their [Germany's] strength in the air and their capacity to wage war on the ground. . . . The tide has turned!" Fighter pilots in the normal pipeline had been sent to England at the expense of units in the 15th Air Force in Italy. The result: seventeen pilots in the 4th Squadron for twenty-seven planes, and those bedraggled and exhausted.[4]

About to undergo a baptism of fire, I was as green as the spring wheat in the fields around us. The pilots in the 4th all looked to be several years older than us greenhorns. Most if not all were college graduates and battle-hardened veterans of the North African campaign. They had moved to the island of Corsica, off the west coast of Italy, and now had pulled up stakes to occupy this field on the east coast of the boot, just adjacent to the boot's spur. In the infantry, as Bill Mauldin pointed out, "Joe" was about twenty-two and "Willie" was ten years older, representing the age range among the average foot soldiers. In the Air Corps, despite at least thirteen months of flight training, in addition to six months of initial Basic, the average age of pilots was about five years younger, or twenty-two to twenty-four. But none of the other eleven replacements for the 52nd were younger than my twenty years.[5]

I was young enough to be chafing at the bit to get into a Mustang and get some of those Jerries, like the pilot of the FW 190 who'd shot down Bob's B-17 resulting in his death at twenty-two. But first there was ground school, and I couldn't afford to doze. At 430 mph, the P-51B was faster than the P-38's 415 and the P-47's 426. By waxing the wings and pulling out the emergency "tit," we were able to add another 5 to 10 mph. In 1942 the Mustang's Allison engine had been replaced by the Rolls-Royce "Merlin," giving it its superior speed. This compared with the two Allison engines in the P-38 and the big Pratt-Whitney engine in the P-47. In addition, the sleek streamlining of the P-51 made it, from the front and rear, a very small target.[6]

My introduction to the 51 included every moving part, taught first in the classroom and then in the cockpit itself. The instrument panel was as much more complex than the AT-6's as that was more than the Piper Cub's. And those instruments were never more critical than when flying in the clouds, with virtual zero visibility. With the monsoon rains approaching the last part of August, further instrument training in the Link Trainer was a must. After putting the 51 through its paces, especially in mock dogfighting with Swede Larson or Ace Burnett, I would be, after twenty hours, presumably ready for combat.

Of the five of us attached to the 4th Squadron, Jack Chidester and Bob Hyde were my bunkmates as we settled down in a four-man tent; Steve Stevenson and Jim Utterback were settled in another tent. With a hearty steak supper under our belts, the three of us sat up exulting in our great luck in getting this assignment, with a big leg up on our 44C and 44D compatriots back in the States. It scarcely passed my peripheral brain contact that maybe we would find this lack of training a decided handicap when it came to simply surviving the fifty missions that constituted our tour of duty.

Reveille the next morning was at 0500 hours. Eager to learn the ropes, we hopped out of our sacks and joined those scheduled to fly the day's mission, posted on the bulletin board the night before. Down to group headquarters we bumped along the dirt roads in a big GI truck, taking our seats in the rear of the briefing room. Before us was spread a huge map of southern and central Europe. Munich, up beyond the Italian and Austrian Alps, was the day's target. Already the big four-engine B-24s had taken to the air from their bases around Foggia, some sixty miles to the south. Our pilots were to rendezvous with them at a given time and place over the northern Adriatic. Our fighters were just one of several groups assigned to provide escort, crisscrossing the skies above the bombers, ever on the alert for enemy fighters diving down from out of the sun. The mission could expect flak as soon as it crossed enemy lines in northern Italy, getting heavier as it approached the target area: the marshaling yards and the aircraft factories that were now turning out the new jet fighters the Luftwaffe was adding to its fleet. The operations officer, after answering questions from the assembled pilots, ended with a hearty "Good luck!" There was little question but that these pilots would need all the luck they could get, I figured, as the five of us made our way to a lecture on armament by a squadron officer. Our P-51s, we were told, were equipped with .50-caliber machine guns, two in each wing, each gun with two hundred armor-piercing, incendiary bullets converging at three hundred yards. Every tenth bullet was a tracer, leaving a white path so we could see where our bullets were going and correct, if necessary. Every time we pulled the trigger at the top of the stick, a camera would automatically take movies of our intended targets. Powering this P-51B was a Rolls-Royce Merlin engine, more efficient than the former Allison engine above fifteen thousand feet, whereas the Allison engine did a better job below fifteen thousand feet, ideal for strafing missions.

After lunch the five of us met the returning pilots as they made their reports in debriefing to the intelligence officer. In the 4th we had registered five kills without losing so much as a man. Exhilarated by their victories, the pilots, back at the 4th, described with sweeping gestures the chaos of dogfights high in the skies over Munich, where Jerries had jumped the bombers from out of the sun. In a matter of seconds, formations were broken as the Mustangs took on the invading ME-

109s. Tracer bullets filled the sky and fighters as well as bombers became "flamers" as they spun into the ground below, leaving a trail of black smoke behind them. With each dramatic description of a kill by one of our pilots, my blood surged. No doubt about it, this was a hot outfit! Here, we were convinced, was seventh heaven!

I couldn't wait to join them on a mission. But wait I must. Buckner, I learned, one of our "twelve disciples," pranged on his first training flight. Coming in for a landing on the single dirt strip that ran downhill, parallel to the coast, our substitute for a runway, he'd tried bucking a stiff crosswind, lost control, and ran off the strip. He not only totaled the plane but struck an Italian laborer who'd scrambled from his work on the runway, but not fast enough. It cost him a leg. Lucky for Buckner, he had his shoulder harness secure and emerged from the cockpit in a cloud of dust but none the worse for the wear. I was coming to appreciate just how much training I'd need in that bucking Mustang before I could "tame" her for battle.

In contrast to the formality of training back in the States, I was struck by the utter informality of the men, regardless of rank. Aside from the occasional "sir," to the colonel who headed the 52nd, there was little evidence of a pecking order. There was no saluting except in awards ceremonies, when a top pilot from the 306th Wing Headquarters was on hand. Nicknames were common and in the 4th included "Snake" Morris, "Buck" Gassman, and "Monster" Ward, each a tribute to the size and presumed potency of one's private member. When it came to the relationship between the pilot and his crew chief or his assistant, Bill Mauldin put it well: "No man who depends on those below him—not only for his success but for his very life—is going to abuse his men unnecessarily. Not if he has good sense."[7]

The morning Buckner pranged found me learning to taxi, my crew chief perched on the end of my right wing, directing me. Unlike the P-38, the nose-up attitude of the P-51 prevented my seeing the runway directly ahead of me. So I resorted to the hand signals, a new language for me.

That evening I scrounged scrap lumber from the crates used to ship our wing tanks to us and improvised primitive furniture, including a bench, a table, and a chest of drawers. Then I made the mistake of bragging about my workmanship, so others came to inspect it for themselves, leaving with the advice that my flying had better be better than my carpentry or I wouldn't last a week in combat.

It wasn't till June 11 that I finally got my chance to take the Mustang aloft. While others were off on another mission, Ace Burnett, dolled up in his Texas cowboy hat, boots, and drawl to match, checked out Fred and Jim. Then, lunch over, Jack and Bob had their turns. The four of them raved about their rides. My mouth was watering.

At last it was my turn. On takeoff I jumped that bronco off the runway, but unlike the horse, it stayed aloft. I climbed to twelve thousand feet and tried some stalls. It was handling so beautifully! So I tried a barrel roll, then a slow roll. Then I executed a split-S and within seconds the airspeed indicator hit 500 mph and was climbing toward the red line at 550 before I climbed back up, almost stalling before I completed my loop. But, using my trim tabs, I was able to level off in an Immelman. My aerobatics may have been sloppy, the ball on the instrument panel jumping back and forth across the center, but this was a mind-altering experience! It was an epiphany in the heavens I would never forget. I checked my watch. An hour had whizzed by. I now had to land, and eyes in the tower would be scrutinizing my every move as I entered the traffic pattern. But here, on this dirt strip running downhill and almost invariably in some crosswind, I'd have to grease 'er in. I took note of the wind sock to try and compensate for the crosswind coming in from the west. This meant I'd have to turn into the wind a bit and only straighten it out seconds before my wheels hit the dirt. For if I landed the least bit sideways, as Buckner had done, I'd probably lose control and, like him, run off the runway, endangering the Ities who always seemed to be working there.

Determined not to hit the hill above the strip as I came in to land, I overshot and heard the tower operator: "Go around, Curtis. Try again." I gave 'er the gun, climbed back up, and came around for a second try. It was a winner, with only the slightest bounce. I heaved a sigh of relief as I turned off to taxi, stopping to let my crew chief hop on and direct me. But first he gave me a "thumbs-up," meaning he was satisfied that I'd made it. But was Burnett? As I climbed from the cockpit there came the familiar drawl from the ace of San Antonio. "Curtis, good show!" Just those three words sent my spirits soaring. Was it conceivable that this klutz, this budding flier who seemed always to have his head up and locked, would extricate it long enough to become a combat pilot?

That night I joined the rest of the group's pilots in the briefing room to watch the most recent combat film. Here was no Hollywood make-believe. I found myself swallowing hard as I watched one Jerry after another get lined up in the crosshairs of our men. The tracer bullets showed the machine guns were finding their mark as flame and smoke belched from the bogeys and they began spinning toward earth. Sometimes a wing came off. Other times the entire plane disappeared in a burst of flame, meaning the gas tank had been hit by one of our incendiary bullets. Sometimes I caught sight of a Jerry bailing out, his chute in danger of being hit by planes engaged in the turmoil of multiple dogfights at the same time. And sometimes I made out one of our bombers trailing smoke and flame as it descended in a spin, with little chance of the crew getting out. Then my thoughts went to Bob, who did manage to bail out, only to drown in the frigid waters of the North Sea. When one of our Mustangs did register a hit and the enemy fighter headed for the ground, the

P-51 pursued it, catching the crash and fireball on film to justify a kill. How long, I wondered, before I'd be joining them on such a mission?

I had a lot to learn, both in ground school and in the air, and it soon dawned on me just how important this additional training would be. The next day, June 12, I listened to lectures on the engine, on the radio, and on plane identification. That afternoon I learned of a British pilot in a field just north of us coming in to land in his P-40, stalling, crashing, and catching fire. He was badly burned, yet better off than the crew of the B-17 that crashed in an emergency landing at our field. Crippled, it wasn't able to maintain altitude and hit a tree, clipping off a wing. Crashing and burning, its fuselage became a crematorium for the crew of ten. The site of the crash, just a quarter mile from my tent, served as a daily reminder of three things: this war was a deadly business; this war was intensely personal; and I was lucky to be flying fighters.

There was no question but that what I was learning in ground school would help ensure my safe return to the States. But just as important were the tips I was picking up from these veteran pilots who were each day waiting for the five of us greenhorns to relieve them of having to fly every day. The easy banter of pilots about to leave on another dangerous mission, or silently mourning the loss of a buddy, couldn't hide the fact that, whether escorting or strafing, all was reduced to that bare-bones equation: *kill or be killed.* All the propaganda, all the slogans, all the Hollywood movies that glorified the heroes, all this that hooked youngbloods like me, all the idealism that marched alongside the bands and parades were, in the last analysis, reduced to that simple, stark choice. If anybody understood that, Burnett did, even when he pretended to be the quintessential frontier cowboy for the benefit of photographers and home consumption back in San Antone.

On Tuesday the 13th, I got more bad news. It appeared that the thirty or more of us pilots aboard the *Frederick Lykes,* plus others in other shiploads, were already paying dearly for stepping into combat planes from the AT-6s. The latest casualty I got wind of was none other than Joe Hawk, the first lieutenant who'd become so infatuated with flying that he'd transferred to the Air Corps. Perhaps he was thinking of his family when he came in for a landing. One thing for sure, he wasn't thinking about the two requisites for landing safely: lower your wheels and be sure your shoulder harness is secured tightly. If you forgot to lower your wheels but had your harness secured, you had a good chance of escaping serious injury. And if you forgot to secure your harness but did lower your wheels, you'd probably be OK. But if you forgot both— as Joe did—you were in for a peck of trouble. Hitting the runway on the belly of his plane forced his head to shoot forward and strike the gunsight, shearing off the top of his skull as though he'd been scalped. Hustled from the plane to a waiting ambulance, he underwent extensive surgery as a team of flight surgeons placed a silver cap over the top of his head, then took skin from his body and grafted it over the cap. It was a miracle that he survived to return to the States and his family. But he never flew again. This was sobering news, for Joe and I had become good friends after graduating from Aloe Field.

As more and more of our tenderfeet clobbered themselves in P-38s, P-47s, and P-51s, at last General Twining issued an order that all further training by this select group would be done in P-40s, the very planes we would have stepped into after leaving the AT-6s back in the States. In a few days I'd learn for myself how much slower and more sluggish the Warhawk was than the Mustang.

The next day all pilots gathered at group headquarters to listen to two MIAs who'd been shot down in their Spitfires when the 52nd was stationed at Corsica earlier in the year.

Both had eluded capture, but wounded, had slowly, painfully threaded their way back to the Allied line in Italy and to their base. Now they were visiting to give us some pointers in the event we were shot down and captured. We were all ears.

The gist of their advice was this. Before starting a mission we must check to make sure we have all our emergency equipment. This should include a map, a compass, and Italian money, for the Italians would not part with their food if they could sell it. As for weapons to defend ourselves, we should be sure to have our Colt .45 automatic pistol strapped on, with at least three magazines of seven bullets each. In addition we should see that we have a trench knife attached to our belt, and a smaller pocketknife. To protect our ankles in bailing out as well as hiking through rough terrain, we should wear our paratrooper boots, ten inches high with rubber soles. The Mae West life preservers, strapped beneath our chutes, and the dinghies we sat on, would come in handy, whether bailing out over sea or land. They would have made it back sooner, they insisted, had they been able to travel on water along the coast at night. If possible we should keep our chutes, for the beautiful white silk could be cut into scarves, each bringing a dozen eggs in barter.

What should we do if captured? If by Germans, we could usually count on their abiding by the international rules of war. These included giving name, rank, and serial number. But we were under no obligation to reveal anything else. If, however, we were captured by the Italian Fascists who'd thrown in with the Germans, we could expect rough treatment. For they had taken a vow that they would never take an Allied prisoner. One pilot they learned of had crashed his plane and emerged from its flames, only to be thrown back in it by enraged civilians. Another, parachuting to earth, was killed by rifle shots as he descended. And still another, landing safely, was set upon and clubbed to death.

If, on the other hand, we were lucky enough to make it to

protective woods, we should realize our troubles were just beginning. They had met other escapees in occupied Italy, some of whom had escaped and been recaptured several times, yet had managed to keep body and soul together for months at a time. Some they'd met, though but twenty-five or so, who looked to be sixty, their hair turned gray, their eyes sunk deep in their sockets, their skin covered with sores from vitamin deficiency. Almost all suffered from hookworm as they plodded along in shoes that were falling apart, exposing their bare feet. And some had resorted to improvising shoes of cardboard or animal skin. But worse than these were those who had contracted the deadly malaria.

Always, they cautioned, we should keep our uniforms, even when threadbare, for the Italians instantly recognized an American in borrowed or stolen civilian clothes by his erect stance and snappy gait. I confess I had trouble envisioning these MIAs and prison escapees with either an erect stance or a snappy gait. But perhaps these were possible their first few days on the run. A further paradox appeared when these two escapees told of two other pilots who'd bailed out of their Thunderbolts, been captured by Italians behind enemy lines, and faced curtains for sure until they somehow convinced their captors that they were simply fellow Italians flying American P-47s. At that, they must have spoken Italian fluently. One of their captors then asked how many times New York City had been bombed—a commentary on the propaganda being handed out by the Axis. We must be sure, the two escapees reminded us, that our first aid kits contained the new sulfanilamide that had been developed to treat wounds to prevent infection.

They then turned from giving advice to describing in graphic terms the life of the typical peasants that they'd become familiar with. Making up over 90 percent of the population of southern Italy, their lives stood in sharp contrast to the lives of the typical landowners. Shuttered behind their windows in majestic white villas set atop the hills, they could check on the stoop labor of the peasants working the fields below.

The "serf and share" system was all that the average Italian had come to know from one generation to the next. His house was little more than a small hut, rarely more than three rooms, reeking of sweat and garlic as well as human waste from the outhouse nearby or from fields it fertilized. Instead of milk and other dairy products, he made do with cheap wine. Instead of fruits and vegetables, his diet consisted, in the main, of potatoes and bread, pasta, spaghetti, and macaroni. It was no wonder that he was short of stature, with shoulders rounded from hour after hour and day after day of stooping over in the fields. Unless he lived by the seashore or a lake or stream, he seldom bathed, especially from October to April.

Now destitute from the ravages of war, mothers as well as daughters sold themselves to the invading GIs. There were no less than ten thousand girls in Rome, they pointed out, who applied for jobs with our military to serve as waitresses and maids and were rejected, nine out of ten of them for being infected with VD. Even the upper classes were selling their females to the brothels that abounded. "Buyer beware" was the warning from these two, even as they conceded that some pilots managed to escape only because protected by prostitutes.

For more than an hour these two escapees talked, concluding with two suggestions. First, if shot down, we should travel by night in Germany and by day in Italy. Second, we should learn some stock Italian phrases, for gestures often proved fruitless. Two questions nagged me as I left that meeting. Could this Italy be the descendant of the great Roman Empire that ruled the then-known world for five centuries? And, if I had my choice, would I prefer capture to death? To both questions I gave a qualified yes.

The latter question, though seldom voiced, always seemed to lie just beneath the surface, even as the 4th lost Crawford on June 16. A good-natured pilot who sported a "Swede" mustache, he lost control on an escort mission over Hungary when he was spooked by a P-38 attacking him. It appeared that the Germans had repaired one or more downed Lightnings and were now flying them against us. What grated, in addition, was that in losing Crawford we'd registered no kills, whereas the 2nd Squadron laid claim to no less than ten. Supper that night was unusually quiet as most of us ate mechanically, pondering a fate that could be ours any day.

But it was not this question that gave me a fitful night's sleep. For that afternoon I'd joined Burwell on a makeshift raft out in the breakers rolling in from the Adriatic. Between the sea and the sun the two hours did me in, and I was suffering from a persistent headache and fever, along with the chills. By morning I was wet with sweat, so I turned the sleeping bag inside out and hung it from a tree.

Though my headache refused to leave me, I managed to complete ground school, including a final test on aircraft recognition at 1/100th of a second. There were final lectures on briefing and security, and on decorations, awards, and promotions. My headache persisted, so I sought out our squadron flight surgeon, "Doc" Curran, an affable captain from Boston. His diagnosis was not assuring: either a touch of dengue fever or a mild case of malaria. That night and all the next day I wet the bed with sweat, so Doc pulled around in his jeep to take me to the hospital, only to find my temperature—at long last—back to normal. Relieved but weak, I took some replacement salt, along with water, raw lemon juice, canned pineapple juice, and a laxative. Within an hour or so I'd heaved everything on my stomach and was weak in the knees and exhausted. One look in the mirror gave me the shudders. What had become of the swashbuckling fighter pilot, eager and ready to take on all comers? But my fever was gone, so I paid a visit to our squadron barbershop, run by a young Italian entrepreneur. For a shave and a haircut I forked over fifteen cents, plus a nickel tip—all in the new lira we'd been issued. Then, not willing to let well enough alone, I hiked the mile or so to the beach and back, enough to send my temperature back up.

As the days slipped by and I was in no shape even to step into a Piper Cub, I wound myself into a perfect funk. Here the other eleven were racking up transition and combat training while I was playing cat-and-mouse with dengue fever or malaria or God-knows-what. Increasingly it appeared that I was the odd man out. Sleeping fitfully at best at night, I tried catnapping through the day, only to be awakened again and again by hammers and saws from the direction of our squadron headquarters. For there local Ities were patching together from crate plywood an "officers' club." What they lacked in tools and expertise, they made up in zeal. Soon there appeared a mess hall, divided into kitchen, bar, and dining room. Then, for good measure and a few extra lira, they added a rec room, where we soon improvised a Ping-Pong table.

The next evening at group headquarters we were treated to a show sponsored by the local Red Cross girls, most of them real lookers to remind us of what we were missing back home, and to whom we could return if we were careful—and lucky. Invariably they lifted our spirits as they met our pilots returning from their missions, providing doughnuts and coffee from their Clubmobiles. Chuckles and wisecracks also greeted the returnees, sometimes prompted by the pilots, after torturous hours of confinement in the tiny cockpits, having to relieve themselves from the wings of their planes, as soon as they emerged from their cockpits. Now we were introduced to a skit, "Clip Joint in San Severo," dedicated to a village nearby where we spent some of our off-hours. The drama featured an all-Italian cast, including a dazzling blonde, almost unheard of in southern Italy. Though I was still weak, listless, and unable to hold anything on my stomach, this play buoyed my spirits. The next day they got an additional boost when Doc okayed my flying the next day.

I awoke that day fully expecting to take a ride in the P-40, for whatever it was worth, but nowhere could I find the group ops officer, Major Chapman. Then I learned the Warhawk was undergoing a major inspection. I figured the day was shot when, with mail call, I found four letters from Myrt, the first I'd gotten from my fiancée since leaving the States. Flying or no flying, it turned out to be a red-letter day!

May 19, 1944

My darling,

We may not have been together as long as most couples but we sure did crowd a "heap o' livin" in the short time we were together. To me, that's life—to fill each and every minute with just as much as possible—that's what makes for both happiness and success. Right? Gee, Dick, do I ever love my ring (haven't had a pair of gloves on since I got it).

By the middle of June, Myrt had gotten my letter suggesting I was at last doing some serious thinking about the future.

May 28, 1944

My darling Myrt,

If, for some reason, I should be taken from this world to the greater one beyond before we can enter into Holy Matrimony, I want you to know, dear, that I would consider it no greater compliment if everyone rejoiced in my passing—affording me the enjoyment of knowing that others who knew me had enough confidence in my earthly existence to rejoice at the opportunity awaiting me in the world beyond. Believe this, dear.

It wasn't till June 23rd that I finally checked out in the P-40. As I took my seat in the cockpit, MacDonald, Chapman's assistant, gave me a rundown on the instruments, confirming what I'd read in the official handbook on the ship. Since I'd already checked out OK in the P-51, I figured this would be a walk in the park. Alas, it was anything but. It seemed to take forever to reach ten thousand feet, was sluggish to the touch and much worse in the maneuvers of my aerobatic regimen.

Nowhere did its sluggishness affect me more than on landing. The first time, as with the 51, I overshot, so circled around and tried again. Again the voice of the tower operator instructed me to go around again. By this time I was disgusted and embarrassed that those in the tower saw me unable to put this crate down safely. So I resolved that the third time I would not overshoot. I'd set 'er down in the first few feet of the runway if it killed me. And, as it turned out, it almost did. Instead of making it to the runway, I came in so low that my wheels hit the hill before the runway. This collapsed one of them, so that when I did settle the plane down on the runway, landing on one good wheel sent me spinning around like a top in a cloud of dust, sending the Itie runway workers fleeing for their lives. As luck would have it, I ran off the runway but missed the laborers. But I'd managed to total the plane, leaving the only P-40 in the group good just for parts.

I feared the most as I came face to face with our new group CO, twenty-six-year-old Colonel Levine, Chapman by his side. I needn't have worried, for the CO asked if I'd checked out OK in the 51. Chapman assured him I had, so Levine allowed me to return to the P-51. To top it off, it would be the new P-51D, with six guns instead of four, synchronized to fire through the spinning prop without shredding it and a 10 mph increase in speed. Above all, its new bubble canopy permitted me a 360-degree unobstructed view of the sky around me, a significant improvement over the B's 300-degree view, with reinforcements blocking some of that. Again, as luck would have it, our squadron won when straws were drawn, so the first Ds to arrive would go to us. By the 24th we had twenty-three of them, the envy of the rest of the group. After my accident with the P-40 I had to have a recheck of my depth perception and distance reading. Everything was OK except for a slight headache that came when I shook my head. Would I ever get back in shape?

I awoke Monday, June 26, to an absolutely gorgeous summer day, the deep blue of the sky reflected in the Adriatic. I shook my head. No more headache. Everything was turning up roses. Then I looked in the mirror as I took out my razor and I winced, for my upper lip was puffed out. My ordeal on the Liberty ship over was coming back to haunt me. If the swelling didn't appear in one place, it did in another, threatening to interfere with a tight fit of my oxygen mask. Again Curran had no more idea of what was causing this than he did of my earlier visit, diagnosed as dengue fever or malaria. But he permitted me to fly, assuring me I'd get enough oxygen even with an imperfect fit.

So that afternoon I took to the skies again, this time with the P-51D. After dancing with a few clouds blowing over, I put 'er into my aerobatic regimen, then dropped to the deck to scatter the bathers along the shore. Tired of that, I headed out to sea and encountered some fishing boats equipped with sails. As I buzzed them I waved in greeting, only to find them shaking their fists and scrambling to prevent my prop wash from capsizing them. So I returned to shore and tried buzzing one town after another.

My buzzing was cut short by the sight of another P-51, a B belonging to the 2nd Squadron. The pilot was waggling his wings, obviously eager for a mock dogfight. I was game, but quickly realized just how green I was when, not once or twice, but a dozen times he outmaneuvered me, coming in on my tail. Had he been a German, I'd have been blown out of the sky. Finally we broke off, and I executed a split-S and dove down from twelve thousand feet, greasing 'er in for a smooth landing—of all things. In this, my second time in a 51, I came quickly to understand that I had a whale of a lot to learn if I was to return to escort my bride down the aisle.

I returned to my outfit to discover that the 4th had inherited seven more pilots, while the other two squadrons divided up an additional twenty. Graduates in 1943, they'd racked up the standard transitional time in P-40s, then P-47s. So with but four hours in a Mustang, I figured that soon I'd be eating their dust. I also learned that our squadron had registered eighteen kills that day—undoubtedly to impress these newcomers. No doubt about it, the 52nd was racking up its share of the kills. On June 27 we bagged thirteen more. Sully Varnell of the 2nd was now high man with twelve black crosses on the side of his ship. The 4th's CO, Capt. Tim Tyler, had bagged two more. That evening the excitement was palpable as we sat on the edge of our chairs for the showing of the combat film. There it showed one Jerry after another exploding in midair or spinning down in flames. Some of the gang even bagged a few on the deck, big puffs of black smoke all that was left of plane or pilot.

The next day it was formation flying—*tight* formation flying. So snuggled up were we in each other's wings that we could almost count each other's teeth as we smiled. When we got to twenty-four thousand feet, the flight leader did a quick split-S and, diving almost wingtip to wingtip, we executed a series of maneuvers, with the airspeed indicator often flirting with the red line. The end result for me, apart from the delightful exhilaration, was a nasty earache. For the life of me I couldn't seem to clear my ears with the rapid changes in altitude, no matter how hard I blew, with mouth and nose shut. As I wrote in my diary that evening, "Nearly blew my brains out but finally cleared my ears." I could only hope that this would not become a common problem.

Myrt's letter of June 4th caught up with me, showing her excitement at getting my cablegram.

> June 4, 1944
>
> Well, dear, if I were to try and express the joy—the thrill— the wonderful feeling I got when the phone rang this morning and a voice said, "I have an overseas cablegram for you," I would be at a loss for words. It's been 17 days since I heard from you. . . . Gee, it was wonderful. I didn't know whether to laugh or cry.

After a few more hours of gunnery practice, using an abandoned lighthouse on an island in the Adriatic as a target, I joined others of our "twelve disciples" in ferrying our P-51Bs to the 332nd Fighter Group just south of us. You'd think that was duck soup, that nothing could go wrong. But it did. For George Isaac, my buddy from Aloe Field who'd lent me ten dollars to see me home to Worcester after graduation, forgot to lower his wheels and bellied in. Fortunately he didn't compound the mistake, as Joe Hawk, another Aloe buddy, had done, so George wasn't hurt, even though the 332nd was now short a plane. To prevent others from landing and smashing into the wrecked plane on the runway, the tower operator shot off enough red flares to make it look as though we were in the midst of an Independence Day celebration a week early.

The 332nd was the fighter group that became known as the "Tuskegee Airmen." Having enjoyed the autobiography of Booker T. Washington, *Up from Slavery,* telling of his founding of the Tuskegee Institute in the South after the Civil War, I was impressed when I learned that all of these airmen were college graduates. The group owed its existence to the persistent intercession of Eleanor Roosevelt with her husband, our commander in chief. She rightly observed that if we couldn't integrate our armed services, we ought at least to permit them to form their own fighting units. These Negroes were, without doubt, every bit as good as we were with the Mustangs. Yet to show how deep-set was our prejudice, we referred to them as "Jigs." Later, flying our missions, I heard an occasional dig at our neighbors to the south as one of our pilots would get on the radio with another and, imitating a Negro dialect, would complain that he had a faulty generator or radio or was encountering too much static interference and was returning to base.

One of the lasting stories, sworn to be true, had it that one member of the 332nd, having claimed three kills for the day's mission, returned to the field to celebrate the traditional slow roll off the deck of the runway for each victory. We all knew that any slow roll was bound to lose altitude. The first one went OK, and in the second he managed just to clear the deck. But the third found him running out of altitude and—as we tactfully put it—"that Jig augured in, spreading himself all over the landscape!" When word of this reached General Twining, he issued an order that there were to be no more victory rolls. And of course it was never enforced. After all, a victory was a victory, and that was what we were there for. Why deprive the men of a little show-off? In reality, the 332nd racked up, even as the 52nd did, such an impressive record of victories that it, too, earned a Presidential Unit Citation. This allowed each pilot in the group to wear a ribbon of deep blue, framed in gold, over his right pocket. Not until later, when we engaged the 332nd in Ping-Pong and basketball, did we get to know some of them well, and accredit them as good guys and good athletes as well as good pilots.[8]

June 10, 1944

My darling Dick,

Yesterday's paper brought us the story of the invasion and guess what? It also told of our engagement. I would pick D-Day, wouldn't I? It will be 3 weeks tomorrow since I had a letter from you. Boy! You don't know how glad I was that you sent a cablegram, dear. Although it was sent "sansorigine," I at least knew you weren't in transit. Look, honey, I want to send you a package every now and then and, as you probably know, I can't send anything without a letter containing a request, so-o-o, will you please oblige?

If we knew little of the Negroes who dwelt among us in the States, how much less did we know of the Soviets, our allies in this war? On June 27 the 52nd played host to a Mustang outfit based in England. This was their first leg in the triangular run we came to know as the "shuttle run." Thus when our planes escorted bombers to the Ploesti oil fields, they would land in Russia, only to take off, bomb Berlin, and land in England then, to complete the third leg of the shuttle, they would bomb enemy targets in France and land in Italy again.

Although I arrived too late to participate in these shuttle runs, I was eager to hear from our pilots on their return from England. I could scarcely believe my ears when one of our pilots told of an event he witnessed in Russia. Put up in a tent overnight, he listened as one of his tentmates complained that he couldn't find the bar of soap that he was sure he'd packed. It so happened that a Russian pilot was passing by and, understanding English, immediately sought out his CO and told him what he'd heard. Right away the CO ordered a search of all tents in the area. Coming up with the soap—no big deal for Americans—the commander accosted the sneak thief, who confessed. Immediately he was taken out and, with not even a semblance of a trial, was shot dead. This would serve as an example to the rest of the men. The face they put on communism had to be squeaky clean. Our pilots returned, more thankful than ever that they were not a part of the Soviet air force.

I envied the newcomers to the 4th their last training in P-47s when they started flying combat on June 30—until I heard of Kurtz. On this, his first mission, he was clobbered by an ME-109 attacking from the rear. He managed a belly landing in Germany and was apparently taken prisoner, the first of many casualties among our last arrivals. As low man on the totem pole, flying number four position in this flight of four, it was his job to protect the rear of his element leader. This enabled number three to have a shot at the enemy without having to worry about an attack from the rear, the most likely place for an attack. Attacking in pairs, this meant that the cover man was vulnerable, rather than his leader, from an attack. The same held for the number two man protecting the flight leader. The strategy of the finger formation had been gradually developed since World War I, and had proven to be most efficient, at the same time limiting those who would attack to numbers one and three.[9] Apparently Kurtz, in concentrating on staying on the tail of his leader, failed to see the ME-109 on his own rear. Whatever else was drilled into us newcomers, we were never, *never* to leave the tail of our leader. Whatever else we forgot, we must remember this cardinal rule. To violate it opened one up to a court-martial.

The same day I learned of Kurtz I got in a couple more hours of mock dogfighting with Utterback against Bourne, a veteran. My job was to protect Utterback's rear as Bourne maneuvered to come in on my rear. I had a dickens of a job keeping one eye on Utterback and the other on Bourne as he tried putting me in his gunsight. I then learned that if my element leader in combat registered a kill, and I'd helped him by protecting his rear, I'd get credit for an assist.

Just how grueling this practice could be came home to me on the afternoon of July 1, when I spent three hours tangling with four P-38s, a P-40, and a P-51, all ganging up on me to "shoot me out of the sky." It was a good thing it was only a practice—and I set to wondering if Swede had put them up to it. Still, though a practice, my knees were shaking uncontrollably, my nerves were shot, and I was exhausted. Fortunately, in combat dogfighting seldom lasted more than a few minutes.

June 12, 1944

My darling,

Got tickets today to a War Bond Rally at the Auditorium. Well, I finally got a letter from you after 3 weeks. Gee, was it ever swell to hear from you! Written on board ship— when I don't know—the censors did a good job of cutting the date out. I've been writing 3 or 4 times a week and re-reading all those you sent me since last August. Now that our engagement has been in the paper, congratulations have been extended whenever I step out the door. I've never been so happy and the only thing that would make me happier would be to have you with me. Remember the night when you were home you asked about the way I'd put the stamps on my letters (upside down)? It meant "I love you," dear.

July 1 was notable as we welcomed seven more P-47 pilots at the 4th, making fourteen since the five of us arrived on June 6. As it turned out, we would need every last man by the end of the month. Now that Italy had surrendered and its soldiers disarmed, Hitler was convinced that his most vulnerable front was Italy, which he was determined to shore up. At the same time he understood, ever since the Battle of Britain four years before, that the nation that controlled the skies controlled the progress of the war. He could no longer count on Kesselring holding the line without air superiority. So in the month of July Hitler threw in every fighter plane he could scrounge from other fronts in order to stop the bombers, including the dive-bombers at the front. He was most concerned about Ploesti, Romania, and its oil fields, his major source of fuel for his war machine. He was also concerned for the aircraft factories in Germany, especially those turning out jets in Munich. As a result, the 15th Air Force during that month lost more than any of the other Allied fighting units fighting in Italy. Chuck Yeager, another P-51 pilot, flying out of England with the 8th Air Force, complained that "the summer of 1944 was a dry gulch for those of us eager to mix it up with the Germans."[10]

Instead of taking to the skies on the 2nd, I took to nearby towns to do some bartering, for I'd collected a stash of cigarettes, the coin of the realm. With two cartons a week issued us, and me not smoking, I was all set to haggle with the Ities, especially a wizened old woodcarver. For sixteen packs and seventy cents I got from him a beautiful carving from cherry-wood of the symbols of the 15th, of the 52nd, and of the 4th—each of my units. And there, in the middle, was a place for a photo of my one and only. Stained and shellacked, it fairly glowed as I returned to display my treasure to the gang. Since the cigs cost me only four cents a pack but fetched thirty cents on the black market, the $5.50 the woodcarver figured he'd pocketed cost me only $1.34. I may not have been bettering my career as a pilot, but I seemed to be improving as a haggler.

That was a better deal than I got with the officers' club where, though I didn't drink, I still had to fork over $15 a month, most of which went for booze. My pay was only $150 a month, plus 50 percent flight pay and 10 percent combat pay. Sending home $150 a month to Dad for war bonds left precious little to spend, and having another $15 taken out represented a big hit. Some comfort I scrounged from the fact that I wasn't being sickened from the hootch the Ities were passing off to vulnerable GIs. This rotgut consisted of anything these enterprising natives could throw into the brew, including aftershave lotion and kerosene. Realizing the toll this was taking on the 52nd, Colonel Levine dispatched a twin-engine bomber to the south of France to pick up a good supply of fine wine, along with a few fine "ladies of the evening." The wine fit better in the wing tanks than the ladies, but all brought surcease from boredom and the funks that the brass complained about. After all, Levine must have reasoned, nothing was too good for the 52nd, and particularly its officers of field grade rank or above, starting with the majors who could wear scrambled eggs on the visors of their caps.

After lunch the next day I trundled down to the flight line, climbed into one of the new Ds and took off for a couple hours of mock dogfighting and gunnery practice. It seemed to go better than usual, and I returned, satisfied that I was making progress. That is, until I came face to face with Ace Burnett, now acting squadron CO while Tyler was on leave. Burnett minced no words. "What the hell, Curtis, did you think you were doing, taking up a plane without permission? Don't you realize that's a court-martial offense?!" With that he grounded me till further notice, presumably to give me time to reflect on how often I'd come to being busted. I counted them, and concluded this was my fourth try. All in all, it wasn't my best day.

June 15, 1944

Dearest Dick,
Sure was surprised to find you were in Italy! In one of your letters you spoke of "post-war plans." It may be hard to tell which career will be your choice, but remember this, my dear, your plans are my plans.

The next day, Independence Day, was, if anything, worse. For the previous night I'd checked the bulletin board, there to find that both my tentmates, Chidester and Hyde, were scheduled to fly a mission the next day. They had successfully passed the ultimate test for combat duty to climax their twenty hours. That was a high-stakes chase with Swede Larson. Using every maneuver in the book—and some that weren't—he tried losing them and coming back in on their tails. They'd passed, so now they were being introduced to the big time, a mission over the marshaling yards of southern France.

But when the mission returned, there was no sign of Chidester. The word was that in an effort to catch up to his element leader in a dogfight with ME-109s, he got in a dive and passed the red line on his airspeed indicator. His right wing peeled off as he tried pulling out at eighteen thousand feet and down he went, unable to bail out in a plane that was out of control. Hyde, relieved that he'd returned from his first mission, fed me the details. There we sat, dejected, mourning the loss of one we'd gotten to know well, even as we pondered our own fates. The three of us were now two. I could see in my mind's eye Jack's folks getting the same telegram from the War Department that my folks had gotten when Bob was shot down about thirteen months earlier.

Yes, the 4th had lost one, but had bagged four Jerries. Meanwhile Allen in the 5th had shot down four himself. The group seemed to be resting easily, knowing that we'd bagged far more than we'd lost. But we in the 4th, especially Bob and I, felt the loss of Jack deeply, even as we wondered who'd be next. Was it Bob's folks who'd be getting that notice from the War Department, or would it be mine?

June 18, 1944

My darling,

I had to laugh when some of the speakers at a 25th wedding anniversary party told about quarrels and misunderstandings which, they said, are bound to creep into married life. I said to myself, "we'll show 'em!" You'll never know how much I look forward to your letters. I awaken in the morning wondering if I'll get a letter, and all day I look forward to reading a letter when I get home.

My grounding didn't last long, for the next day I was ordered into the air with Utterback to practice flying wing to Stevenson. Already I'd racked up close to the twenty hours I needed, and could scarcely wait to get a crack at those Jerries. But wait I would. Another couple hours of practice that day put me over the minimum, and I was ready, even eager. But apparently neither Swede nor Ace thought so. When the day's mission, escorting bombers over Toulon, in southern France, returned, I was eager to learn the details. It seemed that a German pilot made the mistake of attacking a flight of four Mustangs single-handed, and paid for it with his life. I wondered, on hearing this, if Hitler's War Department sent similar telegrams of condolence to the parents of German fighter pilots. One thing for sure; if war was hell, then this was one hell of a war.

On July 6 Hyde was scheduled again, this one a long escort job over France. The 4th spotted no bogeys, but the 2nd and the 5th not only spotted them but shot several out of the skies. The next day Bob was again scheduled, this one another escort job up over Germany. The 5th lost a pilot who made the mistake of overshooting an ME-109 he had in his gun sight and, rather than turn or dive, he stayed right there so the German had nothing more to do than open fire on his rear. As Bob put it, "The Jerry ran right up his tail and— poof!" So here we were, Stevenson, Utterback, and Curtis, each of us stoking more hours until that lucky day when we'd be scheduled. That day soon came, and we exchanged excited congratulations, only to find, the next day, that the mission had been canceled, due to the target being socked in with bad weather.

As the first week of July passed, I read in *Stars and Stripes* that our infantry in Normandy was betting the war in Europe would be over in another month. After all, they noted, since D-Day they'd been making remarkable progress, pushing through hedgerow after hedgerow as they advanced toward the German border. Soon they'd be joined by other units moving north from the south of France, in a pincer movement that was bound to trap many thousands of the enemy. What those GIs were overlooking was the fierce loyalty of the Wehrmacht to their Führer which, coupled with a strict discipline that had been drilled in them, left them a formidable force. Especially was this so when they had their backs to the wall—namely the border of their own nation, a nation that in the "Great War" had never been invaded before an armistice was signed. So while the Germans in the Appenines of Italy were dug in, refusing to budge an inch, so were the Germans in Normandy putting up stiff resistance.

Nowhere was this fierce resistance more pronounced than in the air over Germany. Hardly a day passed that our escorting fighters didn't encounter enemy flak and/or enemy fighters. On July 8 another of our pilots from the 4th, Grewe, was killed when he caught a direct hit from flak and his plane exploded over Vienna. Another of our boys, Gassman, was hit but managed to return to base.

Casualties or no casualties, I was chafing at the bit. Perhaps I'd never have flown a combat mission had the brass known what I was doing, even on a simple test hop on that day. After putting the plane to be tested through my usual aerobatic regimen, I dropped to the deck to follow a river up through the Appenines, buzzing one town after another en route. I waggled my wings to the kids as they came running out to wave. Climbing, ever climbing, I was taking in the sights even as I lost track of my speed until I found myself in a narrow valley, hemmed in by mountains ahead and on both sides, and in imminent danger of stalling out—and auguring in. Slowly, ever so slowly, I kept it just above the stalling speed as I held my breath and hoped I'd miss the mountain-sides. Gradually the Mustang reversed course. I heaved a sigh of relief as I headed back down the mountain. At this point I neither knew where I was nor what I was doing there, except sightseeing. So I put in a call to our homing station, "Steelmill," and got directions to base. There I soon learned I'd been assigned to Tribbett's flight of eight Mustangs, com-pleting the four flights making up the thirty-two in the squadron. It looked like it was only a matter of days—or even hours—before I'd be scheduled for a mission. Combat was fast approaching!

On Sunday morning the 9th we celebrated by installing our first electric lights, with a fifty-watt bulb assigned to each tent. Here was luxury indeed, meaning no longer would we have to squint by candlelight in the evening to read our letters from home. That afternoon six of us went after each other in some exhilarating mock dogfighting, not only with each other but with interlopers like P-38s invading our air-space. Suddenly we watched a P-38, below us on the deck, disappear into the Adriatic, leaving just an oil slick. So this practice could be deadly stuff, too. But for the next few days I kept at it, determined to convince our squadron brass that I could—that I should—be scheduled for combat. One eve-ning, after the regular showing of the combat film, while the projectionist was putting in a regular Hollywood movie, I chanced to meet an ace in the 2nd Squadron named Bob Cur-tis. Even more coincidental, he had a younger brother named Dick. They hailed from Niagara Falls, New York, where some in my paternal line had settled years before. Why I didn't investigate to see if they were distant cousins, I'll never know.

FERRYING MUSTANGS ACROSS NORTH AFRICA

It was Wednesday, July 12, that I discovered I'd spend the next couple weeks ferrying P-51Ds across North Africa, from Casablanca to Tunis and up into Italy. Perhaps the brass at the 15th had come to realize that the casualty rate among the thirty or more of us shipped over to stanch the bleeding was way too high, and we needed more training before entering combat. Here I had twenty hours or more under my belt, and I'd be adding hours to that. Though I was disappointed that Chidester and Hyde had gotten the jump on me, I surmised that the brass knew what they were doing in upping the transition/combat training time. In any case, I was looking forward to this new venture.

Tim Tyler, our squadron CO, back from R&R, drove Harry McIntyre and me to group headquarters, where three others joined us in a drive—in nothing less than a command car—to the 15th Headquarters in Bari. Bill Buckner, Joe Caruana, and Pete Fulks joined "Mac" in appreciating the painting I'd paid for in cigs to have put on the back of my A-2 leather jacket. For there an Itie had drawn a P-51D in the process of shooting down an ME-109, smoke trailing the Jerry. This, I could only hope, would be a self-fulfilling prophecy. Dressed to the nines in this, over my tailored gabardines, with white silk scarf, leather gloves and paratrooper boots, and my Colt .45 on my belt, I affected a raunchy look with my crushed cap and a swagger stick. No doubt about it, I looked as though I could take on whatever awaited me in the sands of the Sahara.

On the way to Bari we were suddenly stopped by an Itie waving a red flag at a railroad crossing. We waited—and we waited—and we couldn't make out the sound of an approaching train. At last we got out and peered both ways down the narrow track. Nary a locomotive was in sight, so we jumped back in the car and shot past the gatekeeper as he shouted in his best pidgin English, "Are you crazee! You'll be smashed to pieces!" A mile or so down the road we peered back to see a small pony engine pulling a few cars about as fast as we could run.

Before boarding a British transport plane for Casablanca, we came across a B-24 pilot in the Red Cross officers' club, grounded for what we'd come to know as "combat nerves." We could understand that more than he realized for, apart from flying over enemy territory, just becoming airborne with a full load of bombs could be a deadly business. It seemed that every week or so we would be bent over our breakfasts, the mission planning to rendezvous with the bombers at a certain time and place, when we would hear from the south a distant "BARROOM!" This was the sound of a bomber, taking off from an airfield around Foggia, crashing on takeoff, the plane and crew being blown to smithereens. Over the target, it wasn't unusual for as many as a dozen bombers to be heading to earth, trailing flame and smoke in their wake, victims of an attack by fifteen or more bandits attacking from out of the sun. Each passing day seemed to reinforce the conviction that we were the luckiest pilots on earth, to be flying not only fighters, but the queen of them all, the P-51D. At that, we couldn't have known that it was the Mustang that, shooting down no less than 4,950 enemy planes, more than any other fighter in the European theater, would become a legend.

En route to the Orienti Hotel in Bari, we were drawn to a mob of Ities that had gathered to watch a fight. It appeared that an Itie had made the mistake of accusing an American sailor of being a Nazi and had jumped him. In an instant the sailor's buddies had waded in, even as other Ities joined the crowd, and soon there was pandemonium, broken up only when jeeps of MPs pulled up with flashing lights and loud sirens. I fingered my trusty Colt .45, not knowing where or when I might have to rely on it in a jam.

Then I met Shiney Shineberg, special service officer at the 52nd, there for an R&R. Knowing that I carried the reputation of being something of a prude, Shiney joshed, "Hey, Curtis, come with us if you want some action." Born and weaned as an action addict, I was game, only to find Shiney and company heading up the stairs of what turned out to be a bordello. There in the anteroom were perhaps a dozen girls waiting to talk us into a quickie in one of the several rooms in the rear. Joe Caruana, another pilot from the 52nd, joined me in insisting we'd wait in the anteroom while the others indulged in "R&R." Curious, I asked the girls who remained why they were in the business of selling their bodies. Their parents were dead, and each had a child to support, as well as a brother and two sisters, so they'd turned to the only business that could come close to providing for them. Now, twenty and sixteen, each of them looked ten years older. How many customers did they service? Their average take was twenty, at four dollars a clip, some of that going to their pimp/landlord. Their eighteen-year-old brother was sitting in a corner, concentrating on his studies. Suddenly an MP appeared and threatened the sixteen-year-old with jail if she kept this up. All this I was jotting down in my notebook, sensing I'd have plenty more to add when I reached Africa.

En route, our C-47 touched down in Corsica, and the fifteen of us ferry pilots aboard had lunch and took in the variety of enemy planes stuck there, including an ME-109, a Stuka dive-bomber, and a tri-motor Italian Re.2000. Then we meandered over to several huge scrap piles, the remains of scores of planes destroyed by Allied planes. There too were huge hangars, now so precarious that it looked as though a stiff wind would blow them over.

Our next stop was Algiers, and it was the 14th of July, Bastille Day, their Independence Day. While loudspeakers were trumpeting the French national anthem, the five of us from the 52nd descended the steps of the Club Bosphore. The joint, restricted to "Officers Only," reeked of tobacco smoke, booze, and raucous laughter as prostitutes cadged drinks and money for "services rendered." Then a curtain was drawn on a stage and a little orchestra struck up a tune that, borrowed from the Germans, had become a favorite of the Allies, "Lili Marlene." Out pranced a trio of what looked like middle-aged women, singing as they tried toe-dancing. It was pathetic, we all agreed. But no more so than the succumbing of one guy after another at our table to the charms of the girls, as the champagne softened the backbones of any resolutions they might have had. Finally, at 2300 hours, Mac returned to the table from his soirée and chided me: "Curtis, what the hell's wrong with you? Don't you know that girl propositioning you said she liked you so much she'd do it for free?" Free or not, I had other things on my mind, like the chance of becoming infected with VD, and the pact I'd made with Myrt back in New York.

Back on the street, a bleach blonde sidled up to Buckner with a proposition she figured he couldn't refuse. She'd shack up with him for the rest of the night for "fifty hundred francs," or about a hundred bucks. Buckner's answer must have startled her—"Say that again and I'll kill you"—even as he made a move for his sidearm. She took off like a scared jackrabbit, only to return when she concluded he must have been kidding. "Look," he said, "we'll give you the money if you take all five of us." Again she took off, and this time she didn't return.

By the afternoon of the 15th we finally touched down at Casablanca, where we drew our rations and mess tickets, then boarded a bus for the former Italian consulate, now housing ferry pilots. The next day I sold my three cartons of cigarettes for five bucks apiece and we took a bus tour of the city, courtesy of the Red Cross. As we toured the new and old medinas, or native quarters, we were told that only Muslims were allowed to live in the old section. My senses were assaulted with the din of traffic, the piercing cries of hawkers selling water from mule-drawn kegs, and above all this racket an overpowering stench.

Who among the five of us could forget what happened when the bus pulled up in front of massive iron gates leading to a fenced-off building? For there were housed eight hundred to a thousand whores who'd been picked up on the streets but couldn't pay the fine. Now, confined to this place, they were required to take on all comers for one hundred francs each. Brits and Yanks were prohibited from doing anything more than looking at the girls advertising their wares with varying degrees of undress. But as soon as one of our guys pulled out his camera to get some pictures, the girls turned tail and fled, succumbing to their superstition that this would bring bad luck.

Leaving this massive bordello, we headed for the palace of the sultan. Along the way we saw food markets abuzz with swarms of flies and incessant haggling, barbershops consisting of nothing more than a spare piece of canvas hung between two poles, with a makeshift seat and everything but broken glass used for shaving. What a contrast, we thought, as we entered the palace, enclosed by a twenty-foot wall and topped with electrified wires. This, we were told, was but one of five such palaces strung across French Morocco to accommodate the leader and his seventy wives. The opulence of the palace and its magnificent landscaped grounds and gardens was a study in contrasts with the filth and poverty of the masses. I could only conclude that the problems we faced back in the States were as nothing compared to this degradation.

My utter naïveté came through loud and clear when I

chanced to meet a little Arab kid on the street. Sidling up to me, he gave me a peek at a ring he had hidden in tissue in his hand. Softly he asked, "Hey, mister GI, how much you give for this fourteen-carat gold ring?" He'd stolen it, he confessed, "to help my poor sister." I was curious. How much? Only 1,500 francs, or about $30, surely a giveaway price. I was no sucker. How did I know it was pure gold? I wanted a closer look. He couldn't allow that, for the MPs were after him. Seeing I was losing interest, he let me look at the inscription on the inside of the ring. "You look, mister GI. It says right there fourteen-carat gold." Of course it was in Arabic. This was Greek to me, so I gave him my final offer as I hopped aboard a bus: 300 francs. I was off and, I figured, rid of him. No such luck, for there, as the bus pulled up to the next stop, was this kid, who'd run fast enough to keep up with the bus. Well, a deal was a deal, so I swapped him 300 francs for the ring, even as I felt a twinge of remorse for taking the ring for what was certainly a steal. After all, the little ragamuffin had a sister who was in tough shape. Some two weeks later I displayed my prize to the guys at the 52nd, expecting they'd be green with envy. Alas, the only green was on my finger as I slipped off the ring for them to examine. Of course it was brass, and I was the ass! Was it Barnum who said a sucker was born every minute?

On July 21, I was assigned a P-51C to fly to Tunis. There below me as I flew were caravans of camels plodding their way across the desert sands, their paths marked by little dust devils—or sand-devils—beneath the baking sun. Suddenly I found myself in the middle of a thunderstorm, its turbulence lifting, then dropping my plane two hundred feet or more and, even with my shoulder harness secure, knocking my head against the canopy. The rest of the trip got so boring that I buzzed every bomber or transport I came across, then took to aerobatics when I caught myself dozing.

Arriving at Tunis, all I could make out were a couple airfields, sitting side by side, and one of these was deserted. After making three calls on the radio for landing instructions and getting no answer, I landed on the one showing some signs of life. I overshot, not touching down until I was half-way down the runway, then braking so suddenly that I swerved and almost collided with a couple B-26 twin-engine bombers parked next to the runway. Then, as I saw the run-way ending and the danger of running off the end, I braked it hard and almost nosed over. I expected to see someone run-ning out in a jeep to show me where to park, but nobody ap-peared. So I taxied over to what looked like an operations office. Still I could rouse nobody, so at last I decided to park the bird. I spotted a likely place and pulled in, only to fall into a deep ditch, hidden by the tall grass. The prop dug into the ground and the engine stopped cold, bending one of the blades. Exiting the cockpit, I stood on a wing, looking in vain for some sign of life. So I headed for the nearest build-ing where, at last, I found someone who, in his French-accented English, told me this was a B-26 training school for French pilots, trained by Americans. Suddenly a jeep pulled up and a French lieutenant apologized for not sending a truck out to show me a parking space. Then he apologized again, this time for running the wheel of his jeep over my foot as I was parking my gear in it. The fact that it was only a jeep, plus my paratrooper boots, prevented serious injury.

He then drove me over to the nearest American field, where I phoned El Aouin airport, my destination. Yes, they'd send a jeep over the next day to pick me up. So that night I hit the hay in a cot and some borrowed bedding in a resplen-dent mansion that had been commandeered by the French, and was now packed. It was hot, stuffy, and noisy. Yet I slept soundly and awoke to a fine breakfast and the French lieu-tenant eager to return me to my injured plane. There a couple dozen GI mechanics helped pull the stranded bird from the ditch.

As I filled out my report at the Ferrying Transport Service, I realized this was no tribute to my flying. Here I'd succeeded in ferrying a single 51, only to land at the wrong airport, where I wrecked the prop and possibly the engine itself. It was all too obvious I was a lousy ferry pilot. Yet, as I chatted with the regular ferry pilots there, they were envious of my flying fighters—and particularly the P-51. More than one said, "I'd give my right arm to fly a Mustang!" Little did they realize just how incompetent I was. And the day wasn't over. For I looked high and low for my orders, and finally had the clerk cut me another set of papers, so I could board a C-47 for the return trip to Casablanca. The next morning I awoke to find the 47 had already left. The clerk who'd promised to awaken me at 0600 hours had forgotten. Not to worry, he assured me, for another 47 was due to leave at 1600 hours. That time came and went and no 47. Not till the next day did I return. By that time I was wondering what I was doing overseas. Ten days had passed and all I had to show for it was one snafu after another. I concluded that if the rest of the war was being run in the same haphazard manner, we'd never have taken the Italians, much less the Germans.

Still, I was better off than the two Negro pilots who left Casablanca ferrying P-47s and who, two days later, were still missing. Perhaps they'd gone down somewhere in the sands of the Sahara that had already claimed the life of another 47 pilot. The word was circulated that he'd augured in at such speed that several days later they were still trying to dig him out.

After watching Joe Louis, the heavyweight boxing champion of the world, in an exhibition match at the Vox Theater in Casablanca, I picked up a copy of *Stars and Stripes* to learn that Hitler had just squeaked by with his life when a bomb, planted by dissident generals, exploded beneath a big conference table. Only the size of the huge table prevented him from the death that had been long plotted by some of his generals—including Erwin "The Desert Fox" Rommel, who had become exasperated with the monomaniacal Führer. Most of the plotters were shot, Rommel escaping their fate only because of his victories in North Africa. And Hitler continued doggedly on his course of destruction—for his nation as well as himself.

On July 27 Buckner and I took off in 51s for Algiers. From the start my plane had trouble, conking out momentarily on takeoff, then leaking oil that splattered on the windshield till I could barely make out the runway at Algiers. At that, I was better off than Buckner, who couldn't start his engine for the next leg to Tunis. So I left without him, thankful that the crew chiefs back at the 52nd were a cut above those who'd been working on these planes. I also left without my A-2 jacket, for, returning to Casablanca, I found it missing, more probably stolen than strayed.

July 28 was my last day in North Africa. Landing at the 325th Fighter Group at Lasina, I boarded an amphibious jeep—or "Peep"—for a long, winding drive through the mountains to the 52nd. There I discovered that the 4th Squadron, while downing five Jerries in my absence, had lost Bob Hyde, my tentmate. His engine had quit over Germany and he'd bailed out, so was probably a POW. Irvine had lost a wing while flying on the deck and crashed. Peterson had leaked gas and, not knowing it, had run out and crash-landed in enemy territory.

So here I was, with not a single mission, and three weeks after Chidester and Hyde had their first on July 4. I drew no consolation from the fact that Chidester had "bought it," and Hyde had bailed out and was probably in a POW camp in Germany. Nor did I draw any from Stevenson being grounded, on the verge of a nervous breakdown, not having flown his first mission. Perhaps he, too, had been studying the list of casualties suffered by the thirty or more of us pilots who'd landed in Italy on D-Day. Alone in my tent, I pondered my chances. They were far from bright. Still, I was hopeful. With eight letters coming from Myrt since I left for North Africa, I simply had to get home to fetch my bride. Those letters only served to stiffen my resolve. I was also determined to complete my tour of duty of fifty missions. Together they appeared to be a big order, especially when I considered that, of the five of us assigned to the 4th, Utterback and I were the only ones still flying.

5

COMBAT AT LAST!

"Sorry, Curtis, but Pete Fulks was hit by ground fire.
He managed to bail out but is officially MIA."
—Intelligence officer, 52nd Fighter Group

Of the five of us tenderfoot pilots assigned to the 4th
Squadron, none of us with more than thirty hours of transition flying or combat training since graduating with our
wings, two of us, Utterback and Curtis, were still flying at
the end of July 1944. Chidester was KIA, Hyde was MIA,
and Stevenson, spooked at the number of casualties of our
thirty or more pilots on the *Frederick Lykes,* was grounded.
This was about on a par with the other seven assigned to the
52nd. A few were still flying, but that would soon change.

On the first day of August, I was roused from the sack by
the CQ at 0500 hours. At the last minute I was replacing a
scheduled pilot who was sick. Like so many of our recent
missions, we'd be escorting bombers over the Ploesti oil
fields. But at briefing, "Infallible" Pope, our meteorologist,
announced the target was socked in with heavy cloud cover,
so the mission was canceled. I couldn't believe it! It was almost two months since I'd arrived at this Mustang outfit and
almost a month since Chidester and Hyde started flying
combat, and here I was, still cooling my heels, waiting for
my chance. Somewhere in my reading I'd stumbled across
the psychological "Law of Set." It said that once we're set to

do something, to be hindered or stopped in attempting it was a painful experience. I was now in pain.

It was a different kind of pain I experienced that afternoon as I swam from shore and proceeded parallel to the Adriatic coast. For there to welcome me every hundred yards or so were jellyfish, innocent-looking blobs of translucent white, about five inches in diameter with a dark ring in the middle. But they packed a wallop with their stingers, and it was hours before I was no longer conscious of the pain. That was due to my seeing my name on the bulletin board scheduled for the mission the next day. I was to fly Straut's ship, a big black *B* painted on the vertical rudder, and fly wing to McCampbell, flight leader. I'd be identified as "Cockney green number two." "Cockney" designated our 4th Squadron, "green" our flight of four, and "number two" my place in the flight. Could it be that, at long last, I'd get a crack at the Jerries that had done in my brother?

My blood was racing the next morning as we left the breakfast table, hopped into a big GI truck, and bounced along the narrow dirt road to headquarters. I marveled at the composure of the other pilots as they cracked jokes, knowing full well that one or more of them could "buy it" in the next few hours. Again we took our seats on the rough wooden benches in the briefing room as the group operations officer pointed out our target on the huge map before us. It was the marshaling yards in southern France, with us providing escort for B-17s, some of the twelve thousand produced during the war. By damaging or perhaps even destroying those railroad yards we could help prepare the way for our GIs invading another part of this "soft under-belly" of Europe. We could expect flak as well as enemy fighters as we approached the coast. If we spotted Jerries we were to notify our flight leader of their location on the basis of a clock split by the horizon. Thus if I made out Jerries to the right of us, diving down from out of the sun, I'd notify McCampbell over the radio, "Cockney green one—bandits attacking from two o'clock high." He, the rest of the flight and the squadron, all tuned to the same channel, would get the terse message.

Pope announced the weather was clear with the exception of a few cumulus clouds, so we were ready to go. I picked up my chute and emergency kit, hopped in a truck and was greeted by Straut's crew chief, who helped buckle me in. Already he'd warmed up the plane, checking out each item on the list he'd come to know in his sleep. If the plane had been flown on a mission the previous day, the armorers had checked to make sure each of the six guns had its allotted two hundred machine-gun bullets.

The crew chief drew the bubble canopy shut, climbed down and hopped on the leading edge of my right wingtip to direct me with his hand signals as I taxied out for takeoff, directly behind McCampbell. When I got to the runway the sergeant jumped off and gave me the thumbs-up to wish me well. I quickly revved up the engine, checking the mags to make sure the tachometer showed full power. I then pulled out on the runway, taking my position to the right and just behind the flight leader. We'd take off together, requiring the full width of the runway. Getting the OK from the tower, we shoved the throttle to the wall and were soon airborne. Retracting our wheels and throttling back, we climbed to the left. The number three man, the element leader, and his wingman, joined us. In a moment we'd joined the rest of the squadron's planes, to merge with the other squadrons in the group. The group, in turn, continued to climb to rendezvous with the Fortresses at twenty-five thousand feet over the Mediterranean just south of the beaches of France. At twelve thousand feet I attached my oxygen mask, thankful I wasn't pestered by the swellings that would make a tight fit problematic.

Once we met the bombers, we started to crisscross the skies above them, alert for Jerries. We saw none, but we did see a virtual wall of black flak, angry puffs of exploding shells, above us, between us, and below us. And when one exploded too close, I could feel the plane bounce, and held my breath. Then the skies cleared as the bombers headed on straight for their target. As we closed in, the flak reappeared, intent on destroying those bombers on their bomb run. The bombers, in turn, were bent on destroying those marshaling yards. As they released their bombs I watched, transfixed, as small shoots of flame and black smoke arose from the target some five miles below. We'd struck pay dirt.

Of the one hundred or more bombers, none appeared to have been hit by flak, and we sighted no Jerries as we headed for the coast and home. As we passed the southern coast, the German antiaircraft batteries got in their last licks, desperately trying to hit something—anything—but in vain. I saw no bandits as we completed the mission. Once past the coast, we began our descent and were soon over Corsica. My formation was so tight that my wings extended between the wings and tail of McCampbell's ship. I watched as he removed his oxygen mask at fifteen thousand feet and took out a cigarette, relaxing now that we'd left enemy territory. I also removed my mask, but was hardly relaxed with a bladder about to burst. So I reached for the relief tube I'd been told was available for just that purpose, and was in for a nasty surprise. For instead of the contents of my bladder dropping harmlessly into the sea below, it returned with a vengeance, in the form of a fine spray, filling the cockpit and covering my face. It was now obvious that there were a few things I still had to learn about the Mustang.

As we approached the field we maintained the four-finger formation, buzzing the dirt strip perhaps twenty feet up, then pulled up and to the right, forming a single file as we flew parallel to the runway, then swung around and down to land. I had a pretty good landing, and when I reached the end of the runway and pulled off to taxi, there was the same crew chief hopping on my wingtip to direct me back to my parking place. He then helped me roll back the cockpit canopy and release my shoulder harness, and a jeep took me to headquarters where our squadron was reporting to the intelligence officer. And there, to my pleasant surprise, was Colonel Levine, commending me for a good job on this, my first mission.

Yes, I'd been frustrated for almost a month since Jack Chidester started flying combat, all the while racking up close to thirty hours of transition while he had only twenty. But, unlike Jack, I'd completed my mission, safe and sound. Of course, it might well have been different had we been bounced by Jerries, as Jack had been. I took a measure of comfort in that a few hours later as we met to watch yet another movie, *Dangerous Blondes,* in our makeshift theater. Maybe, after all, there was more danger in consorting with blondes than with confronting Jerries in the sky.

The next day it was a "maximum effort" mission. This meant that all four flights of our squadron, plus two spares to take the place of early returns, would rendezvous with two hundred B-24 Liberators over the northern Adriatic. Again I was number two man, flying wing to Tribbett. It was a five-hour-and-fifteen-minute mission, just ten minutes shy of the job the day before, August 3. Up over the Po Valley in northern Italy, over the Italian and German Alps, we flew to our target, just north of Lake Constance, separating Germany from Switzerland. We had to be careful about invading the airspace of this neutral country, much less confusing our target with one in Switzerland! Again we flew through thick flak, but saw no Jerries and no bombers flaming as they spun in below. Again the flak missed us and, as the bombardiers gave their "Bombs away!", I watched as they fell to their target below. I began to wonder where all the Jerries were. Were the rest of my missions to be "milk runs" like my first two? The only casualty, as far as I was concerned, was an oxygen mask biting into my nose, an aching rear, and a bursting bladder.

Almost every evening, following supper, I'd retire to the orderly room where, bent over a trusty Underwood upright, I'd translate my diary scribblings into something I hoped would be coherent prose. Each week I'd mail a few pages to Myrt who, in turn, tried translating them into neat, polished prose in the impeccable typing she'd learned in high school in Worcester. During her lunch hour, or in slack hours, or after hours, she was performing yeoman's work for her fiancé. And I was more grateful than she could know.

July 23, 1944

My darling,

You could have knocked me over with a feather, dear, when I got home from work and saw a big box from you. Not having heard for almost two weeks, I wasn't expecting a package. Gee, honey, those things are beautiful—that little white leather draw-string bag would make a beautiful evening bag.

After two missions in a row, I had more than a week till my third, leaving time for my nose, butt, and bladder to recover. There was plenty to do. In between softball, volleyball, and Ping-Pong there were letters to write, books to read from the group library, and movies to watch. And there were deals to be struck, not only in the surrounding villages but with others in our outfit. I struck a bargain with an enlisted man, paying him $100 for a German Luger and a Belgian Malger with a shoulder holster, with 250 rounds of ammo thrown in. I figured adding these to my Colt .45 might come in handy if I were to bail out or crash-land in enemy territory.

The amenities in our daily existence weren't much to brag about. Meals usually included powdered eggs and powdered milk, vegetables and fruit juice in cans. The only fresh fruit were the melons we bartered for with cigarettes. In one trip to Termoli five of us squeezed into a jeep and added eight muskmelons and four watermelons to make a cozy ride. Sanitary conditions included an outhouse, lying of course on the leeward side of our bivouac area. When the wind conspired against us we'd have an Itie throw some lime into the brew. Cold water in helmets perched on tripods served to awaken us and help scrape the whiskers off, with the lucky pilot using a whole mirror. Baths were taken in the Adriatic in summer and in a jerry-built shower, with hot water, in cold weather. GI-issue canvas cots with sleeping bags that were aired out when we could stand them no longer served as sleeping accommodations. All manner of insects and rodents also craved the warmth and privacy of those sleeping bags. One night we were awakened by a petrifying scream from Bob Hosey, who'd come to make up the fourth man in our tent. He swore that a mouse had just crawled across his face. Rather than argue with him we suggested he keep his pistol under his improvised pillow.

It wasn't till the 12th of August that I flew my third mission. With our GIs just one hundred miles from Paris, it was time to open a second front of the beaches of southern France. On this escort mission our bombers were to single out railroad marshaling yards, bridges, oil storage tanks, and any other targets of opportunity that would tie up transportation in and around Marseilles. Heavy flak again as we approached the coast and our target, but still no Jerries sighted. What was going on? Was Goering's Luftwaffe running out of planes? Or pilots? Or fuel? Or were they concentrating on Normandy? Or on the eastern front with the approaching Soviets?

One thing for sure, as I learned of conditions facing our ground troops in Italy and in France I was doubly thankful to be flying above the painstaking, treacherous, and dirty work below. At least I could return from a mission to quarters that were usually dry, to meals that were a cut above K-rations, and to a few creature comforts. By contrast, these men were often holed up, day after day, in conditions not much better than Dad had to put up with on the Western Front in World War I, where trenches collected the rain and all was mud and where trenchfoot and other afflictions took their toll.

When Ernie Pyle switched from the infantry in Italy to an A-36 dive-bombing outfit, he contrasted the conditions.

A man approached death rather decently in the Air Force. He died well-fed and clean-shaven, if that was any comfort. He was at the front only a few hours of the day, instead of day and night for months on end. In the evening he came back to something approximating a home and fireside. He still had some acquaintance with an orderly life even though it might be living in a tent. But in the infantry a soldier had to become half beast in order to survive.[1]

Returning from the Marseilles mission, I found we were again playing host to Mustang pilots from the 8th Air Force. These shuttle boys from bases in England had struck at targets in France, now in support of ground troops. Little did I imagine that, some fifty-five years later, these P-51s would be immortalized as "tank busters" in the movie *Saving Private Ryan*. For at the end of the film two Mustangs are shown skimming the rooftops to attack German tanks pinning down our GIs in a French town. Not only were the bombers glad to see us; so were the infantry.

Yet these strafing missions were increasingly taking the place of escort missions, and were exacting a heavy toll. On August 13, I returned from a shopping trip to find I'd been scheduled at the last minute for a strafing mission the brass had pulled out of its hat. But since I wasn't there, they scheduled somebody else in my place. It was a keen disappointment, what with me so far behind in racking up missions.

Furthermore, I was eager to move from the milk runs to something more exciting.

A SIDE TRIP TO ROME

One would think I'd stick around if I was so eager to accumulate more missions. But when our group chaplain, Chester Bishop, asked if I'd like to go with him and a few other pilots to Naples and on to Rome, I couldn't resist. With so many more pilots joining our squadron, I had no trouble getting permission to leave. Before long there were twenty-two of us bumping along in a couple weapons carriers, one pulling a trailer. Everywhere we looked, it seemed, we could find a long nose hanging over a wall, with two beady eyes telling us that Kilroy had already been there and, presumably, done "that." No doubt about it, this plaintive GI was a true pioneer, breaking new ground wherever he went.

When we turned in at Naples around midnight we figured we were in for some sound sleep. Enemy planes rarely ventured south of the front lines in northern Italy. So we were shocked awake by the wail of air raid sirens. We snapped on the lights, only to snap them off when shouts were heard above the turmoil, "Shut off those damn lights!" Then Chappy suggested, "Let's head for the foxholes." "Forget it," I said, and turned over on my cot, determined to snag some sleep before dawn. As it was, we were up at 0545 hours for a grubby breakfast and a flat tire on the trailer.

Our first stop was Pompeii, just fourteen miles southwest of Naples. Here, we were told by our tour guide, was the city that time forgot, until it was unearthed in the sixteenth century. Buried in a mud-lava up to sixty-five feet deep by the erupting Mount Vesuvius in A.D. 79, it had been excavated to show its inhabitants caught in the middle of their activities when suddenly buried alive. As we made our way among the ruins we were surrounded by kids selling miniature male genitalia, made of bronze or silver. They were guaranteed, the young hawkers promised, to bring good luck if not increased virility. Ominously, Vesuvius was still belching smoke from its recent eruption, as though to warn us that we, too, could be caught in this ancient Gomorrah, where all kinds of sex seemed to be the favorite pastime of these rich sybarites. The volcano caught them, in a phrase, "with their pants down," and my camera was busy exposing this "sin city" for the benefit of the folks back home who contended that the world was getting worse rather than better.

En route north to Rome, we paused to take in Cassino, still appearing and smelling as it did in June. At least Pompeii, after the centuries, was left with only bones. Then on to the Eternal City, where we were divided among four different families, members of the congregation of Pastor Vincenzo Veneziano. His church and mission work were supported by Chappy's Southern Baptist Convention. What little these families had they were happy to share with us, and on Sunday some of us joined them in a Protestant service while others made arrangements for a personal visit with Pope Pius XII in the Vatican.

There was so much to see that we scarcely knew where to start. Deep underground we took in the Catacombs, caves under the city where, by oil-fed torches, Christians hid from persecution in the early days of the Church. Then it was on to the Colosseum where, we were told, those Christians who were caught were fed to the wild animals. These gory spectacles were the "circuses" that the emperors provided for the multitudes, along with the bread. Garibaldi Park, our next stop, featured the statue of Giuseppe Garibaldi, who was largely responsible for the unification of Italy in the nineteenth century. His fame as a patriot and master of guerrilla warfare in conquering the Papal States was such that President Lincoln in 1861 offered him a command in our Civil War. Garibaldi declined the offer, partly because Lincoln appeared not to condemn slavery and partly because he was not offering Garibaldi the supreme command of the Union Army.

The next day I joined Chappy in trying to locate a little Baptist church in a town seventy-five miles away, only to find it in ruins and the congregation elsewhere. With a translator in tow, we set off to find the pastor and his little flock. Up one road after another, we were finally stopped by GIs warning us of mines ahead. But we continued on, careful to keep to the middle of the road, until we found a girl who led us to a little church that doubled as a schoolhouse. There we found the pastor and twelve children, including a number of orphans, scratching out a living on the rocky hillsides. He raised white angora rabbits, selling them for six dollars apiece for their fur and meat. He also raised pigs, one of them being led around with a rope around his neck. But the pastor's main source of income came from his son, about my age, and a few other older boys who worked for the Allies by day.

We could only stand in admiration of this pastor as he eked out a living for his people. Bad enough that they'd been bombed out of their church and their homes. But adding to their woes was the continuing discrimination in their own country. For Protestants, we were told, were excluded from government positions and, despite Garibaldi, they were not considered true Italians by the great preponderance of Catholics making up the country. I was astonished to learn from him that when Mussolini invaded Abyssinia in 1935, the operation was financed by the Vatican. In return, the Vatican confiscated all property left behind by the fleeing Protestant missionaries.

But lest we Protestants become smug, I had only to recall for Chappy that John and Priscilla Alden, my ancestors, had fled the Church of England to land at Plymouth in 1620. Nor was it a comfort to recall Roger Williams fleeing the persecution of the Puritans of Boston to found Providence, Rhode Island. We could only commiserate that religious persecution had figured in virtually every war since the dawn of history.

Before heading back to the 52nd, I managed to pick up a little red piano accordion for $145, including cigarettes and cash, and amused some of the gang in trying to pick out a few tunes en route. In the midst of "Old McDonald," I heard a distinct splat, and looked up to find a tomato had caught a pilot in the back of his neck. We were passing through a village and, we liked to think, the women on the second floor were tossing stuff to us out of appreciation for what we'd done in liberating Italy from the Germans. In any case, there was a roar of laughter as the overripe tomato dribbled down his back.

DOWN TO THE LAST OF THE TWELVE

Back at the 52nd, Shorty Hanes was delighted to know there was another accordionist in the 4th. Except he was an expert and I was a novice. So he started me on the fundamentals even as he told me of the loss of Jim Utterback, shot down in my absence. That left me, alone of the original five assigned in June to the 4th, still flying. As I contemplated my dwindling prospects for returning alive and well to Myrt, I discovered my flight jacket was missing, adding little to my morale. Here was $9.50 gone to the winds, or—in all probability—into the hands of some Itie with more entrepreneurial skills than conscience. I wasn't alone. Others in the outfit told of clothing and equipment that were disappearing at an alarming rate. And this despite one Itie who, for stealing a pair of trousers, was sentenced to prison for three to five years. Bill Mauldin was apparently experiencing the same problem when he wrote, "The Italians haven't given me a chance to give them anything; they have stolen everything I

own except the fillings in my teeth. . . . In spite of the fact
that the Italians consider Americans a gravy train which
came to bring them pretty things to eat, the doggies still pity
them."[2]

It was Sunday, August 20, before I completed my fourth
mission. I flew "Tackle red two" on the wing of the squadron
leader, Abdul, in escorting bombers over Blechhammer,
Germany. But learning that the target was socked in, we were
forced to an alternate target, and were back in five hours or
so, evading the usual flak and spotting no Jerries. Another
milk run. But what we lacked in excitement was more than
made up when a pilot from the 2nd Squadron, executing
aerobatics over the field, apparently got in a dive and, like
Chidester, passed the red line in seconds. Trying to pull out,
he lost a wing, then the other, then the tail assembly. By the
time he'd plowed into the ground less than a hundred yards
from our runway, the wavering screech of a runaway engine
was sending chills down my back and raising the hairs on my
head. I could only think of Chidester as I joined others in
rushing to the wreckage. Looking up from the speeding jeep,
I saw the two wings fluttering down, marking the grave of yet
another pilot from the 52nd.

Mission number five came two days later when I flew wing
to flight leader Evans on my first strafing mission. Here was
no milk run. If tension seemed to run high from time to time
on an escort mission, it ran nonstop as we entered Germany,
hugging the ground to evade enemy radar and catch a German airfield by surprise. There it was, at Blechhammer, row
upon row of enemy planes as tempting a target as we could
hope for. So surprised were they that we made two passes before the gunners reached their ack-ack stations and machine-
gun positions. By that time the guns of the 52nd had left
dozens of planes burning on the ground, while none of our
planes was even hit by the tardy gunners. In addition to the
eight Shorty Hanes's flight claimed on the ground, they got

two in the air. For on the way back they ran into a pack of slow, cumbersome Junkers Ju 88s. Sitting ducks, two of them were soon flamers under the guns of Don Stinchcombe.

After sharing our intelligence with headquarters, we were told that Joe Louis would be stopping by for a visit before an exhibition bout that evening in San Severo. That afternoon we were delighted to meet the man who'd made short work of Hitler's best, Max Schmeling, now exhibiting some of the boxing I'd seen in North Africa. I left, thankful that Hitler's mighty armed forces were now more than meeting their match in a grimmer ring of battle.

Our squadron officers' club got some much-needed sprucing up when some of our guys requisitioned a big truck and took off for Rome, to return with furniture of all kinds. They even brought back a bathtub, a Frigidaire refrigerator, and an old upright piano.

August 18, 1944

Myrt, darling,

You haven't seen squalor till you come over here and see the population starving, amid black markets galore. Actually, the people flock around the GI mess halls and beg for the leftovers on your plate—you dump them into an old tin can they hold out, and they retire to a corner to live for another day.

More and more I want to become a missionary when this is over—but I don't want to study for four years for it—mebbe I can get in on some concentrated course that should take only a couple years. One thing I'm going to be doggone sure about—my family's never going to go hungry, never have too little clothes to wear, never go without a roof over their heads, never have too little education, and never lack a "touch" with God. If these hold true, I'll have felt I'd done my duty as a father.

I wish you could send me a cow, for what wouldn't I

give for a nice, fresh glass of milk! Everything's powdered, including the eggs.

To elude the censor, I took to a code that I knew Myrt would understand.

If you see Wyman's wife [my father's middle name was Wyman], tell her I heard her son was over here flying P51Ds. They're a pretty hot ship, I hear, with a bubble canopy and all. What a lucky guy!

Shortly after writing this, I learned that the plane I was flying was no longer being censored since, in all probability, the Germans knew what we were flying, where we were based, and—very possibly—when and where our individual missions were scheduled.

On August 23, I put in my sixth mission, escorting B-24s in what I figured would be another milk run, in contrast to the exciting strafing mission. My job as number two man flying flight leader Evans's wing, I reminded myself, was to stick to his tail, regardless of the circumstances. Rendezvousing with B-24s over the northern Adriatic, we passed the Po Valley in northern Italy, then the Italian and Austrian Alps as we closed in on our target, Munich. Suddenly a swarm of fifteen to twenty ME-109s pounced on our bombers from out of the sun. Before we could jettison our wing tanks and engage them, they'd shot down as many as a dozen of our Liberators. The machine guns in the 109s' wings, supplemented by a 20mm cannon in the nose, made them deadly for the bombers, especially with the expertise of veteran German pilots. I watched, transfixed, as one after another of the bombers burst into flame, some exploding in midair, falling helplessly to the snowcapped peaks below.

Our element leader broke off from the flight with his wingman to engage the bandits while I stuck to Evans's tail, providing rear cover for him as he put an ME-109 in his sights. Suddenly it disappeared in a cloud, so Evans and I raced around to the other side to watch it, burning and spinning into the Alps below, leaving a dirty mark on the side of a mountain that was otherwise pristine in its matchless beauty in the bright sunshine.

Back up we flew to what was now sheer mayhem as bombers and fighters alike, some German, some American, were flaming and spinning. Chutes filled the air below, many of these airmen tugging frantically at their shroud lines, desperately trying to avoid being hit by spinning planes. One moment I found myself trailing Evans in trying to turn inside an ME-109. The next moment I was diving, following him as we both flirted with the 550 mph red line on the airspeed indicator. And the next moment I was standing on my tail, my nose straight up as Evans fixed another German in his gun sight. I couldn't believe that, between the planes still under control and those disabled and spinning, those men who'd bailed would make it safely to the mountains below.

Over and over I heard the echo of Swede Larson's voice in training, "Now, Curtis, if you forget everything else, remember to stick to my tail, like glue!" My heart was pounding against my rib cage, my long johns were wet with sweat, and my scalp was tingling as I stuck to Evans's tail. I didn't know how on earth I'd make out a Jerry if he came in on my tail, for I had all I could do to stick to Evans in these sweeping maneuvers, threatening to tear my wings off as I momentarily blacked out recovering from a dive, or threatening to stall and send me into a spin when I headed straight up.

Adding to the chaos were the innumerable calls crackling on the radio in high-pitched voices. "Break left, Tempest Two, you've got a bandit closing in!" "Tempest Four, where the hell are you?!" "Gotcha, you son of a bitch!" "Stinch, have you been hit?" It lasted no more than ten minutes, but it seemed like a lifetime had unfolded before my eyes when the

Richard K. Curtis (RKC), taken in Rome, January 1945.

Myrtle E. Fisher marries RKC on July 7, 1945, in Worcester, Mass.

My father, Albert W. Curtis, after his release from the Army in 1919.

Brother Bob Curtis and his new bride Margie, married April 1943. Bob was killed in action as a navigator on a B-17, June 13, 1943.

Curtis Square in Worcester, Mass., named for Bob.

Dana Curtis, a Marine sergeant as gunner on a B-25 bomber, with Midge, his bride-to-be, on his right arm and Betty, his kid sister, on his left arm, Worcester, Mass., December 1944.

Brother Dana's grave marker at Arlington Cemetery. He was killed in Korea on April 14, 1951.

RKC (right rear) as an aviation student at Butler University, Indianapolis, Ind., May 1943.

(From left to right) Ken Doolittle, RKC, Adolph Downing, R. G. Christiansen, and Fay Clark with a PT-19 Trainer at Curtis Field, Brady, Tex., September 1943.

RKC in a Basic Trainer 13, Curtis Field, Brady, Tex., October 1943.

Betty, RKC, Mom, and Dad at home, 48 Beverly Road, Worcester, Mass., April 1944.

Crew chief T.Sgt. Norman Bobcean from Mt. Clemens, Mich., and RKC. Prior to mission to takeoff, September 1944.

Crew chief and assistant checking out "Myrt's Dickie-Bird," September 1944.

Crew chief straps me into the shoulder harness to prepare for takeoff, September 1944.

Crew chief on the end of my wing guides me to runway for takeoff, September 1944.

"Itie" laborers laying new interlocking steel runway at 52nd Fighter Group, August 1944.

"Chappy" Chester Bishop persuades RKC to take a vacation to Rome, August 1944.

RKC with Pastor Vicenzo Veneziano and children in Rome, August 1944.

"Geezer" Gaisser, next-door neighbor in the 4th Squadron, 52nd Fighter Group, October 1944.

Felix "Monster" Ward and friends, 4th Fighter Squadron, October 1944.

"Itie" kids preparing a road before the monsoon rains came, 4th Squadron, August 1944.

Pete Fulks, from Evanston, Ill. Shot down September 3, 1944, and rescued by Tito's guerrillas in Yugoslavia, to return two months later, September 1944.

What happened when pilot Major "Pinky" Brewer of the 52nd buzzed the runway after returning from a mission and pulled up too sharply, October 1944.

RKC in "pinks," dressed for a squadron party in a nearby Italian village, October 1944.

I return to my beloved Myrt to help plan our wedding, Worcester, Mass., June 1945.

Germans broke off and headed for home. By this time my tongue stuck in my mouth so I could barely move it. I was shaking all over. A cold sweat broke out above my eyes, making it hard to see through my goggles.

As we returned to base I was glad I'd stuck to the tail of my leader. I hadn't fired a shot, but I'd get partial credit for the one Evans had shot down. Here was the epiphany I'd been longing for since I began my pilot training—the goal, postponed again and again since I'd arrived at the 52nd—and I was glad when my wheels touched down beneath me back at the base. In addition to Evans's kill, Nash and Frye each claimed one, making three for the 4th, while the 2nd claimed one.

My adrenaline high was just beginning to recede when I reported to Intelligence. Evans's congratulations were music to my ears. I'd stuck to his rear through thick and thin. I hit the sack that evening grateful to be alive, and literally exhausted as I'd never been before. Never had anything taken such a toll on my senses. I awoke after ten hours' sleep still tight as a drum. I had to relax. My body craved vigorous exercise. So I ran down to the beach, a mile or so away, plunged into the breakers rolling ashore, and swam along the coastline for a half mile before emerging from the bracing water and stinging jellyfish to run back to our area.

It was then that I learned more about the previous day's mission. Chuck Hudson, a new tentmate, had failed to stick to his leader, became separated, and would have been reamed out and perhaps court-martialed if he hadn't gotten a Jerry when he dropped down to the deck. At that he was lucky his leader, exposed from the rear, hadn't caught it from a Jerry. Hanes, already an ace, claimed another, while Deckman got his fourth. Our squadron was doing its share. Yes, we were also losing pilots. But for every pilot we lost we were claiming multiple kills. And for every pilot we lost we were getting several replacements. That afternoon five more joined the 4th, all 44C men who'd graduated a month before me yet were only now arriving almost three months after I'd gotten to the 4th. Ed Searles, from New York City, joined us in our tent, eager to learn from us "veterans" just what combat was like. And, of course, we weren't at all shy about telling him. The same day I ran into an old buddy from Aloe Field, a 44C classmate, big, blond Ed Leary, now in the 2nd Squadron. Each of these newcomers had undergone a minimum of eighty hours of transition back in the States, and were now to be broken into the dreamboat of them all. With but six missions to my credit, I discovered that, of the twelve of us rolling into the 52nd on June 6, only three of us were still flying Mustangs. Two others had been "washed" to fly transports, the 51 just too hot for them. Maybe, after all, we should have gotten in that eighty hours before heading overseas?

My seventh mission on Saturday the 26th was to have been playing wing to Evans again on an escort job. But up over the Adriatic my engine started to skip, so I shoved the throttle forward so it was pulling forty inches on my manifold. Still I was falling behind, so I radioed Evans that it was no use. He then told me to head for home and called up one of the two spares tailing the outfit while I reversed course. The sputtering engine then died completely, leaving me to try to coast to a landing spot. Again Lady Luck was sitting on my shoulder. I was high enough and south of the front line enough, to glide down to a repair base along the coast. A mechanic soon found the problem, fixed it, and I returned to the 52nd, glad to be back, even though I'd lost credit for the mission.

I wasn't much help on the last mission, so I figured I'd better be some help in laying down a brick floor in our squadron officers' club. The fall and its monsoon rains were just over the horizon. To clear the floor we tried dumping two less-than-prized possessions on other squadrons. The first, our ancient bathtub, found a new home in the club of the 5th Squadron. The second, our battered piano that was in need of more than tuning, saw no takers, so we deposited it in our squadron dump for the rats to pluck out their tunes.

Not till the 29th did I complete my seventh mission, flying wing to Bob Frye in a strafing mission up over Czechoslovakia, just below Blechhammer and about a hundred miles west of the Russian front. Neither Frye nor I saw any Jerries, but our element leader, Gassman, and his wingman, Chaskin, spotted a couple ME-109s and were lining them up in their sights when Chaskin's engine started acting up. So our flight dropped to the deck and soon ran across an airfield with a dozen or more enemy planes on the ground. Here was our favorite "target of opportunity," and before the airfield's guns could fix us in their sights we were gone, leaving several planes burning.

We then stumbled across a train, chugging its way across an open field, heading west ahead of the retreating Germans. So the four of us lined up in single file to put the locomotive in our sights. As Frye went in, suddenly the sky darkened with puffs of flak and tracer bullets from gun positions on flatbed cars of the train, putting him in their sights. The anti-aircraft fire missed him and he missed hitting the locomotive, but took a last swipe at the cars being pulled, including the gun positions and a car possibly loaded with ammunition. I was next. My eyes were glued to that locomotive as it was centered in my gunsight. Ignoring the flak and bullets on all sides of me, I pulled the trigger and, lo and behold, the engine exploded, sending pieces skyward. Already our outfit had lost a pilot who had run into the remains of his target as they shot upward in his path. Would I clear this mess, accompanied by a huge belch of steam? I held my breath. As luck would have it, I sailed through it without a scratch.

Returning to base, I could hardly wait to watch the day's

combat film. Suddenly I recognized my own film, but now saw for the first time the wall of flak and tracer bullets I'd flown through, in addition to the billowing steam and parts blown skyward by the exploding locomotive. When the film was over, several pilots, including Frye, warmed my heart with their congratulations. It was for this strafing mission that I later received the Distinguished Flying Cross. And it was only my seventh mission, proving that my luck was holding. The only question was how long it would last. Another forty-three missions?

It was Wednesday, August 30, that Chappy gave me the kind of news that made completing my tour of duty seem all the more doubtful. One of our pilots, returning from furlough in the States and taking off from an Italian airport, crashed into a B-17, killing all aboard both planes. Still more bad news as I drove to Foggia to look up Tom Kuykendall's brother, also flying Mustangs. Finding the airfield, I introduced myself and told them I'd gotten a letter from Tom asking me to go and introduce myself to his brother. Sorry, they informed me, but he'd recently collided with another P-51, killing both pilots. I wrote to Tom, my former instructor at Brady, giving him the news I was sure he'd already gotten from the War Department. I never heard from Tom again. Perhaps he was wondering how I, one of his biggest screwups, could still be flying and his own brother be dead. Undoubtedly the parents of these two brothers derived some satisfaction when the telegram bore the standard information that their younger son had been "killed in action," defending his country.

I now became aware of a dramatic development since I arrived at the 4th. Back in June we had all we could do to put seventeen pilots aloft, leaving ten planes unused. Now, facing September and the rainy season, we had all we could do to muster fourteen planes for a mission, with two of them serving as spares. Meanwhile we'd accumulated enough new-comers to make thirty pilots. With bad weather approaching, meaning fewer missions, and a surplus of pilots, I wondered how on earth I'd finish my fifty, especially in view of the many projections that the war in Europe would be over by the end of the year.

That same day I learned that six of our veteran pilots were receiving their second silver bar. As I was congratulating them on making captain, I came to Swede Larson, our oper-ations officer, and recalled he was a second lieutenant, the same as I was, when I joined the outfit. Now, less than three months later, he'd gotten two promotions and within a month or two would be earning the rank of major. How to account for this spurt in promotions? It seems that Jim Wiley, our CO in June, was but a captain himself, and was loath to promote any of his subordinates, including Larson, the second in command. Now that Wiley had returned to the States, he'd been replaced by nothing less than a lieutenant colonel. The lesson: if you want to be promoted, promote those below you. Another lesson: if your testosterone is riding high, stick to the American Red Cross girls. For Wiley had gained the reputation of being a ladies' man. The story of his bedding down with one of the Red Cross girls in her Clubmobile, while our pilots quietly listened to it all as they gathered out-side the vehicle, never failed to draw a guffaw in the outfit. Especially rich was his assuring the girl that she, in giving her all, was serving her country as a loyal American.

The last day of August was a bonanza. When I gathered at Intelligence to listen to the reports, I was sorely disappointed that I'd not been scheduled. For on this, another strafing mis-sion, the 52nd claimed fifty-five enemy planes destroyed on the ground, with twenty-seven or almost half of them, shot up by the 4th. In addition, of the four locomotives exploded by the group, the 4th laid claim to three. But the 52nd lost four pilots, including P. D. Frazier, who'd taken Chidester's place when his plane disintegrated on his first mission almost two months earlier. Frazier, flying wing, was protecting his leader from the rear when an ME-109 came in on his rear—and he was gone. Yes, I could exult with Nash, Gassman, and Lutry in each claiming a kill, but my enthusiasm was tempered by the knowledge that I'd lost another tentmate. And when Lutry, on this, his first mission, approached to land, he overshot and hit the runway at 190 mph. He slammed on the brakes and did a complete somersault, landing on his back. Slightly hurt, he was sent to a field hospital, where this West Point graduate received the Purple Heart.

Even more ominous, in my case, was the news that Tomlinson, one of the original twelve, who'd been assigned to the 2nd Squadron, was shot down and was now classified as MIA. That left just two of us still flying the 51s. Pete Fulks, from Littleton, Illinois, assigned to the 5th, was a big, likable guy. At six-four and 225 pounds, he had all he could do to squeeze into the small cockpit. Though in different squadrons, our paths had crossed often, since we both attended chapel regularly. I liked Pete, but was now set to wondering which of the two of us would be next.

The mission on August 31 won us a Presidential Unit Citation. It had been a banner day, but at some cost to the 52nd. The next day, however, would long be remembered not only by the 4th, but especially by two of our pilots. Again I wasn't scheduled, but learned the news at debriefing. It started out as a typical escort job, with no Jerries sighted. So our CO, Tim Tyler, dropped to the deck for opportunity targets. Sure enough, there was another train. Charlie Wilson blew up the locomotive on his first pass. But flying through the exploded parts, he wasn't as lucky as I'd been. One piece struck his plane and cut through his glycol line, forcing him to crashland in enemy territory. He emerged unhurt from his cockpit to see German trucks, less than a half mile away, bearing down on him. It looked like the jig was up—or was it?

Suddenly there appeared another Mustang coming into the same field, then taxiing toward Wilson. It was Maj. Wyatt Exum, one of our new additions to the 4th. In a flash Wilson ditched his chute and joined Exum, squeezing his long, lanky six-foot-two frame in behind him. How this India rubber man did it, curling up under the canopy above the radio, was a feat he couldn't repeat when Army photographers asked him to do it again. But there he was, pulling the canopy as hard as he could over his frame, almost closing it. Meanwhile Exum, not waiting for the canopy to close, was swinging around his plane and pushing the throttle to the wall as the Germans, now on the field, were in hot pursuit, firing everything they could to foil this daring escape. Slowly, ever so slowly, the Mustang, now overweight, gained speed and lifted its wheels from the rough terrain, just in time to clear a hedgerow, its air scoop picking up enough leaves that you'd think it would clog. But here they'd made it back, just barely. Wilson unscrewed himself from his cramped position, his mind awhirl and the sleeves of his flying suit shredded to ribbons.

For this daring act, skillfully executed, Exum was awarded the Silver Star. But that wasn't his only accomplishment. He'd come to us from the South Pacific, where he'd been flying the P-39 Airacobra and, in his spare time, inventing a new gunsight that automatically took into account both the speed of the attacker and the target plane, eliminating the need to lead the plane. In addition, "Ex," as we got to know him, astonished us with his photographic memory. We watched him carefully as he took a deck of fifty-two cards, shuffled them well, then glanced briefly at each one as he turned them over. Having done that with all fifty-two, he then identified each card before turning it over, with 100 percent accuracy.

We all came to appreciate Ex, but none more than Wilson. That afternoon he popped into our tent to share with us each vivid detail of the daring rescue. That evening we converged on headquarters to watch the combat film of the day, then to learn what America meant to *Rosie the Riveter,* a funny yet touching movie of women at work on the home front.

I tucked my eighth mission under my belt on Saturday, September 2. It was a strafing mission just across the Adriatic in Yugoslavia. I flew wing to Major Trowbridge, another field grade officer who'd joined the 4th. We managed to draw our share of ground fire as we targeted trains, trucks, and anything else looking suspicious. But no Jerries. In three hours or so we were back, there to learn from the *Stars and Stripes* that our ground troops had crossed Normandy and were just fifty miles from the German border. Meanwhile Soviet troops were joining forces with Tito's Partisans in Yugoslavia. Faintly in June, but now gaining in intensity, I could hear the sound of a death rattle in Hitler's throat.

September 3, 1944

My darling Myrt,
I don't think it'll be long before Germany tosses in the sponge and calls it a war—then secretly starts preparing for another one. I just hope the ol' U.S. doesn't try to hide its head back in the sand.

Of the 375 days I spent overseas, no day was more traumatic, no day more seared in my memory than Monday, September 4, 1944. Flying element leader on Frye's wing on this, my ninth mission, I took off from a hastily constructed dirt runway, parallel to the main one now being winterized with interlocking steel mesh pieces before the dust turned to mud. Each of our squadrons was to take a different sector in Yugoslavia and strafe everything that appeared to be a part of the German war machine. Across the Adriatic, flying just above the water to evade enemy radar, we chanced on a locomotive idling in the marshaling yards of a village. We broke formation to attack in single file. Hosey, my tentmate, managed to blow it sky-high. Re-forming, we set out for more prey. And there, pulling another freight train, was another locomotive. Again lining up to put it in our sights, we went in for the kill, led by Frye. This time the Germans were not only ready but lucky. Suddenly I saw Frye's ammo cover fly off his wing, and he began spewing glycol, trailing a white stream in his wake. With but ten minutes at the most to reach the coast, could he make it? Could he land at sea and be picked up by a PBY, a rescue seaplane?

I called Frye again and again on the radio. Was he hurt? Was he dead? Then I saw him jettison his canopy. Could he climb high enough, even to four or five hundred feet, and bail out? No answer. Perhaps his radio had been shot up. I watched his plane losing what precious little altitude he had. Closer and closer it came to the trees below. An opening in the trees and a small field. Could he crash-land there? No such luck. Into the woods beyond the field the 51 crashed, shearing off one wing, then the other. Turned upside down, Frye was held in the plane as he dangled from his shoulder harness. Then the gasoline spilled out, caught fire, and immolated him, even as we flew within a few yards of the plane, helpless to execute an "Exum" even if we tried.

Horror turned to disbelief, then to anger, then to rage as I led the other two planes on a vendetta, now more personal than ever. The radio crackled with curses and shouts of victory as we trained our guns on everything that moved: trains, marshaling yards, trucks, and anything else that appeared to belong to Hitler. At last, out of ammo, I led them to the shore and called the homing station for a fix, knowing we were also short of gas.

Then, for some unknown reason other than to prove mine was dumb luck, I dropped down over the Adriatic until I was just clearing the waves, the spray hitting my canopy. I looked back to see the other two following me, but at a safer fifty feet or more above the waves. "C'mon down and join me— this is good practice!" But they kept their distance, probably wondering if I was really determined to kill myself. When I landed I came to realize just how close I came to doing just that. For my mechanic told me I had less than ten gallons left in the tank, or less than three minutes of flying. Had I run out while I was hugging the waves, there would have been no way I could have aligned myself properly to land on water. I'd have bought it for sure.

Lost in my detailed debriefing for Intelligence was my utter stupidity in putting not only myself but the remainder of my flight at unnecessary risk. Though I kept this under my hat, apparently one or the other of my wingmen let it out. Thereafter I found myself a permanent wingman, unable to lead a flight and thereby earn my captaincy. Still, I was vastly better off than the veteran ace Frye. And I soon discovered I was better off than Fulks. Hit by enemy fire while strafing, he had bailed out and was now officially MIA. In addition to Pete, two others from the 5th failed to return, as did two from the 2nd. In all, the 52nd lost six pilots in that one mission. And I could easily have been the seventh.[3]

So here I was, scarcely a month after starting to fly combat on August 2, with but nine missions to my credit, leaving forty-one yet to fly to complete my tour of duty and return home on furlough. And now, alone among the original twelve still flying Mustangs, I was now entertaining strong doubts that I'd ever get back alive. If I was as good a flier as the rest, it appeared I was succumbing to impulse over reasoned judgment, definitely not the mark of a leader. Here was Frye, a seasoned veteran, an ace, and an able leader, and I'd just seen him burn to death in his plane. If he could get it—just like that—what hope was there for the likes of me? Yet I had to face the fact that sheer chance played a major role in combat, and that luck had been with me in spades. But for how long?

In the solitude of my enveloping depression I was coming to realize that if my klutziness didn't do me in, my stupidity would. Then where would my family, my friends, and especially my fiancée be? Compounding my consternation was my being next in line for the Grim Reaper. Philip died at five days. Then Bert at nine, and his twin brother, Bob, at twenty-two. One after another I'd lost my tentmates. Now I was alone among the original twelve still flying 51s. Of the forty-one missions left to fly to complete my tour of duty, I could count on more and more of them being deadly strafing missions. The odds were definitely not in my favor.

For the first time in my short life I was truly afraid. Oh, yes, fears had popped in and out of my mind before, but here was a pervasive fear that I couldn't seem to shake. How would that interfere with my job as a fighter pilot? Would I bow to caution when it came to attacking Jerries in the sky or targets on the ground? I resolved to be more careful, but would that resolution, like so many I'd made, founder on the rocks of impulse, of forgetfulness, of selfishness? I had to face it. Thrill-seeking was an addiction; an adrenaline high was my fix. Now I wondered how long before my luck ran out.

September 7, 1944

My dearest Myrt,

You'll never know how sweet it is to get back, sweaty and tired, from a long mission, to find a beautiful letter from you, dearest. It's like a fresh, cool breeze as it hits me and leaves things bright again! When I don't get any, I go back and read some of your past ones.

By this time I'd been getting a nudge from Mom that I ought to think about the ministry as a career—or "calling"— as she put it. Already I had been considering it, but hadn't let anybody know except Myrt. At first it was just a hint. Now Mom was pressing. After all, she reasoned, Bob had planned on becoming a clergyman after the war. Didn't I think I owed it to him to take his place? It surely wouldn't hurt my chances to be on speaking terms with the Almighty to assure my safe return. But, I figured, if Bob, with that resolve, should have "bought it" in this war, why should I deserve anything more from the powers that be? I realized my mother was projecting her own dreams on her one son, then on another. For she was the daughter of an itinerant home missionary of the American Baptist Convention who'd been trained at a religious school and had toured the New England–New York circuit with her evangelistic message. Mom had gone to the same Gordon College in Boston with the idea of becoming a foreign missionary, an idea cut short when she met and married Dad right after World War I. I could still hear the soft clack of her old typewriter as she put new words to old hymns, as she memorized Scripture, chapter after chapter and book after book, and taught us children to do the same.

But for me, the ministry seemed to pit two images against each other. On the one hand there was Chappy, a relaxed, casual buddy. On the other hand there was the stiff, staid, and very proper Rev. Cleveland Wilson, all decked out in his Sunday morning coat and tails, delivering sermons I couldn't understand in a voice that, if I wasn't poking Dana next to me, put me to sleep in minutes. As bad as his preaching was to my young ears, his demeanor, with a smile perpetually fixed on his face, was worse. Did nothing ever ruffle him? Was he always like this, even in the privacy of his own home? My emotions were definitely mixed. So I countered Mom's urging with the offer to become a Boy Scout professional. Not good enough. It wasn't simply service to one's fellow man that egged her on. It was enlisting in the service of the Almighty, in the hope that Providence would return this son to her, alive and well. I remembered her telling us kids about the importunate widow who finally got the judge to listen to her plea only because of her continuously pestering him. She'd learned this lesson well—so well, in fact, that I finally surrendered. I agreed—but I struck a deal with her and her Father in heaven. If God would return me safe and sound from this crazy war, I'd train for the ministry.

Learning of my decision, Chappy was impressed, so much so that he asked that I give my "testimony" to a worship service he was to conduct with a Negro transportation outfit nearby. Here we were, fourteen Negroes listening respectfully to two whites, one a Southerner with a distinct Virginian accent, the other a Yankee with a distinct New England accent. The service over, Chappy led two new converts to the shore of the Adriatic and immersed them in the chilly waters. I was so impressed that I set about my missionary work and cornered another pilot from the 4th, Don Stinchcombe, persuading him to join me in the evening service.

That night, as I never failed to do, I took another long and satisfying look at the photos of Myrt pasted on the inside of my footlocker cover, and decided if it took snuggling up to God to permit me, some day, to snuggle up to Myrt—well, it was certainly worth it! All this religion business, as most of the pilots saw it, was simply what a gambler does in hedging his bets. So they paid little heed to it aside from attending services at Christmas and Easter, or more often if they chanced to lose a buddy in battle. But to get serious about it, that was something else. Already I'd managed to queer myself with others in the 4th by my swearing off booze, tobacco, gambling, and womanizing. Now, as I warmed increasingly to Chappy and urged others to attend services, I was increasingly seen as a Puritan. It may not have impressed them, but surely it did Myrt, when I relayed my decision to her. And who was to know? Maybe it would impress the Big Man in the Sky.

But now, as the rainy season descended on us, I had my work cut out for me to add forty-one missions and take the boat back to the States.

6

THE RAINY SEASON
ENGULFS US

"Why the hell, Curtis, are you falling for all that crap?"
—HARRY McINTYRE, fellow pilot, 4th Squadron

"The most important thing I try to do in my classes is to
build in each student an automatic crap detector."
—CARL SAGAN

ITALY, THE FORGOTTEN FRONT

Winston Churchill was counting on General Alexander winding up the Italian campaign victoriously by Christmas 1944. Alas, it was not to be. Having taken Rome, he pursued the enemy northward, hoping that Operation Anvil, the invasion of southern France, would not divert men or equipment from his forces. Best for Italy if the invasion were postponed, if not canceled. That would permit his Allied troops, flush with victory, to press on into the Po Valley.

But as we escorted our bombers north to targets in Austria and Germany, we continued to draw heavy flak from German positions in the Valley. This despite our 15th Air Force destroying all the bridges there to hinder the retreat of Kesselring and his troops. Neither Churchill nor Alexander was happy when seven Allied divisions in Italy were diverted to Anvil. With 100,000 fewer troops, Alexander had his hands full dealing with Kesselring, who was reinforcing his line with fourteen divisions, bringing his total to twenty-six, in addition to two reconstituted Italian divisions. By August 12 Alexander's twenty-three divisions had been stopped dead in their tracks, despite overwhelming Allied air power. We had more than five thousand planes operating in the Mediterranean theater, most of them in Italy. Goering's Luftwaffe, by contrast, had only two hundred, and these had been badly mauled prior to Operation Anvil. But supremacy in the air, while critical to victory, wasn't enough to guarantee it. We still needed ground forces, especially in the snow that was by fall making any advances through the mountains almost impossible. The Germans were dug in, and it would take several more months for the Allies to uproot them.

Churchill, aboard a warship off the Riviera coast, watched as LSTs, filled with seven French and three American divisions, landed with no resistance. An American and a British airborne division had landed ahead of the LSTs to pave the way. The plan was to advance four hundred miles northward and link up with Patton's 3rd Army and its tanks, south of Strasbourg and just sixty miles from the German border. Though Hitler diverted four divisions from Normandy to shore up his southern troops, they were no match for the Allies' superior power on land and in the air.

Operation Anvil was off and running even as, on the other side of Italy, Churchill was meeting with Tito in Yugoslavia to assure himself that the two thousand tons of supplies the Allies were delivering by air were not in vain. Yes, Tito would assist in Allied landings in the northernmost tip of the Adriatic, at Trieste and Istria. But no, he was opposed to the Allies controlling the area. He wanted it to be a part of his Yugoslavia. Churchill, however, holding the trump card in Allied reinforcements of the Partisans, prevailed amid Tito's grumbling. Churchill then asked if Tito would try to introduce communism in his lands, once victory was assured. No, replied Tito, he had no intention of doing so. Would Tito make that public? No way, for that would make it appear that Tito had been forced to do so. Then Churchill, knowing that Croatia had sided with the Germans, warned Tito that the Allies would lose interest if the fighting in Yugoslavia developed into a mere civil war and the struggle against the Germans became only a side issue. Churchill insisted that Tito meet with King Peter and come to an agreement to end the civil strife, and Tito agreed.

Everything seemed to be going well on all fronts, with the exception of Italy. By September 11 Anvil and Overlord would join forces near Strasbourg. But these successes in Europe came at the expense of Alexander's being tied down in the snows of Italy's mountains. Still Churchill held out hope against hope that Alexander would advance through the Po Valley and take Vienna before the Soviets got there. "Even if the war came to an end at an early date," wrote Churchill, "I have told Alexander to be ready for a dash with armoured cars."[1]

As the ground war in the rugged terrain ground to a standstill, we in the sky had no shortage of targets—if only the weather would cooperate. By September 5 the drenching rains were turning our area and our spirits to mud. I unburdened myself to Myrt, complaining that I'd never finish my tour of duty. Increasingly I viewed the war as senseless. Had I known, when I escorted the bombers in blasting Munich's marshaling yards and aircraft factories, that just outside the city was Dachau, one of over two hundred concentration camps in German-controlled territory, the war would have made more sense. For in those camps, unbeknownst to any of us, the Germans were systematically exterminating no less than 10 million Jews, Gypsies, homosexuals, and political dissidents. Neither did we know of Hitler and Himmler standing before large assemblies of Wehrmacht officers to recount in grisly detail the genocide of the Jews, to the enthusiastic applause of the military brass. Nor did we know of Hitler's warning to his people that the collapse of his thousand-year Reich would bring not only personal and national catastrophe, but the ultimate victory of the Jews.[2]

But we were ignorant of all of this. And we were ignorant of the Manhattan Project, in which German scientists who'd emigrated to the United States were helping develop a super bomb that would end the war in Asia in less than a year.[3]

THINGS ARE LOOKING UP?

In all, our Allied prospects the first week of September looked brighter than my own. Would I ever see again Pete Fulks and other MIAs from the 52nd? The 5th brought a ray of hope when Stewart reappeared. Captured and taken prisoner by the Germans a few weeks earlier, he was back among us, eager to share his experiences. On the first leg of the shuttle run, with the oil refineries of Ploesti the target, he'd been shot up by an ME-109 but had managed to bail out. Captured, he was confined to a prison in Bucharest. But when Romania fell to the advancing Allies, the 15th Air Force sent in bombers as well as transports to return some one thousand of our Air Force personnel, including Stewart. So I held out a wisp of hope that I'd see Fulks again. Or, for that matter, Myrt.

My tenth mission was to escort bombers over Hungary, where they unloaded their cargo over the bridges thirty-one thousand feet below. These were critical for delivering reinforcements and supplies to the enemy as well as providing escape routes in their retreats. But as I watched in fascination the flame and smoke rising from below, I longed for just some of that heat to stop my teeth from chattering and my body from shivering. I'd even brought a blanket along to cover my legs over my summer flying suit, but flying at an altitude probably a half mile above Mount Everest, the temperature had to be below freezing. What little heat came from the cockpit heater did little to warm my bones. Again there was some flak but no bandits, and I was back in four hours to thaw out over hot tea and Myrt's delicious Toll House cookies.

Though we had little heat almost six miles up, we were determined to have heat in our tents, so we installed a kerosene stove. With plywood on the floor and the stove in the middle, we were beginning to savor some of the creature comforts. That evening Straut, our next-door neighbor, along with Morris and Bourne, were promoted to first lieutenant, earning the congratulations of us all. As for me, I had little to celebrate in the leg cramps and jellyfish stings awarded me for swimming that afternoon.

Friday the 8th turned out to be another red-letter day. A select group of ten of us, representing the group, were awakened at 0500 hours. At briefing I learned I'd be flying wing to our new Group CO, Colonel Malcolm, who'd replaced Colonel Levine. Comprising just two flights and two spares, we landed at a British base at Ancona for a second breakfast and briefing. Our job was to provide cover for eight British Beaufighters, twin-engine bombers. Soon we were skimming the waters of the Adriatic, just as I'd done four days earlier, in hopes of evading enemy radar. Our target was the former luxury liner *Rex,* now converted to a troop transport, anchored in the harbor at Trieste. Reconnaissance revealed that it was a sitting duck, yet in all probability surrounded by ack-ack batteries and machine gun nests, as well as three enemy destroyers. Our job was to draw enemy fire, forcing the enemy to reveal its gun positions and to permit the British Beaufighters to go in with their rockets, which would hit the ship just below the water's surface. Our second briefing at the British base did nothing to relax us when they said this would be one of the most dangerous missions we'd ever had.

As we approached our target I wondered at the briefing's choice of words. Was this a sitting duck with all the ground fire we could expect, along with Jerries bouncing us from above? In all probability, we could expect casualties. Spotting the big ship off in the distance, we waited for the worst. But to our surprise, ground fire was light, we saw no Jerries, and the destroyers were ten miles away.

It turned out to be a field day. First Tim Tyler's flight put the *Rex* in their sights, strafing to draw out the positions of enemy ground fire. Then the Beaufighters attacked, releasing their rockets—three-inch weapons and six to a plane—piercing the hull below the waterline. Then it was our flight's turn. We raked the vessel from bow to stern, then turned and dropped our wing tanks on it for good measure. Could we set it afire? No such luck. But when we turned to leave for home we saw one sad king of the luxury liners, listing badly as it burned from rocket fire. No longer could it be used to evacuate German troops from Yugoslavia. We returned to base without having suffered a casualty, surprising Intelligence. The mission confirmed just how effective we Allies could be when we worked together harmoniously.

The next afternoon, a sunny day for a change, I was asked to check out a plane that had just been repaired. Meeting Snake Morris in the air, we took turns chasing each other in and around, above and below the sun-washed clouds. It was relaxing, it was fun, and I could report the repair had fixed anything wrong with the ship.

September 9, 1944

My dearest Myrt,

Myrt, how would you like to learn how to fly after the war? I hope to get myself a plane some day. I can teach our kids to fly as well. Really, it's in a class by itself—up above the clouds where I can almost shake hands with God. Away from the hustle-bustle of the crazy world below, to the peace and quiet and hum of the engine throbbing confidently in your ears. You get to realize what is meant by flying "getting into one's blood."

On Sunday the 10th I flew my twelfth mission, taking Straut's place on Hanes's wing. Straut was off to Rome for a visit, leaving his mistress alone next door. Yes, we promised, we'd look after her. But he wouldn't leave until he'd exacted a promise from us that we'd just be looking. Joining the bombers for escort, we found our target socked in so turned to our secondary target, none other than the forsaken *Rex,* now a burned-out hulk ready to capsize. Our bombs helped it along, and by the time we left, the only trace of the once-proud liner was a big oil slick.

Returning for debriefing, I was in for some great news. One of the new P-51Ds was being assigned to me! I could scarcely believe the news. I decided to balance the big, black *N* on the tail with the name for the ship at the front. So I had the group artist paint in script on the side of the fuselage and just in front of the cockpit *Myrt's Dickie-Bird.* What it lacked in ingenuity, I figured, it made up in uniqueness. I could guarantee no other ship, bomber or fighter, carried that name. When others in the 4th wondered at it, I explained that Myrt was my fiancée. Yes, they understood, but what was this "Dickie-Bird"? Well, the plane was a bird, and it was now assigned to the nickname I bore growing up. They usually left, scratching their heads. But as long as Myrt and the folks and my new crew chief approved, that was it. Sgt. Norman "Bob" Bobcean, from Mt. Clemens, Michigan, was obviously not only a dandy mechanic but a man of impeccable taste!

Along with our new planes we in the 4th inherited eight new pilots, two of whom trained with me in 44C back at Brady. Farnkopf was a buddy from college training at Butler, while Easely and I had been together from Preflight through Advanced. Only now, after six months of transition flying, were they joining the 52nd. Yet, with all my head start, here I was with but twelve missions under my belt and less than one hundred hours in a Mustang.[4]

Softball was one of our favorite games. Pitted against

other pilots, we managed to hold our own. But put against our own enlisted men in the 4th, we scarcely knew what hit us. As catcher in these games, I did my share of landing us usually in second place. In a game on September 11, with a stand-down keeping us out of the air, John Lowe, our group adjutant, broke his arm. When Doc Curran examined him, he was convinced Lowe was suffering from shock, so decided to test him by asking him to pronounce a certain word. Sure enough, Lowe was left gasping as he stammered, finally getting out the word. So Doc called for a blanket to comfort the good adjutant and desisted only when Lowe finally convinced him that he was a stutterer.

It was on the 12th that I flew my thirteenth mission, providing low cover for B-24s while other fighters crisscrossed the skies above us. Our vapor trails, intersecting continually, would be visible to the flak batteries five miles below. Reconnaissance had revealed what looked like jet propulsion factories and warehouses in the area of Munich. Hitler was counting on the jets to make the difference in the air war, so he'd surrounded the city with the big guns, fully capable of knocking us out of the sky at our altitude. With a speed at least 100 mph faster than our planes, the ME-262s could shoot us out of the sky like fish in a barrel. So this was a critical mission.[5]

I flew number four on Chaskin's wing while Larson led our "Tackle red" flight. As we approached Munich we saw the Germans had prepared a reception for us, in the form of a thick smoke screen obliterating the targeted factories and a thick wall of black flak puffs so concentrated on us that a couple explosions just below me tossed my plane upward a hundred feet or so. I shuddered to think where I'd be had they hit me. Suddenly I watched in fascinated horror as three Liberators collided in midair and went into their death spins. I saw no chutes, so concluded another thirty men accompanied the flaming, smoking bombers as they crashed into the mountains below.

Then Swede was on the horn with "Bandits at twelve o'clock low!" With that, he executed a quick split-S and we did the same, following him down in a steep dive. But I was falling behind Chaskin, so I quickly checked to see I'd not jettisoned my wing tanks. That done, I had no trouble keeping up. There, at twenty thousand feet, were the "bandits" in the form of friendly P-38s.

Back to base, mail call brought a welcome letter from Dana. He was now training as a gunner on a B-25 twin-engine bomber, the same plane Jimmy Doolittle and his boys used to bomb Tokyo in the summer of 1942. So here were the three Curtis boys, all choosing to fight this war in the air. With Bob, the navigator, KIA, I could only hope that Dana and I would be able to tame the "Wild Blue Yonder" enough to return alive.

September 3, 1944

My darling Dick,

Friday when I got home I found a very beautiful cedar chest standing in the dining room. It's all new and shiny and beautiful. Gee, I wish you could see it now, honey. And now I've gone and bought a beautiful china dinner set! Real china is hard to get now, so when I saw this set I thought it would be wise to get it. Right? I think of you so often, my darling, wishing that you were home, but at the same time realizing that you wouldn't be completely happy here if there was work to be done over there. Remember, dear, "I'll Be Seeing You." A nice song!

Stars and Stripes carried the good news that the Allies were now ten miles inside Germany. My heart skipped a beat. Would the war's end in Europe be a Christmas present? Now that would be an unbeatable gift for the holiday!

September 12, 1944

Dearest Myrt,

I speculate that Germany will toss in the sponge on October 7, 1944, at 3 P.M. and Hitler won't be around. For the German people will have overthrown him, aided by the Army (and against the Nazis), and will have set up a Committee on Armistice themselves. The U.S., however, won't have much to say what happens to Europe after that, for Russia's got it in the bag. Then, I figure, I'll get a crack at the Japs. If they're afraid to meet the old reliable P-40, how will they react to the new P-51?

Savoring the prospect, I hiked down to the flight line to pay my respects to my old P-51B, undergoing a seventy-five-hour inspection. It now looked like an anachronism, the big *K* still emblazoned on its rudder. Still, it was at least a notch better than its former pilot, I concluded, when I took to the Link Trainer to brush up on my instrument flying. There'd be a lot more of it, now that heavy cloud cover was becoming the order for most days. I quickly showed how rusty I'd become since my last visit to the Link in June by spinning in not once but three times. Had I learned nothing? Or had I forgotten so much? Or was the klutz lying just beneath the surface reasserting himself? I checked with the technician at the controls, only to find he'd forgotten to advance the throttle as I was climbing. No wonder I was stalling out and spinning in as I tried to make it to 1,500 feet! He apologized and I climbed back in, managing this time to pass.

BULL SESSIONS AND JAM SESSIONS

By September 14 our missions were being scheduled, only to be canceled because of cloud cover obscuring enemy targets. It was becoming such a habit that card games inside and volleyball games outside our officers' club were filling the hours. Having been burned enough when I'd tried gambling, and being a novice at poker and blackjack, I joined them only when we could face off across the Ping-Pong net or the volleyball net. The rest of the time I was either reading, practicing the accordion—sometimes with Hanes and others in improvised jam sessions—or writing letters. Or I was engaging in heavy conversation with my tentmates and others as they joined in.

With the start of fall just a week away, there was a chill in the air. But inside my tent there was no chill as cigarette and cigar smoke brought tears to my reddened eyes and I had to step outside every few minutes to breathe some fresh air. At last I turned to Smitty, the cigar-smoking civilian representative of the Packard Company, which was manufacturing our new Rolls-Royce engines. "Why on earth do you smoke, Smitty?" At that, Hudson, the cigarette smoker, chimed in. "Why, everybody smokes, Curtis, don't you know that? You're the odd man out!" Rather than quit, or even step outside to blow their smoke, they proceeded to marshal every conceivable argument and parade it before me even as they continued to blow smoke in my face. Certainly anybody who was a real man smoked! Hudson: "Just look at Humphrey Bogart. Look at Clark Gable. Why, even the women are smoking!" Smitty: "Do you suppose, even for an instant, that Uncle Sam would be passing out a couple cartons a week if it was bad for you?"

The flak of their arguments was exploding around me. I reflected on the folks back home. Dad smoked, as did Myrt's dad. All my scout leaders lit up. All the men and some of the women at Norton's carried a pack to "relieve their nerves." But Smitty and Hudson weren't about to let me off the hook. A smoke was "satisfying," as Chesterfield reminded us. And any GI, including Kilroy, would "walk a mile for a Camel!" So I turned to my father as an example. I pointed out that our small house reeked of tobacco smoke as he, his eyes red and his fingers yellow, insisted on a pack of Old Golds accompanying him wherever he went. And when it came to any physical exertion, he was easily winded. So how, I put it to them, could anything that bad for you be good for you? At last, my arguments falling on deaf ears, and my eyes watering, I bolted out of the tent, trailed by guffaws.

In the discussions I had with my fellow pilots, none aroused such heat as when the subject was religion. I recalled the unspoken rule for commissioned officers that they were not to discuss religion or politics if they were to maintain themselves as "officers and gentlemen." I didn't know much about politics except that Dad was a staunch Republican who'd voted for Alf Landon in 1936, convinced by a "scientific poll" conducted by *Liberty* magazine that he'd win in a landslide over Roosevelt. Except it was FDR who'd won in the landslide. For the poll had been done by phone, and it was the affluent Republicans who had most of the phones during the Depression. Now, in 1944, twelve years after being elected to his first term, and still my commander in chief in his fourth term, FDR looked like he was running out of steam. But beyond this, my understanding of politics was minimal.

It was when our discussions turned to religion that I could count on plenty of fire and smoke, if little light. And no one could bring the fierceness of verbal battle to the fore like Harry McIntyre. Older by a year or so than I, Mac was a Harvard man and son of the editor or publisher at Little, Brown, in Boston. In fact he claimed his father owned 49 percent of the business. Mac's eyes widened as he breathed fire along with his cigarette smoke when we talked religion. Raised a Roman Catholic, he'd come to see the light at Harvard when he was introduced to William James's *Varieties of Religious Experience*. I soon realized I was out of my league. What little I knew of politics I'd imbibed from my father, and what little I knew of religion I'd imbibed from my mother. A strict fundamentalist, she took literally, it seemed, every word of the many she was memorizing from the Bible. If a little learning was a dangerous thing, I was in danger of being swamped by Mac's flood of information as well as invective. I'd just picked up a copy of Henry Link's *Return to Religion,* the story of a businessman who'd left the fold, only to return to it when he found the alternative unable to sustain him in crisis. Mac, now a professed "born-again atheist," scoffed, but agreed to read it if I'd read his copy of James. As he left the field of argument he couldn't help but leave a parting shot. "Why the hell, Curtis, are you falling for all that crap?!"

In later years I learned of Carl Sagan's standard answer when he was confronted with the question of what he tried to do for students in his classes at Cornell. "The most important thing I try to do in my classes is to build in each student an automatic crap detector." But on that day, as Mac took his leave, I could only think of those I'd met whose religion seemed to sustain them, especially in times of crisis. There was Mom, arousing the admiration as well as the sympathy of the neighbors as she took refuge in her religion when confronted with one after another of her sons dying. And there was Myrt, thoughtful, kind, outgoing, wise beyond her years, and a staunch Christian. And here in Italy was Chappy with his ready smile and quick wit, thinking nothing of putting on his boots to help push jeeps out of the mud, even buying another glass of booze for Malcolm when, by mistake, Bishop knocked over the CO's drink at the bar. So I had some living exemplars to confirm me in my choice, and I wondered who Mac had. Atop all this, I explained to Mac that John and Priscilla Alden, my ancestors, had fled England on the *Mayflower* because of religious persecution. Again Mac scoffed. I had my nerve claiming to be a direct descendant of the Aldens. "Curtis," he said, "you're no Pilgrim, but, sure as hell, you're a Puritan!" With that, we broke off debate, and I took some solace from a book I'd taken out of the library, Somerset Maugham's *The Summing Up:*

> It may seem arrogant that I should not be content to walk in the steps of men much wiser than myself. But much as we resemble one another we are none of us exactly alike. . . . and I see no reason why I should not, as far as I could, choose my own course.[6]

Later in the book I learned of the author's complaint that, now in his sixties and in failing health, he would not live long enough to write so much more that he wanted to write. He deeply regretted the habits he'd cultivated that were now shortening his life. So I resolved that not only would I steer my own course, but try to guard my health so I'd live long enough to undertake my life's work and complete the body of it. Here was serious thinking and resolving, something more foolish mistakes could drastically foreshorten. First on the agenda was simply surviving this war.

If I wasn't challenging Mac or Hudson or Smitty to a debate, I'd find release in my piano accordion. The pilots of the 4th didn't have to look far for an occasion to break out the booze and celebrate in style. On the evening of September 14 it was the celebrating of Smith and Larson making their second silver bar. Hanes and I fetched our accordions and soon the rafters—such as they were—were ringing with one song after another—such as *they* were. It was a toss-up as to whether the singing or the accordion playing was worse. At any rate, the more booze was consumed, the more boisterous the outfit became, until they had Exum on the floor, removing his pants. It wouldn't have been a big deal except for the presence of several Red Cross gals, who seemed to enjoy it as much as the rest of us. As we tossed his pants to one another, with the good major in hot pursuit, he finally bolted for the door and returned, dressed in another pair. By the time I left for my domicile, Hosey and Bofinger had passed out cold.

The next day who should come to the door of my tent but Exum. Nope, I didn't have his trousers, and I had no idea where they were. Come to find out, that was not his concern. Apparently he was so moved by the accordion music the night before that he was determined to learn how to play. All I knew, I explained, were a few fundamentals and a few simple tunes. That was all he wanted, so I taught him what little I knew. And that night, as Hanes and I returned for a little more harmonizing, with the singing boisterous enough to be heard above the pounding of the rain on the roof, Ex was scrutinizing my fingering as I plunked out the tunes.

CAUGHT BETWEEN THE RUNS AND THE RAINS

The next day was a trial and a half. I awoke to the drum of raindrops on the roof, a light spray descending from the ceiling with each pelt of a drop. But I had no time to examine the leaky roof. I had all I could do to thrust my feet in my boots, grab my poncho, and head for the privy, slopping and sliding through the thick mud. Not only had I vomited during the night, but I was now possessed with a fearful case of the runs. Forgoing breakfast as too much of a good thing, I took to the accordion again to practice boogie-woogie but soon quit as shouts from nearby tents hinted that I was making too much of a good thing.

By afternoon the sun was shining, prompting me to invite "Nails" Ludwig, a new 44C graduate living next door, to join me in a run to the beach. The chill of the water did more than shock me, and it took the return run to thaw me out. There, waiting for me, was a letter from old pal Al Barrios, now a copilot on a B-17 in England. George Arnberg, another fellow Worcesterite, was now flying a B-26 bomber. I was happy for them, but happier that I was flying fighters, and the queen of them all.

It was Sunday, September 17, before I racked up my four-teenth mission, a super-secret deal, with just twelve of us, and Morris the spare. Escorting only two B-17s, we were to make no radio contact, under threat of court-martial. Hardly had we started out than three turned back, apparently with engine trouble. At that point I gave special thanks for Bobcean, my crew chief, and his assistant, for rarely did I ever find less than a purring engine in *N*. When Ernie Pyle visited the A-36 dive-bomber base in Italy, he found pilots with unbounded praise for the enlisted men who cared for their planes:

> These men took a terrific pride in their planes, and they worked like dogs to keep them in good shape. Being trained technicians at least 25 [years old] . . . these mechanics were fully aware of three things about their jobs: that their lives were immeasurably better than that of the infantry men and they should be grateful; that the pilot that flew out to battle was the one of their family who really took it; and that the pilots' lives often depended on their work. The result was that they were immensely conscientious. When a favorite pilot failed to come back the enlisted men took it as hard as the officers did. A mechanic whose plane was shot down was like a boy who'd lost his dad.[7]

Soon our secret mission was up over Yugoslavia to Hungary, where the big bombers set down in a small airfield of grass. There, eagerly awaiting them, was a band of Allied escapees, including some big brass. Before the bombers left the country, they left their calling card in the form of bombs on the marshaling yards of Budapest. Leaving orange flames and black smoke billowing behind us, we made for home, surprised that no Jerries attacked us. The flak, however, was especially heavy, yet missed all of us. Hardly had we left Budapest than we ran into squalls and thunderstorms so fierce that bombers and fighters alike were bobbing up and down, hard put to keep from running into each other. All the way back to the base the nasty turbulence did its best to do us in, so it was with a sigh of relief that we finally descended through the thick cloud cover and rain to land back at the 52nd. No doubt the escapees were even more relieved when they emerged from the bombers at Foggia. At debriefing I learned that Smith, whose captaincy we'd just celebrated, lost his engine back in Hungary and, in trying an emergency landing, overshot and, pushing down too hard on the brake pedals, turned end over end. Only later did we learn he'd been captured and was recuperating in a prison hospital.

In *Stars and Stripes* I learned that the Allies had invaded Holland. But there was nothing in the paper about the 170 B-24s that the 15th Air Force was converting to transports. Their job: to ferry our various units to northern Italy to be closer to the enemy. This would enable us to range farther and farther up into enemy territory, particularly Germany, to hit the heavy industry there. But it also would make us more vulnerable to enemy attack at our new bases.

It was Monday the 18th that I dressed in my best bib and tucker for an awards ceremony at group headquarters. There I would be reacquainted with standing at attention, sirring, and saluting, as a bird colonel from Air Force headquarters in Bari pinned an Air Medal on me and several others. That was for completing just five missions, and here I'd almost completed ten more, earning me an oak leaf cluster to attach to the medal. Purple Hearts and Distinguished Flying Crosses were also handed out. But the one that did more to burst our buttons in the 4th was the Silver Star pinned on Exum. No one felt he deserved it more than Charlie Wilson. Ex joined me the next day for some more lessons, apparently as appreciative of what I was trying to teach him as he was for the third-highest award given for valor in battle. That afternoon I joined Steinle and Deckman in commandeering a truck to haul back a load of sand from the beach to provide an island in the rain covering the bivouac area and threatening to inundate the floor of Deck's little shanty. That night, as I turned in, I again realized how lucky I was that I was no longer flying the old P-51B, for that day its undercarriage buckled on landing, leaving old *K* in dire straits.

On September 20, I completed my fifteenth mission, flying wing to Morris until Knepper developed engine trouble and returned to base. Then Morris and I both flew wing to Gassman, the flight leader, as we escorted Liberators to targets in Czechoslovakia. No Jerries sighted, but heavy flak followed us as we left giant fires in our wake. On the return trip a flight from the 2nd Squadron dropped down to strafe, only to lose a man to ground fire. The memory of the deadly accuracy of German machine gun fire, taking out Frye, was still painfully fresh in my memory. I experienced a different kind of pain as I parked *N* back at the base and raced for the nearest privy.

By this time I was exasperated with the runs as well as with the swellings that kept emerging on my face. Was it something I was eating? Drinking? Could it have something to do with the gallons of fruit juices I was emptying from the big #2 cans I'd gotten in exchange for my cigarettes and beer? Adding to my consternation was the steady drumbeat of the monsoon rains pelting the roof of the tent, of the officers' club, and of the privy. If I tried reading in bed, the drops that were now falling from the ceiling formed puddles on my sleeping bag and spattered on my pages. Then I learned that the guarantee of the canvas being leak-proof held only as long as nothing touched the inside of the canvas. Others were experiencing the same leakage, and we all sought refuge in the club, making it a crowded, stuffy, and noisy place to do any reading, much less serious thinking. The dirt roads had now become canals, to be forded at the risk of drowning the engine, if not the riders. To take to the land and pioneer a new road risked getting stuck there.

The dust of summer was now the goo of mud. Yet, game to the challenge, Farnkopf, Gaisser, Hanson, Dzurnak, and I requisitioned a 2½-ton truck and were soon fording the waters to the beach to haul back a load of sand so heavy that, when we tried driving up and over the railroad tracks that ran parallel to the beach, the truck threatened to flop back and over, until four of us stood on the front bumper. It worked, as did the much heavier truck on its return trip, even with the water up over the axles. Back at the 4th, we spread the sand out as a subfloor-island, then filtered it with twelve gallons of 100-octane aviation fuel to exterminate the crabs, insects, and other denizens of the shoreline. If the raw gas didn't get them, then they were doomed, we figured, when we tossed a match to it. Then and only then was it fit to put a cover over to form a floor. And what did we use as a cover? Well, it so happened that there appeared to be an extra pile of steel matting next to the runway, and soon we'd loaded twenty pieces and tied them together atop the sand. It was a good thing we weren't accosted by some "wheel" to investigate what we were doing. But with the rain and all, we figured—correctly—that others were tending to their own escape from the rain. The job done, we took some satisfaction from lugging sand without getting stuck, purloining matting without getting caught, and laying it all down without interference from the big brass. We were drenched to the skin, chilled to the bone, and nursing big blisters. And in my case, I'd had to take breathers all too often to make for the privy. Yet we derived some satisfaction that we'd bested the elements and any nosy superiors.

On Friday, September 22, the mission was a go, and I

found myself back in old *K*, now presumably repaired, flying spare on a mission to Munich. By the time we passed Ancona I saw I wasn't needed, so dropped down to the deck to buzz the shoreline back to the base. Luckily, there were no bathers forced to duck to avoid losing their heads, as had happened to a native when a P-38 clipped him before he had a chance to duck. I never did find out what happened to that pilot, but it was taken for granted by us that American lives were many times more precious than Italian lives. So much for prejudice and screwball pilots like myself. I returned to find we were being issued—at long last—winter flying gear. The heavy leather and fleece-lined flying suit and gloves, along with fleece-lined rubber boots, meant I could shed the wool blanket I'd been using to stave off the shivers.

It so happened that some missions were "barn-burners"—the kind you never forget. Others were "butt-burners"—the kind that, at most, were mere blips on the memory screen. My sixteenth mission was of the second kind. It could well have been of the first kind had our target, Blechhammer, not been invisible because of heavy cloud cover. Now that Ploesti had been laid low as an oil producer for Hitler, we turned our attention to this city, the number one target now in the European theater, producing some fifty-seven thousand tons of gasoline each month. But there it was, hidden below heavy cloud cover, so the bombers found an alternative target, again escaping the flak that peppered us repeatedly across enemy territory.

At the debriefing I learned things at the base had been more lively than this 5′25″ mission. A Heinkel 111 German bomber had crash-landed at the 332nd. Emerging from the wreckage, no worse for the wear, were a German general, two colonels, and a Hungarian ace and his wife. Taken into custody for questioning as POWs, they were thankful to be alive and out from under Hitler's heavy thumb. Within an hour of the crash-landing, the Heinkel had been stripped clean of everything that could possibly be a souvenir.

September 27, 1944

As you probably know—and if you don't, my folks would readily vouch for it—I've always had a sort of crazy bug inside me. Whatever I drove—a car, truck, or bicycle—I always wanted to see how fast I could drive it. Really, living to me has always been to see how close I can get to breaking my neck—without doing it. So far I can say I've been more than fortunate, for flying the P-51 on strafing and escort missions soon takes a pretty good portion of that crazy feeling out of you.

Come October 1 and with it five more pilots for the 4th. By this time the only thing we could guarantee them was that the sun rarely shone by day nor the moon by night. But they were always welcome to the crap games that, lubricated by ample booze, took their toll. One night Tyler lost $1,500 while Ex walked away with $2,000. Heavy money was changing hands beneath a roof newly tarred. For at supper, night after night, leaking rain was diluting too much of our grub. Before long the canal-roads were too deep to ford, so we had a bulldozer carve out new roads through the fields. As the water began lapping our floors, taking the sand out from beneath the plywood, we grabbed our GI shovels— small enough to carry, big enough to dig a trench—and went to work.

September 19, 1944

My darling,

I hope, Myrt, that they all realize soon that it's about time to call this thing quits. Life's too short to spend it fighting. I only hope and pray, dear, that when our sons grow up they won't have to meet with the same experience as the children of World War I heroes.

It wasn't till October 7 that I was able to take to the air on another mission, this time as wing to our group CO. Was he checking out the rumor that must have been circulating that Curtis was too dumb to fly anything but wing? He had ample time to discover it, for this was another butt-burner and bladder-buster, just fifteen minutes shy of six hours. We were four flights and two spares, with no radio use in this, another top-secret mission. On up into Czechoslovakia we escorted just five bombers, converted to transports. There, in a remote airport, were thirty POWs waiting to flee the country. I didn't know if Malcolm was scrutinizing my flying, but I was certainly studying his. Never had I flown with such a nervous leader. Here this chicken colonel was jockeying the throttle back and forth in tandem with the stick. Up and down, slow then fast, until we could barely make out our base through heavy squalls, a stiff crosswind, and clouds below one hundred feet, prompting the tower operator to light up the sky with red flares. I had all I could do to set 'er down without pranging. At debriefing I got a pleasant surprise, for Smith, who'd been shot down and, in an emergency landing, had gone head over heels and landed on his back, was among those rescued.

September 23, 1944

My darling Dick,

It's no wonder the cookies were old. It took them all summer to get to you. I made some more last night and they'll be off to you tomorrow. Margie was up Friday night. She talks so much about when Bob comes home. It's hard to know what to think—she believes so definitely that she'll see him again.

The following Monday I was nudged awake at 0530 hours by Chappy. In a weak moment I'd promised him I'd try to sub for him while he was in Palestine for his R&R. South to Foggia I drove him and watched as he and several other chaplains took off for Jerusalem. As I contemplated my additional duties during the coming week, I thought that we were more and more resembling policemen or firemen, with long stretches of tedium broken by full-throttled emergencies. I was soon settled in Chappy's office at group headquarters, set to "punch the tickets" of malcontents, whatever their gripe. As the week wore on, however, I had few takers. Yet I had much to do simply to prepare for the service on Sunday morning. As I set about piecing together something that would pass for a sermon, I felt the prick of conscience in my denunciations of Wilson, the preacher back in Worcester. Could I hold the attention of the congregation here, five thousand miles away, any better than he had? Would the group CO and the rest of the big brass give me the cold shoulder—or worse, fall asleep? The thought of their sitting before me, waiting for some sign of heaven's benediction, was daunting.

THE PILOT BECOMES THE PREACHER

More daunting, however, was my mission on Thursday. The dawn brought the news that we were at last in for a clear day. At noon I took off as number four on Morris's wing for a strafing mission in Czechoslovakia, only to find him complaining of a rough engine and returning home. Then Dzurnak's engine conked out and didn't restart till he was down to nine hundred feet, whereupon he thanked his lucky stars and headed for home. That left me and a spare flying wing on either side of Nash as flight leader. I knew we were approaching some vital target when, it seemed, all hell broke loose, with flak and machine gun fire targeting us. So Nash took us through some violent evasive maneuvers until we cleared the gun positions.

Suddenly we spotted an enemy train, the locomotive trailing black smoke. Here was the kind of sitting duck that made my mouth water. Except that it suddenly turned dry as I followed Nash in and ran smack into a wall of flak and tracer bullets coming from the flatcars that mounted the gun positions. Some flak explosions were bouncing my plane as I got the locomotive in my gun sight. Suddenly it exploded, sending its shrapnel skyward. Once again I was lucky and waded through the mess without my plane being hit. That done, we headed for more "opportunity" targets. Soon there appeared before us an airfield, loaded with German planes lined up in neat rows. As we formed a single file and went in, again all hell visited us. So, with but a single Junkers Ju 52 bomber-transport in flames, Nash must have figured one pass was enough. Hardly had we left the airfield than I looked up to my left, there to see a cluster of ME-109s, crossing us close enough that we couldn't miss them, nor they us. I counted fifteen of them and got on the horn to Nash. "A swarm of bandits at ten o'clock high!" No answer. I repeated it. Still no answer. "Nash, are you there?" Not a word. So I waggled my wings to get his attention and pointed, frantically. Here was a golden opportunity going to waste! Nash ignored me, even as he was ignoring the bandits, now disappearing in the west. Were these fledgling pilots, putting in transition time as I'd done in North Africa, flying their fighters closer into the heartland? Were they so short of fuel that they had only enough to make it? I could only guess why they didn't take advantage of their fifteen-to-three odds. Was Nash dubious about those odds? I pondered leaving his wing and taking them on myself, but thought better of it—striking a note of caution, something I'd rarely done in my short life. This, together with Swede's admonition to stick to the tail of my leader, managed to prevail.

Returning to debriefing, I put it to Nash. Didn't he see the 109s? No. Didn't he hear me on the radio? No. Didn't he see me waggling my wings within a few feet from his own cockpit, and pointing toward the bandits? Never. I could only conclude that this was one of the reasons Nash was earning his captaincy, leading flights, while I floundered as a flunky second looie.[8] Nevertheless, it had been a banner day, with Tyler claiming two kills and Hudson and Wilson each claiming one. Altogether the 52nd laid claim to four in the air and no less than forty-nine on the ground, in addition to trucks, barges, and locomotives.

October 12, 1944

My darling Myrt,

Thanks for the big, beautiful box of cookies! They're "multo bene," as the Ities would put it. And they go tip-top with a nice juicy cantaloupe or musk melon, 19 of which I got in trade with an Itie farmer nearby. He'd have given me more, as they're just rotting away in his field. But I'd rather they not rot here under my table in the tent, so I only took 19. Should last a week, what with 2 new pilots moving in with Chuck and me.

By the way, 2 of the 8 new fellas coming into the 4th Squadron were in training with me, as well as 2 others who came over earlier. They all wonder how I got over here so early!

The next day was Friday the 13th. On the GI truck to briefing we kidded each other, all the while wondering if one or more of us would fail to return. Looking around, I saw a couple of the guys with their fingers crossed. Another was wearing his lucky rabbit's foot. How strange, I thought, that down through the years people from around the world had developed ways of averting the evil eye. At headquarters we were told that this was a "major effort," meaning that our group would be putting into the air everything that would fly as well as holding the spares throughout the mission. I was a spare, but took the place of Bourne's wingman when he developed engine trouble and headed for home. As predicted at briefing, enemy flak was leaving almost as much black smoke as was pouring from the refineries of Blechhammer below. One burst of flak almost got the four of us, jouncing us in our seats. So we spread out and left the target area in flames.

Come Saturday and, not scheduled, I was asked by Major Chapman to take up Exum's plane, in which he'd installed his new gun sight, to see how well it worked. The 8th Air Force, sold on it, had it installed in all their fighters, but the 15th had not, despite Ex's joining us. So I tried it out in a few passes at a B-26 that happened along but, unable to use live ammo and the tracer bullets, I depended only on the camera shooting some footage. I reported that if it did all that Exum said it would, it would certainly be a great lifesaver. At the mission's debriefing I learned that the 2nd Squadron had lost a man. Shot down, he'd managed to bail out, so who could tell? Maybe he was a POW. Also learned that the 2nd's CO, Major Watkins, lost his canopy to ground fire. At that, he was lucky he'd not lost his head when bullets pierced his headrest.

October 14, 1944

My dearest Dick,

To say that I am very proud of you would be a gross understatement. To say that I am very happy for you and that I'm "walking in the clouds" would also insufficiently describe the thrill and the joy I got when last night I leisurely turned the pages of the *Gazette* and saw a piece telling of your award. None of us had any idea it would come so soon. After sharing this news with your family, I got dressed to go to what I'd been told was a farewell party for my former boss. And you know what, honey, it turned out to be a belated engagement party for me—and was I ever surprised! Oh, Dick, you ought to see the beautiful mahogany tray they gave me. It's simply grand!! Mr. H. spoke of our meeting in N.Y., and of your picture in the paper last night. Many compliments were made in your direction.

The next day, Sunday, I mounted the platform in the chapel with far more trepidation than I'd registered on any mission. For there before me, in the front row, were seated Colonel Malcolm and other top brass, waiting—I figured—to see if my preaching was any better than my flying. As I questioned "What Price Peace?" and proposed that this war seemed to be but an extension of the war Dad had fought in, I seemed to have the eyes of most of the forty officers and enlisted men before me. But when I turned to the "spiritual lesson" and the need to "get right with God," the eyes were suddenly glazed over. It was apparent that they'd heard that song before. At the end of the half hour homily I had precious few still with me. Yet, gracious to a fault, there was Malcolm, "Curtis, a good job!" That was undoubtedly more than he could say for my flying. Or, for that matter, than I could say for his flying.

There could be no doubt that I was hot for at least one convert, and none more so than the avowed atheist, McIntyre. Just the night before, in need of reinforcements, I'd cornered Hugh Ottley and a couple others and we'd descended on Mac, determined to show him the error of his ways before he chanced to meet his Maker. It was no use trying to persuade this godless Bostonian as he bobbed and wove, jabbing at us with the names of James and other freethinkers he'd imbibed at Harvard. We left his tent agreeing that this Irishman was not only godless but hopeless. By this time I was convinced that my missionary skills needed as much if not more burnishing than my flying skills.

MUCH RAIN—FEW MISSIONS

My twentieth mission I finally concluded on October 16, escorting B-17s to Brux, Czechoslovakia, which was producing thirty thousand tons of oil each month for Hitler's war machine. Having knocked out the refineries at Ploesti and Blechhammer, we were now concentrating on the smaller centers. As we approached what was to be the target, we found it completely obscured by thick cloud cover. Some of the bombers dropped to the deck for a clear view while others climbed to thirty-five thousand feet. Unfortunately those we were escorting preferred the heights. With my cockpit heater on the fritz, the subzero temperature was invading my heavy flying suit, setting my teeth chattering. Lucky for them, Hanes's flight dropped to the deck where they thawed even as they spotted an enemy train and lined up to pepper it from locomotive to caboose. Except the last car was no caboose but an ammo car. Suddenly it exploded in one huge sheet of flame and debris that caught Hanes, lifting him in a split second at least five hundred feet. Not only did it leave gaping holes in his wings and tail, but bent one of his props and blistered his canopy, leaving him with all he could do to see. It was a miracle that he was still able to fly. And an even greater miracle that he was able to make it back to base as he scrunched his head from side to side to try to make out other planes and the horizon.

Shorty was a shaking case by the time he got to debriefing. I was still shaking from almost freezing to death and he from almost burning to death. Instead of dragging out his accordion and inviting me to join him in a spontaneous concert, he sat at the bar, still shaking but downing one drink after another as he related his close call with the Grim Reaper.

"Scared shitless," as he put it, he'd "had it with this guerre." He'd be flying no more missions. We knew better. All he needed was to get back to his squeeze box and belt out a few more tunes. He'd be back in harness once he'd shaken the shivers. And he was.

My twenty-first mission the next day was long, uneventful, and cold. While the bombers left fires raging in Blechhammer far below, my hands were all but frozen, six miles up. For, true to form, I'd forgotten my heavy, lined leather gloves. Of the 120 hours I'd now racked up in the Mustang, none were colder than these where we left vapor trails crisscrossing each other high in the sky and, we hoped, out of range of the antiaircraft gunners below. As it was, we weren't, but apparently none made a hit and we all returned to base safely. With another twenty-nine missions to fly to complete my tour, I wondered, as I strapped myself into the cockpit each time, if Lady Luck would continue to be with me.

October 18, 1944

My dearest Myrt,
Some nights I barely have enough strength to crawl into the sack, especially after these lo-o-ong missions. With the cold weather and the rain, I figured the pesky insects would favor us by going elsewhere but no, they love our tents and worse, our sleeping bags. Now, with the war almost won, as far as the Nazis are concerned, the 15th AAF, instead of providing good missions for us, is engaged in making more aggravating rules to lower morale.

With no letup in the rains, and six more days to my next mission, I had to make do with reading and writing, interrupted by Ping-Pong games that substituted vigor for finesse. Sometimes my atheist friend, McIntyre, was my partner, and I marveled at his coordination and speed when stashed. Sober, he was contentious, even cantankerous. But well lubricated at the bar, he was both funny and skillful. I also had recourse to my accordion, joining with Hanes from time to time in a songfest in the officers' club. Evenings we usually spent at group headquarters, watching combat film, usually followed by a Hollywood movie. Then, while others busied themselves with cards, I found great comfort in reading and rereading the forty-four letters I'd gotten from Myrt.

Yet along with the comfort of knowing wedding bells were in the offing was the regret that I might well not finish that fiftieth mission. If I didn't finish it, I would have the chance of doing so in the Japanese war theater. Finish it or not, the prospect of the Allies invading the Japanese islands would call on every available weapon at our disposal, and even then at great cost of lives.

The waiting, the continual waiting, scrounging up things to do, was often broken by defensive measures to keep from drowning in the deluge of the monsoon rains. An example of our desperation occurred on Friday, October 20, when a gang of us devised our own mission. The target: a bombed-out railway station by the tracks running alongside the beach. The purpose: to knock down one of the remaining walls and collect enough brick to cover the club floor. For the plywood we'd laid atop sand was sinking as the sand was being washed away. Having learned from my previous fiasco to be sure the truck was far enough from the wall we pulled down, I joined the others as, soaked to the skin, we harvested something like 3,500 bricks and forded our way back to the 4th through our canal roads. Out went the window screens and in went the bricks. Before the day was over we had Monster Ward pronounce the benediction in the best Italian he could muster, *"Molto bene!"* With that we had something else to celebrate that evening, amid the yelps and cussing at the card games, the clatter and hustle around the Ping-Pong table, and the serenading of still others around Shorty and me with our squeeze boxes. Then a number of us joined Dzurnak to roast chestnuts over the fire in the stove they'd just rigged up in the middle of the tent floor, burning 100-octane gasoline. As Ludwig, a tentmate of Dzurnak's, hit the sack, we hoped he'd enjoy a full night's sleep. For the night before he'd awakened us up and down the line with his unearthly screams. Investigating, we found him swearing that he'd been bitten on the face by a centipede. Of course we laughed him to scorn. If centipedes had one hundred legs to gad about with, why on earth would they resort to stinging—and least of all the innocent Ludwig? Far from being reassured, he spent the rest of the night standing guard over his sack, pistol in hand, determined to do in any predator invading his quarters.

With Sunday morning came chapel and our chance to give thanks for still being alive to fly the magnificent Mustang. Chappy was in Foggia to take his turn over the English-speaking radio station, so we were introduced to Chaplain Terry, lent to us by the 332nd next door. Only gradually were we coming to know and appreciate the Negro fighter pilots there, and overcome some of the latent prejudice that had come to us so naturally that it was habitual. Chappy had returned from Jerusalem armed with Christmas gifts. For me to give to Myrt was a beautiful silk lounging robe and a silver bracelet inscribed "JerUSAlem." Not especially practical, but as they came from the Holy Land, she would surely appreciate them.

October 23, 1944

My sweetheart Myrt,

It's hard to realize, perhaps, just how much your letters, photos, and packages mean to me. It's bad enough when we're flying missions regularly, but when ol' man weather makes for stand-downs aplenty and we sit around and bide our time, the old morale is apt to drop a bit. As I write this, I have my half-shelter, or pup tent, rigged up over my bunk to strain the water sieved by the outer tent!

I've discovered that about 95% of our Squadron is planning on staying in the Army. For a commissioned officer—with flight pay too—in a peace-time Army, is a very substantial job, as far as security is concerned. Yet in itself it is purposeless, in my opinion. Not much more than a parasite, with too many things in this world that need tending to. I'm casting a wondering eye at China as a missionary's stamping ground. At home in the States religion is all but shoved down your throats. Meanwhile in the rest of the world are millions of potential Christians. All they need is a salesman—that's the job!

The next day was a butt-burner of a mission to the Skoda Manufacturing Works in Czechoslovakia. The dismal overcast persisted all the way to and from the target, with the beautiful exception of a break for the sun to shine through and onto the magnificent Austrian Alps below. There, in this oasis in the desert of rain clouds, I could invariably plan on making out black scars pockmarking the brilliant snow-capped peaks, the graveyards of the hapless crews of bombers we'd escorted. Returning, we found our field socked in right down to the deck, so we landed at the 332nd. Though our fields were separated by no more than a couple miles, theirs was open, showing the fickleness of Mother Nature. Even as we were setting down at their field, a crippled B-24 bomber managed an emergency landing at our field, testimony to the remarkable skill of the pilot confronted with two engines gone, clouds down to the runway, and landing on instruments on a runway hardly long enough to accommodate our fighters.

Returning to the squadron by jeep—an open jeep—I hit a big puddle in the cow path we called a road, traveling at about 15 mph. This lifted the whole pond up and over all of us, covering us with goo. Five minutes later I was still trying to wipe it from my face. When I finally got the wet engine started, the windshield was so plastered that I had to look out the side to see, only to be plastered more by the mud churned up by the front wheels.

Not till October 25 did the weather permit our retrieving our planes from the 332nd. Even then we had to wait a half hour or so while Spitfires interfered with our landing pattern as their British pilots landed at their base just north of us. Finally landing after buzzing everything I could see in the air and on the ground, I learned that Exum's new gun sight, called the K14 and equipped with gyroscopes, was being installed on all our planes. Whether or not my endorsement had anything to do with it, I felt that these would add just a bit more to my chances of returning alive.

From October 23 to November 4 the constant cloud cover over prospective targets kept us grounded. On the 26th we learned that our navy had finally flushed the Japanese fleet out into the open and were now in the third day of the Battle of the Philippines. We also learned that a cyclone was due to hit us that evening, so Hosey, Hudson, and I got busy laying a floor of wing tank crate ends, then weather-stripping the intersection of the floor with the wood walls. Then my tentmates installed the classiest door in the outfit, using for a window a Plexiglas window they'd scrounged from a German bomber that had crash-landed a couple weeks earlier. With this door, weather-stripping, sand, bricks, plywood, and heavy metal matting, together with a stove we'd installed, we could relax, we figured. Alas, if the streams of water weren't continuing to wash away the sand, or the roof leaking like a sieve, then it was the stove threatening to incinerate the three of us. But, we rationalized, *c'est la guerre,* and let it go at that.

If we craved relief from the problems in our tent, we could always retire to the problems of the club. With just five 25-watt bulbs and an unreliable generator to light us, it was a wonder we could make out the speeding Ping-Pong ball as it whizzed past us, or get out of one another's way in doubles. So we put our heads together and concluded what the joint needed was a coat of white paint on the inside. That done, we could be assured that when Mac heaved his plate of spaghetti into the face of the pilot opposite him at the table, it would be his intended target, Gassman. It wasn't unusual that we'd have to step in between a couple pilots who, thoroughly smashed, would rise from their crap games with accusations of cheating, threatening to mop the floor with each other. What we all hoped was that, sobered up, they'd either forget these clashes or forgive, since they would once again have to depend on each other for their lives on yet another mission.

As sorry as we began to feel for ourselves, with the rain continuing to pelt us, we felt even sorrier for the Ities who continued working, day and night, laying the heavy steel matting on the runway, lest our wheels sink in the mud and flip us stem over stern. Having spread some of that matting on our tent floor, I should not have been surprised when, reaching up to pull the light on, as I related to Myrt, WHAM! and I quivered like an aspen in a March wind. So I wrapped a handkerchief around the metal chain and tried it again. WHAM! At last I took off my shoes, changed into dry socks, stood on a wooden bench, and presto! The electricity went to the bulb rather than through me.

While the Ities labored for perhaps a couple bucks a day, there in the miserable cold, rain, and mud, we accepted an invitation from the 332nd to join them for what was billed as an "International Review." Whatever the thirty-two Italians copied from Hollywood, it wasn't the performance as much as the hype. Still, it was a cut above some we'd been exposed to.

Gathering for mail call the following Monday, I was tickled to get a letter from Tom Crull who, with Red Crowder, had gone out of their way to circulate a petition and save my neck in Basic. Now Tom told me he was flying P-47s right here in Italy with the 450th Fighter Group. Ironically, I, the screwup, had graduated a second looie, and here, both of them had graduated only as flight officers. I could only hope they'd also return to the States in one piece. There were, however, no guarantees. For months now I'd watched as one pilot after another from the 4th, all but three of them veterans with many hours racked up, failed to return from a mission. This meant that Crowder, Crull, and Curtis, training mates back in Texas, had at best a slim chance of returning safely to the States, our tour of duty completed.

October 16, 1944

My dearest Dick,
Going over your letters from Texas, a lot has happened in a year. I don't think I could be any happier than I've been since then—except, of course, to have you home.

If it were only our flying that put us at risk, that would have been bad enough. But there were other risks, not the least of which was our sleeping in tents heated with gasoline stoves. That afternoon I learned that a large shack housing Itie laborers, also heated with gasoline, had caught fire and burned to the ground. Luckily no one was hurt. But we took the hint and soon Hosey, Hudson, and I were busy chopping down anything that would burn, green or dry. That evening was a ringer at the club, especially so for Hosey. So much so, in fact, that come morning he awoke pleading with us to put him out of his misery. No such luck. We finally pried him from his lair, bent him over his washstand, and doused his face with icy water. Then, to make sure he was sober, we led him to the kitchen of the club for black coffee. By noon we figured he was coherent enough to join us at the skeet range. Shooting at clay pigeons was a poor substitute for shooting at Jerries, but gunnery practice it was—or so we were told.

September and October had come and gone, most of it

flushed down the boot of Italy by rains that showed no sign of letup. After five months at the 52nd, and only twenty-two missions under my belt, I figured it would be close to a miracle to complete my fiftieth before the war in Europe ended. Still a lowly second looie, I was rummaging the attic of my mind for profitable ways of spending my time. The single constant, the single lodestar guiding my course was some five thousand miles away, in Worcester.

7

COUNTDOWN TO 1945

"M.E.F. to R.K.C. 12–25–44"

—Inscription inside a black onyx ring, my Christmas present from Myrt

PETE FULKS, THE MIA, RETURNS TO BASE

It wasn't until Wednesday, November 1, that the weather finally cleared enough to schedule a mission. But I wasn't included. In fact, with the rains and the new pilots inundating us, I was lucky to get a mission once a week. I had twenty-eight to go, and at this rate I'd not be returning till the summer of 1945. When our boys from the 4th Squadron returned, I learned that, though they had to climb above thirty thousand feet to get above the clouds, they tangled with ME-109s and Barney Chaskin nailed one when it attacked a bomber.

That afternoon I borrowed a set of "pinks," as we called these gray gabardines, from Jake Klerk. Mine were at the cleaners—a distinct improvement over the 100-octane gasoline that had been our "dry cleaning." Assembling at headquarters, we waited for a half hour in the raw chill for Colonel Taylor from Wing Headquarters to make his appearance. But it was worth it. He not only presented me with my first Oak Leaf Cluster to add to my Air Medal, but pinned on DFCs, with the 4th garnering two thirds of these, plus a Silver Star. I was certain I wasn't in the class of those being given these high awards, for I wouldn't learn until another year had passed that I'd won my DFC back in August. And I may not have been featured, as was Charles Boyer as he romanced Ingrid Bergman in *Gaslight* that evening, but I had my own beautiful Swede back home waiting for me.

The next day, as tower operator, I returned late for lunch to find out Ities who worked for the 4th all seated, eating in our "dining room." Seeing me coming for my lunch, they immediately stood and disappeared with their food into the kitchen, despite my protests. I was truly feeling sorry for these pathetic people who'd become accustomed to exaggerated deference to their landlords, then to the Germans, and now to the Allies. At times it seemed that they would almost grovel to remain in our good graces and be employed for perhaps a couple dollars a day.

By Friday our resident electrical genius, Knepper, had rigged up a new and reliable generator, and had replaced the dim 25-watt bulbs with 100s which, with the newly painted white walls, permitted our recognizing each other across the room. If the 4th couldn't boast of bright pilots, it could boast of a bright club!

Mission number twenty-three came on November 4, escorting B-17s to Regensburg, Germany. Another milk run? Far from it. Taking off on his leader's wing, a pilot from the 2nd lost control and smashed into a Mustang parked on the side of the runway, shearing off a wing from each plane. It then careened into two armorers from our squadron, killing the first and seriously wounding the second.

And that was just the beginning. On our return from the target, our flight, led by Deckman, was escorting a bomber crippled by flak. Despite our moving into friendly territory, we were suddenly bounced from above. Anxiety turned to relief when we saw they were P-38s—and not being flown by Germans as had been the case in a previous mission. These Lightning pilots, like us, were possessed of itchy trigger fingers, emphasizing the importance of our plane identification tests. Had they clobbered us, it certainly wouldn't be the first time our men were casualties of "friendly fire."

The mission wasn't over. Returning to buzz the runway, sweep up and back to land, we were interrupted by the tower operator. It seemed that a B-26 twin-engine bomber, being flown by the Brits, had tried an emergency landing at our field, had crashed and come within inches of taking out a string of Mustangs parked near the runway. So, while ground crews hauled away the wreckage, we circled the base, only to watch, mesmerized, as a crippled B-24, its crew having bailed out and now on autopilot, crashed into a field no more than one hundred yards from the edge of our base. Had it struck us, there would have been more than planes destroyed. Again a case of friendly fire. Just how many American casualties in this war were the result of friendly fire will never be known.

Apart from combat losses, it wasn't only friendly fire that was doing us in. Our wild parties were doing their share. After morning services the next day, Chappy and I moseyed over to headquarters for lunch, to find the joint reeking with stale booze and Ities trying to repair the so-called furniture. It seemed that the top brass had flown a C-47 to Rome, not for R&R, rest and relaxation, but for B&B, booze and broads. Guaranteed to take the minds of these men off the war, the nine Roman beauties would keep them company over the weekend at the 52nd. Colonel Malcolm, the CO I'd found to be a "nervous jervous" in the skies, awoke to find his jeep wallowing in a muddy ditch, and on it in bright yellow paint, "Fish Wagon." This was undoubtedly the work of those, like myself, of lesser rank, disgruntled that the chief honchos would refuse to share with them. Two of our own, Bill Parent and Buck Gassman, not to be deterred, had crashed the orgy, had gotten stoned too, then got in a fistfight over who was to drive Chappy's jeep back to the 4th. They ended up wrestling in the mud and were still out cold by noon on Sunday. After all, our reputation as swashbuckling fighter pilots, honed over the years, had to be upheld, regardless of the cost. And the cost would come through to us grimly during the following week.

The next day, November 6, Gassman, barely recovered from his wild weekend, almost bought it. I was flying wing to Deckman on this, my twenty-fourth mission, escorting B-24s over targets in Germany. Suddenly ME-109s bounced the bombers from out of the sun. Returning fire, one of the bombers missed the Jerries but hit two of our boys from the 4th, Gassman and Farnkopf, the bullets piercing Farn's radio, just inches behind his head. Two others from the 4th, Carson and Dean, found their formation on the return flight so tight that their wings collided. Fortunately the damage was minor, and they landed safely.

On November 8 a headline in *Stars and Stripes* caught my attention. FDR, our commander in chief, had been elected for an astonishing fourth term. Was he about to become our president-for-life? If he entertained such dreams, his days would be numbered. He may have been a horse in the middle of a stream, as he never tired of telling the voters, and therefore should not be switched, but as I looked at his photos, I seemed to see not a young racehorse, chafing at the bit, but an old swayback, about to be retired to pasture, prey for Stalin, the predator, in further summit meetings.

It didn't take much of a pretext to provide an occasion for celebrating. The next day Colonel Malcolm returned to the 52nd sporting a full bird colonel's rank. This called for a "major effort" celebration. So fifty of us from the 4th dolled up in our best "pinks" and took off for San Severo and its Club Negative. There five nurses and an equal number of Red Cross beauties, fueled with the best booze money could buy from the Ities, engaged in nonstop dancing as long lines formed for eager pilots to take their turn. I'd hardly cut in and taken a couple laps around the floor before I was, in turn, cut in on. I couldn't begin to match the antics of Dzurnak and Gaisser in their jitterbugging to Glenn Miller's "In the Mood." But then, my Coke was a poor substitute for the high-proof stuff that diluted their inhibitions. At least, that was my rationalization. In less than a month I'd learn that Miller had been lost flying over the Channel from England to France. Still, at forty, he'd outlived Bob by almost twenty years, when the North Sea claimed his life.

The next day, November 10, who should return to the 52nd, just tickled to be back a lowly flight officer, but Pete Fulks. It was more than two months since he'd been shot down over Yugoslavia, leaving me the last of the original twelve still to be flying P-51s. That evening he was invited to tell his story to all the group's pilots at headquarters. Missing from the assembly, however, were three pilots from the 4th, Callahan, Dzurnak, and Hanes, still recovering from the previous night's bash. Before we left early Sunday morning, those of us still reasonably sober went around and collected bodies from beneath chairs and tables, loaded them on the back of a truck and returned them to the 4th.

It was too bad they missed Pete's story. Like Frye, he'd been hit by ground fire while strafing. But, unlike Frye, he'd found a safe field for an emergency landing. Out of the cockpit he'd stepped, to be surrounded not by Germans but by Tito's Partisans. Night after night they'd shielded him from the enemy as he gradually made his way north to Trieste, then across the Po Valley and down Italy's boot to our base. He would be leaving for home shortly in Littleton, Illinois, next to the state featured in the evening's movie, *Home in Indiana*.

A TRAGIC ARMISTICE DAY CELEBRATION

By the 11th of November, Armistice Day, twelve more pilots had been assigned to the 4th, bringing the total to fifty-eight. This was more than three times the seventeen the five of us greenhorns found when we arrived the first week in June. It looked like I'd have to be lucky just to be assigned to fly my missions, much less to return unscathed.

Armistice Day was especially memorable for me. Dad, a radio operator on the Western Front back in 1918, took a wire from Marshal Foch on that day, announcing that an Armistice had just been signed, and fighting was to cease at 1100 hours. Now, twenty-six years later, we gathered for a briefing to hear "Infallible" Pope report that heavy clouds and rain were our lot en route to Brux, our target in Czechoslovakia. But apparently the brass in Bari figured we just had to celebrate the day with a "major effort" mission to remind the Germans that they were once again on the losing end. The 52nd was heading north to the rendezvous point over the north Adriatic when General Headquarters changed its mind and called off the mission.

By this time our own base was so socked in that visibility was reduced to one hundred feet. Back came the pilots, relieved to be able to set down their planes without pranging. All returned except the flight led by Callahan. The alarm soon spread when another half hour elapsed and still no sign of them. From across the field pilots converged on headquarters to await their arrival and debriefing. At last, forty-five minutes late, a single plane emerged through the fog, rain, and snow to land safely. The pilot's report was grim. Callahan, leading the flight on instruments, suddenly executed a split-S and went into a dive over the Adriatic. Trained to follow their leader, the other three executed the same maneuver. In the last minute Callahan realized he'd succumbed to the deadly peril stalking all pilots on instruments—vertigo— and bailed out. Two of the other three, however, Dzurnak and Farnkopf, continued straight down into the cold waters of the Adriatic. The reporter had barely managed to pull out, clipping the spray above the waves, and had returned safely, but so traumatized that he was shaking badly—just as Hanes had done after his close call with an exploding locomotive. These two were my next-door neighbors. Dzurnak and I'd been tossing the football around just before leaving for briefing. They were good buddies and now they were gone, along with Callahan. For despite an extensive search of the Adriatic the next few days, there was no sign of the three.

It was a bitter loss for the 4th, made all the worse by the fact that it was not a result of enemy action, that it was easily preventable. For those with alcohol still in their system, we'd been told, were especially susceptible to vertigo. Callahan and Dzurnak were two of the three we'd carried back from our big party thirty-six hours earlier. None of those who'd gotten stashed should have been flying on the 11th. I shuddered to think of the reaction of the parents of these three on receiving the telegram from the War Department that my folks had gotten on the death of Bob. The mood in the 4th was somber for a week or more. No one wanted to speak of this calamity. Maybe we'd need all these additional pilots, after all.[1]

MUCH TO GIVE THANKS FOR

Thanksgiving was just a couple weeks away, and the parents of these three pilots would find it hard to be festive on this annual holiday. But just a hasty reflection on my part served to remind me of a missionary who'd returned to the States years before and who'd become the Sunday school teacher for several of us early adolescent boys. One day he'd put it to us. "What is the most common sin of all?" I immediately thought of the times I'd lied, sworn, picked up cigarette butts in the gutter to stuff in my corncob pipe, and filched a nickel or more from Mom's purse. Then I thought of the times I'd left Jim Fallon's Community Store without paying for goodies I'd taken. I thought of the Domino sugar bag I'd stuffed with coins when I'd cashed the dollar bills I'd filched from the chain letters Dad was getting in the mail. Yes, it must be theft that was the most common sin. So we offered our suggestions. Nope. None of these. In fact, he said, it was not a sin of commission but, rather, a sin of omission. This term was news to us. But he surprised us all when he said the most common sin was simply ingratitude. Wow! That had never occurred to any of us. Now, about seven years later, I definitely had much to be grateful for, and as the days passed, my reasons for giving thanks multiplied.

After services on Sunday the 12th, I headed over to the 5th Squadron to learn more about Pete's escape. I was as eager to take in more of the details as he was to relate them. Yet twice we were interrupted. The first time it was by the sound of a light plane taking off. It was an artillery reconnaissance job, a "Grasshopper," rising from a fifty-yard clearing near the road, reminding me of the small Piper Cub I'd started with back in Indianapolis and of my instructor's sentence of doom for my flying career. So much had happened in the eighteen months since then—so much to give thanks for.

Hardly had we resumed our conversation than we were roused by the mighty roar of a huge B-24 bomber buzzing our runway, leaving the tower as well as the trees quaking in its wake. I wondered if this was the work of another frustrated bomber pilot who really wanted to fly fighters. And here I was, not only flying despite Joe Webb's indictment, but flying the queen of the fighters. How lucky could I be?

Then Pete and I hiked down to the flight line where I got some snapshots of him standing in front of *Myrt's Dickie-Bird.* This served to remind me of Myrt, the one and only, waiting faithfully back in Worcester to receive me and join me in a walk down the church aisle. I could only conclude with the ancient King David that "my cup was running over."[2]

All of this stood out even more as it contrasted with the

calamities that seemed to be afflicting others around me. On November 15, I took off ahead of the rest of the mission since I was a spare, and flew over to the 332nd to see the remains of four Mustangs that had crashed the previous day. The lead plane was burned to a crisp and the others badly damaged. Apparently the 52nd wasn't the only fighter group in the 15th Air Force that was fouling up this side of the enemy lines. Joining the others on this, my twenty-fifth mission, I was soon flying element leader with Billy Starmer leading the flight and three returning home with engine trouble. One of these, Hudson, my tentmate, had his engine simply quit on him at thirty thousand feet, not to catch again until he was down to six thousand feet. There, with Hanson still on his wing, he spotted a lone ME-109 and made short work of it. Meanwhile, at thirty thousand feet and 50 degrees below zero, we stuck with the bombers until they'd released their bombs, turned around, and reached friendly territory. There was the usual flak, but no hits that I could make out, and no Jerries. So we returned to base, with one more kill chalked up to the 4th.

Always eager to drum up one thing or another, I posted a notice of a Ping-Pong tournament with a sign-up sheet right next to a photo of a local Italian girl, obviously a "friend" of one of the men, advertising her "all" beneath an uplifted skirt. There was no sign-up sheet for her, but I guessed she probably didn't need it. Furthermore, I figured that there was less chance of becoming a casualty avoiding each other in a four-man game of table tennis than in sporting with this girl.

To sharpen my skills at my sport, I took to the table with McIntyre, always a prime opponent, when suddenly I was aroused by shouts from down the tent line. There at the door of my tent, I saw through the smoke guys rescuing stuff that looked dangerously like mine. Racing as best I could in the thick mud, I found the charred remains of my A-3 bag, gas mask, flying gear, a bag of laundry, and—worst of all—my precious Kodak camera. Apparently the gasoline-fed stove had gotten to burning too hot and too close to my gear. I was disgusted, yet thankful that it didn't happen when I was sleeping. So there was no shortage of things to give thanks for.

In all the hubbub I forgot my Link appointment, a more serious offense since the 4th lost three men to vertigo. So Don Stinchcombe, another delinquent, joined me in three days of tower duty, our just punishment. Here, Stinch agreed, was not so much absentmindedness as mere preoccupation. In either case it wasn't as deadly as Joe Hawk's failing to lower his wheels and strap himself in the cockpit. Nor was it as potentially fatal as the forgetfulness of the South African pilot who, flying a Spitfire at the British base just north of us, took off and encountered trouble trimming his ship. He glanced in the mirror and there, holding on to the leading edge of his left wing for dear life, was his crew chief. The pilot had forgotten to stop to let him off before turning on to the runway and giving 'er the gun. Now, keeping the plane just barely above the stalling speed, the pilot nursed the Spitfire down on the runway and this time stopped to let the relieved mechanic off the wing. In another hour or two, when it suddenly dawned on him how close he'd come to the Grim Reaper, the crew chief fainted on the spot.

It was Sunday the 19th that I joined others at headquarters to watch Pete Fulks replace his flight officer's bar with the gold bar of a second lieutenant. Then I relieved Stinch in the tower to shepherd the mission coming in from a strafing mission at Lake Balatin in Hungary. Barney Chaskin's flight from the 4th, however, didn't land. Was it another case of auguring in on instruments? I was relieved to learn they'd made an emergency landing north of us and were safe. Not so the 2nd Squadron, with three of their men shot down by ground fire and, presumably, MIA. One of them, Beard, was last seen bailing out, so perhaps he was OK, though probably a POW.

Monday started out a bummer. In what should have been my twenty-sixth mission, I was again confined to the tower with Jennings, the regular tower operator. Our job was to assure a smooth takeoff, flying in pairs, for fifty planes in eighteen minutes, so timed that they would meet the bombers at rendezvous right on the nose. Instead of eighteen it took us twenty-three minutes. Within another minute there was Major Chapman, group operations officer, chewing us out. Was there nothing I could do right?

Ah, but there was. For six months earlier I'd made the "rightest" decision of my young life when I'd asked Myrt to marry me. And this afternoon at mail call I found a small package from her, obviously a Christmas present. Curiosity may have killed the proverbial cat, but in this case it saved my day. For despite there being more than a month to the holiday, I tore it open to find a magnificent gold ring, sporting a large black onyx. I made out the inscription on the inside of the band, *M.E.F. to R.K.C. 12-25-44*. I'd long since removed the "gold" ring I'd fallen for in North Africa as well as the green stain. Now I gladly took off the Mexican silver cadet ring I'd gotten at the PX back at Curtis Field, and on went a Christmas present that must have set Myrt back at least a couple weeks' pay. I later learned that when Myrt confided in Dad that she was going to send this to me, he'd scoffed. If it didn't stray, it certainly would be lost or stolen en route. Fortunately she was a trusting soul and persisted. Within minutes I was displaying my prize to my buddies, to Bobcean, and to Chappy, just as I'd imagined Myrt had been displaying her engagement ring earlier. My spirits soared in this climax to a banner day!

Two days later another six pilots made their appearance in the 4th, making more than sixty, even with the loss of three on the 11th.[3] Taking up the fourth bunk in our tent was Bruce Solomon. Was there no end to our reinforcements? There in the *Stars and Stripes* was the good news that the war seemed to be winding down. The Allies were punching holes through Germany's western front, after a prolonged stalemate, even as the Soviets were advancing, cutting through Germany's eastern front. In the South Pacific MacArthur was fulfilling his promise to return, made when he was forced to retreat from Corregidor. The only front on which the Allies seemed to be making no progress was right here in Italy. Despite clear superiority in the air, our infantry was stuck in the deep snows of the Appenines in northern Italy, south of the Po Valley.

Solomon arrived just in time for Thanksgiving the next day. I rounded up a couple of the guys who appeared to be more thankful than the rest, and we jumped into a jeep and headed for a thanks service in the chapel. But we didn't get far. Stuck in the mud, we finally pushed the jeep out, getting as much mud on us as was on the vehicle, and arrived twenty minutes late, but still in time to recite our reasons for thanks. Then we started back to the 4th, only to get mired down in foot-deep mud once again. Finally we made it back to the dining room where we dined on cold Spam, intentionally served us, I was sure, to contrast with the feast of the evening. And what a feast it was, with turkey and all the fixin's! We in the 4th didn't realize how good we had it until we learned of the celebration at the 5th. For, as Pete described it, they were seated at the table anticipating a feast as good if not better than we were enjoying in the 4th. They waited. And they waited. At last they devoured the fixin's and finally the great bird made its appearance, but far too rare to eat. Whether it was a tough old bird, an ignorant cook, or a cold stove I never did find out.

To work off the thousands of calories we'd absorbed, the next day Chappy and I drove a truck over to the British airfield at Campo Marino. Armed with shovels, we figured it would take the afternoon to get one or two loads of sand for the new chapel we were building. But, to our pleasant surprise, there was a steam shovel to do the heavy lifting. Load after load we trucked back to the 52nd, and onto the chapel floor, covering it with plywood, with a raised platform at one end. To reward myself I broke out three more of the precious eggs I'd gotten in barter, boiled them on our heating stove, and soon Solomon, Hudson, and I were feasting on an impromptu snack of eggs à la tomato juice and Myrt's Toll House cookies. How much better could it get?

With stand-downs over the weekend, it wasn't till Monday that I took to the air again, this time to turn instructor in combat training for Solomon. It wasn't long before he signaled that he wasn't hearing me on the radio, so we landed, only to learn that he'd not turned up his volume! Shades of RKC! Back in the air, I tried getting him in tight formation, so his wings overlapped mine. Gradually he nudged in until I signaled OK. Then, spotting a P-38 in the distance, I told him to stick to my tail as we took on the Lightning in some mock dogfighting. That done, I showed him the rudiments of strafing a train, as well as introducing him to some violent evasive maneuvers, such as I had encountered back in August. Once he'd corrected his radio volume, I confess I found him a quicker study than ever I'd been, and told him so.

That afternoon I joined Chappy and Ward, his new assistant, and we made the rounds of the squadrons, showing the guys the plans for our new chapel. We hoped they'd not only pay us a visit some Sunday but actually dig down and cough up a few bucks to help pay the Ities for all their hard work, especially their work with stone and brick for the walls.

Finding mortar for the job was another story. With more miserable weather the next day, a number of us who were former Scouts borrowed a truck and headed over to East Marea to join our British counterpart, the former Rovers, in discussing the similarities and differences between the youth groups. We then shared our plans for the chapel with them, only to find them volunteering some mortar. Soon we had six big wing tank crates full, enough to complete the job. We'd already met with them a couple times, and were finding the Limies a cut above what we'd heard of the British reception for American forces that had "invaded" their island: the Yanks were "overpaid, oversexed, and over here."

Come Thursday and some good news via Hosey. I was to trade my gold bar for the silver bar of a first lieutenant. To prep for the occasion, I paid a visit to the local Italian barbershop at the 4th. Here was an Itie no older than I, telling me he'd managed to escape from his duty as a soldier while but twenty miles from the Austrian border. Back through the German lines he'd threaded his way, and here he was, an entrepreneur in need of basic equipment for a barbershop. So I scrounged a couple chairs and a broken mirror and he was in business, clipping and shaving me for twenty cents.

That afternoon I figured it was time we moved to the sport of basketball, so we met with a couple of the enlisted men from the 4th to see if we could drum up a gym for practice and play. Also we needed competition. Soon we had six officers and four enlisted men lined up and ready to take on the 332nd, whom rumor had it was itching for some competition. To find a gym big enough, warm enough, and bright enough was a bigger challenge. I went so far as to promise the 332nd I'd bring along a generator so we could at least see the ball. But as for the heat, the best I could promise was enough competition that they'd have to move around. Still, we couldn't scrounge up a gym, so at last I phoned Lieutenant Wyatt, the special services officer at the 332nd, and got his permission to use their gym at Serra Capriola for practice. Then I requisitioned a weapons carrier, rounded up our fledgling team, and took an hour to drive the half mile to the gym, again getting stuck en route. Chilled from the ride in the open vehicle, we relished the thought of getting inside, until we discovered it registered only 55 degrees. To keep from shivering we simply had to move around—and fast.

Leaving, and eager for our first game, we wondered how we'd fare against this all-Negro squad.

Meanwhile, I had missions to fly, if only I'd be scheduled. On December 2, I found I was scheduled—but for the Link Trainer. To keep my reputation intact, I forgot the appointment, then groveled before Chapman, vowing to end my ways. He chuckled and turned me over to his assistant, none other than my former buddy in the 4th, Stevenson, given ground duty when on the verge of a breakdown. Good old Steve had mercy on me and promised not to tell our squadron ops officer nor our CO.

Then Steve related a story I'd not soon forget. It seemed that an enlisted man in the 4th, "Duke" Cashmere, a short, stubby, redheaded truck driver who brought to mind Higginbotham back in Indianapolis, was recently killed by a pilot named Flynn who, taking off, lost control, veered off the runway and collided with Cashmere's truck. Flynn was not only fined $40 a month for six months but had to spend that six months in the Army stockade in Bari. I fell to wondering whether if Flynn had done this back in June, when the 4th was so short of pilots, he would have suffered such punishment.

At last, on Sunday December 3, I flew my twenty-sixth mission. My luck had held for the first twenty-five. Would it hold for twenty-five more? It didn't help that my forgetfulness was putting in overtime. I took off with neither my sunglasses nor my dog tags. Then, arriving at the rendezvous point, I made out a few straggling bombers in the thick overcast. These we escorted to the target and back, encountering neither Jerries nor flak. Here was the milk run of all milk runs. Flying element leader on Nash's wing, I proposed that we drop to the deck and seek out targets of opportunity. Nash wasn't interested. Maybe he was still brooding over his best friend, Callahan. As we returned to base, I wondered if I was the only one looking for some action.

As it turned out, the only action I saw that day was my confrontation with a mouse crawling over my sack each night—maybe the same critter that had driven Hosey bananas. So I set a trap consisting of a bit of cheese on the end of a small stick, dangling over my water-filled helmet. The rascal surely would lose his balance and drown—so I thought. As it turned out, the next morning the cheese was gone, and so was the mouse. It was tough to admit the mouse had the edge on me. But there it was.

A CHRISTMAS PARTY TO REMEMBER

That evening I had better luck catching about forty men and hitting them up for a buck apiece to join our newly formed Christian club. My pitch: we'd need that—and then some—to host a bang-up Christmas party for the local Itie kids. Already we had some Brits and South Africans on board. Then, to show that some good deeds go unrewarded, I returned to my tent to find that the four of us had been stolen blind by some stealthy intruder. Gone were eight blankets, six pairs of shoes, an officer's blouse, a set of greens, and an A-2 jacket. Our only conclusion: the Ities had made off with it while I was out drumming up enough cash to throw a gala party for the kids. No wonder Bill Mauldin held on to his tooth fillings!

A noble motive, St. Augustine wrote, is the most important factor in determining the value of a given deed. The aim, the method, and even the result pale in comparison. So I was saved from what happened next by what I thought was the purity of my motive. I rounded up a few of the guys to help provide more bricks and stones for the chapel. Requisitioning a big 2½-ton truck, I drove us down to the bombed-out railroad station next to the beach. Soon we were wrestling a big chain around a wall still standing, and attached the other end to the back of the truck. Then I gave 'er the gun. If

Gideon could level the walls of Jericho with a few marches and a blast on the trumpets, I ought to be able to level this wall with that truck. Sure enough, down came the wall, in a crash that must have been heard back at the 4th, a mile away. The top third of the wall landed on the back of the truck, some of it rattling the cab where I had ducked my head. A good thing there was a thick screen covering the rear window. I exited the vehicle to survey a sad scene. Yet it appeared it could be driven, so we piled it high with the rubble, figuring that weight, along with five guys, should get us back. Alas, we didn't travel fifty yards before we were axle-deep in mud, our wheels grinding but going nowhere. Over to the transportation depot I walked, requisitioned another truck with a winch, and soon we were out and over to the floor where the chapel would stand. Chappy was as delighted as the head of the transportation pool was miffed. "Why the hell, Curtis, didn't you have sense enough to measure the height of the wall and make sure you had enough room for it to hit the ground!?" I figured that was a rhetorical question that needed no answer, and simply pleaded good intentions. Good scout that he was beneath all the bluster, he went so far as to lend me a couple jeeps that evening to carry our team over for another basketball practice.

The next day, after more searching for a suitable gym for practice, I returned to find—I couldn't believe it—five more pilots attached to our squadron. Was there no end to this assembly line? How could I ever complete my tour of duty? The following night there was more action onstage by the USO than I'd seen all day. The site was a giant Quonset hut into which Special Services had shoehorned more than a thousand of us, all loaded to the gills with testosterone. Hearts were thumping, mouths were watering, and feet were tapping to the latest hits from home as these lush American beauties danced and pranced and blew kisses at us. That was too much. A number of the men made for the stage, only to be blocked by big, burly, mean MPs, assigned to protect the innocent maidens. When the gals made their exit to wild applause and piercing wolf whistles, out stepped a couple guys to take our breath away, this time by their thirty-foot return shots in a fantastic game of table tennis. What a difference between us duffers and pros like these!

Before we knew it, it was December 7, the third anniversary of Pearl Harbor. Were the Germans, as well as the Japanese, regretting their involving us in this mess, now that we were boxing them in? Almost overnight we Americans had assembled a truly formidable war machine, the likes of which no nation could match. In P-51s alone, we were cranking out some 15,000 at $85,000 each, together with at least twice that many pilots to fly them. In 1938 we'd manufactured just 1,800 warplanes, but in 1944 that number was 100,000, more than fifty times as many. Italy had surrendered. Could Germany be far behind? Still, invading the islands of Japan promised to be a costly business, with casualties being projected into the millions for the Allies. When and if I concluded my single tour of duty, I'd be scheduled for another tour in the Japanese theater. The prospect was not especially reassuring that, after marrying Myrt, I'd be heading overseas again. But war was war, and there'd be no respite until the Axis—all three—had surrendered.

On the 8th the transportation officer winced as he saw me coming to requisition yet another truck to haul more rubble from the railway station. To make sure he'd get his vehicle back in one piece, he assigned a Negro driver, and four of us pilots hopped aboard. This time I was all caution. Not only did I not drive, but we donned our flying goggles to protect us from flying debris. Then, surveying the fourth wall, I noted that in falling there was a chance it would cut the phone lines, bad enough for the civilians, worse by far for the military. To drain my last ounce of prudence, I urged the driver to forgo the old road, still deep in mud, and carve a new one through the field north of us, near the RAF unit nearby. Success! The driver was happy. We were happy. Chappy was happy. But none was more happy than the transportation officer, his truck back and none the worse for the wear. This called for a celebration, Curtis style. So I broke open two delicious fruitcakes I'd just received from Myrt, and we washed them down with canned fruit juice.

The 9th of December brought some distressing news. In the last three days the 52nd had suffered the loss of two pilots and four planes, three of them in the 2nd Squadron. One pilot, a redheaded captain, passed the redline in a dive and, pulling out, lost his tail assembly and augured straight in. A second pilot was lost to weather in a reconnaissance mission. A third fell below the minimum speed in the traffic pattern, stalled, and fell off on a wing, hitting the ground at a sharp angle. Luckily, he had fastened his sturdy harness, and emerged unscathed. The fourth bellied into the Adriatic but managed to get out, his Mae West keeping him afloat until a PBY came and rescued him.

What was especially disheartening to the brass was that not one of the four was engaged with the enemy. All betrayed the same freshman status of our gang of twelve some six months earlier. And these pilots had enjoyed the luxury of an additional eighty or more hours of transitional and combat training before leaving for Italy. I was coming to understand why, in the 8th Air Force, they required two hundred hours just in the Mustang before they could engage in combat.[4]

On December 11, I was scheduled for what I figured would be another milk run, escorting Liberators to Vienna to complete mission number twenty-seven. It proved to be something else again. Prodded awake by the CQ, Nash went back to sleep, so I was nudged awake to take his place as element leader on Swede's wing. Everything was quiet until we approached the bomb run. There we were greeted with everything the Germans could throw at us. The flak blackened the sky around us. One explosion hit a B-24 and sent it in flames on its deadly spin, crashing into the marshaling yards below in a burst of flame to match the bombs bursting in the target area. Suddenly we confronted a massive explosion in midair. Another B-24 had been hit while still holding its bomb load, obliterating plane and crew in a split second. I couldn't make out a piece of either plane or crew and quickly came to understand why the explosions as these bombers crashed on takeoff sixty miles away could reach us at the 52nd. Suddenly Burton, my wingman, called to complain that his right mag was cutting out on him, so he was losing power fast. Swede told me to accompany him back to base, so we reversed course and headed for home, only to find him unable to make it. So we made an emergency landing at Viz, a small island just off the coast of Yugoslavia.[5]

While the mechanics went to work on Burton's plane, we were treated to sandwiches. An hour and a half went by and they were still at it, so I decided to return to base. As I took to the runway, the clouds were so socked in I immediately found myself in them, barely missing a mountain. I chanced to spy through the heavy mist across the Adriatic to base, cutting through the overcast just in time to make out the runway below. At that, I was better off than another returning pilot who overshot the runway and crashed into a truck, demolishing both plane and truck and almost killing its driver. The pilot, however, emerged from his cockpit without a scratch, testimony to both a great harness and a sturdy fuselage.

Meanwhile, back at Viz, I later learned from Burton, there was pandemonium as one bomber after another tried landing on a runway just long enough for fighters. The first crashed at the end of the runway, only to be plowed into by a second, then a third, and so on. And this despite each pilot releasing his braking chute to slow the runway speed. Ambulances were scurrying to and fro, trying to extricate the wounded without being demolished themselves by more bombers. All in all, it was hardly the 15th's best day.

It wasn't till December 15 that I completed my twenty-eighth mission, escorting bombers to Salzburg, Austria, home of Mozart. As we cleared the Alps below, all we could make out was a sea of overcast so thick that bombardiers had to rely on radar to try to locate their target—a hit-and-miss affair at best. By the same token, the ack-ack batteries below couldn't see us, so we saw little flak. Returning, we let down through as thick a pea soup as I'd encountered, made up of rain, snow, and mist, and all of it right down to the deck. It would be a major accomplishment to set down safely. Two pilots from the 2nd pranged on the runway, destroying both planes but emerging unhurt. I was beginning to think the Germans had no better ally than the weather.

Back at the 4th I arrived in time for mail call and a gift from Betty in the form of fur-lined gloves, just the ticket for the increasingly frigid days. Then, donning my fatigues and heavy jacket, along with my new gloves, I borrowed Chappy's jeep and was soon haggling in the marketplace of a nearby town. I returned with two paintings. The first, a beauty, framed in a magnificent hand-carved frame, set me back $3 in Allied currency, ten packs of cigarettes, a bag of candy, and some pipe tobacco. The second painting, less fetching, I got for another ten packs. By this time I was haggling almost as well as the Arabs back in Oran, Algiers, and Tunis, five months earlier.

The next day brought my twenty-ninth mission, escorting B-24s in a long haul to the oil refineries at Brux. By the time I returned I had a case of an aching butt, complicated by a bladder about to burst. At that, I was vastly better off than the crew I'd watched as, hit by flak, they'd tried to bail out of a spinning bomber. Flying element leader on Nash's wing, I'd been on the receiving end of one blast on the radio after another, all to the same effect. "Curtis, get the hell up here and quit dragging your ass!" Part of my problem was my having to keep jockeying my plane with Nash, almost as nervous as Colonel Malcolm had been. Before long I made out the voice of Swede, our squadron leader, bawling out Knepper, my wingman, for falling behind. Nash and Swede were reaming our butts for at least two good reasons. They wanted to make sure that if we were jumped by Jerries, these leaders would be protected from the rear. Also, laggards were especially juicy prey for Jerries bouncing us from out of the sun. It was not that much different from lagging wildebeests as inviting targets for the cheetahs on the plains of the Serengeti.

It was tower duty for me the next day. Nash would make sure I'd regret my falling behind. At headquarters I learned that a P-38 reconnaissance plane that we'd escorted recently had tried making it back to make an emergency landing at the 332nd, but had crashed and burned in the field separating our two fighter groups. So near and yet so far. One's luck could be either good or bad. I could only hope that I'd remain on the side of the angels.

December 18th came and with it my thirtieth mission, when I would sorely test my side of the angels. At 0800 hours I was in the briefing room listening to the group ops officer describe our mission, escorting B-24s to Blechham-mer. It seemed that we'd already done in this target as well as the oil refineries at Brux, only to find that the Germans were repairing them in a matter of days, putting them back in op-eration. This would prove to be a costly mission. Taxiing out to the runway, I suddenly found my radio silent, so I returned to the line and, forty-five minutes later, was pushing my throttle to the wall in an effort to catch up. I was only a spare, but maybe they'd need me. Before long I had "Snuffy" Moore on my wing. Over Lake Balatin we replaced "Cock-ney green three and four," who returned home with engine trouble. Moore, a new pilot, kept falling farther and farther behind, as Knepper had done recently, and was so far back that he lost us and returned to base, flying much of the time over enemy territory, a sitting duck for bandits on the prowl.

Suddenly, before reaching our target, our group leader turned around and headed for home, the rest of us following him, but all wondering why the sudden departure from the bombers we were supposed to escort right to target and back until we reached friendly territory. Ours, however, was not to question why. Later I learned that minutes after we Mustangs quit the bombers, they were jumped by no less than thirty ME-109s. Within seconds five bombers were burning and spinning, while twenty-nine others remained missing on return. This meant that if all the crews of ten on each of those thirty-four bombers had been killed or captured, it would total 340 fliers. Here was a Christmas present the 15th would just as soon have passed up. Never did I understand why Colonel Malcolm, leading our group, had suddenly aborted our escort mission. Were his nerves so shot that, somehow learning of the thirty bandits about to jump us, he'd turned tail and run? Did he suffer so much as a reprimand? That a full colonel had privileges we could only imagine seemed the case since he remained at the helm of the 52nd.

It looked as though our outfit had thrown in the sponge on that day's mission. That evening our basketball team threw in no sponge as we went at it against the 31st Fighter Group. But try as we may, we continued to uphold our growing reputation after this, our fifth game, coming in second every time. Not satisfied with the humiliation of five losses in a row, I managed to get our weapons carrier stuck in a small pond, its carburetor wet from barreling through the water. Since I was driving, it fell to me to get out in knee-deep muddy water, hike to the nearest transportation pool, and relate our sad plight. They took mercy on us, pulled us out, dried the motor, and sent us on our way. By the time I pulled into the 52nd I was in need of a stiff shot of something to brace my sagging morale. And there it was! Nothing could rescue me from Pilgrim's "Slough of Despond" like a letter from Myrt. And here were two of them. Ever faithful, ever cheerful, with a handwriting as graceful as her poise, she never failed to give me a boost. And that evening I needed that boost more than ever as I learned that Ward and Hosey, both of whom had arrived at the 52nd long after I had, had been promoted to first lieutenant.

Not to worry. For the next day Tim Tyler, our squadron CO, who himself had just been promoted to lieutenant colonel, pressed in my hand a silver bar with his congratulations. Just in time for Christmas! Chappy, a captain himself, gave me an additional three bars so I'd have enough for two uniforms.

My thirty-first mission, on December 20, was another escort job for Liberators to the oil refineries and marshaling yards at Blechhammer. Flying element leader to Stinchcombe as flight leader, I listened to Ottley, my wingman, complain that he was losing his right mag, so Stinch asked me to accompany him back to base. But by this time Ottley had fallen so far behind that I couldn't make him out. So, alone and in some clouds, my heart jumped as I did make out what looked like a bogey far below. With a quick split-S, I was diving down to take him on, only to discover it was a wounded B-24 with one of its engines out and its prop windmilling. So I snuggled up next to the pilot and waggled my wings to let him know he had company. He gave me a thumbs-up and a big smile, relieved to have an escorting fighter, especially a P-51. I accompanied him down through heavy overcast past enemy lines, waggled my wings to say "so long," and dropped to the deck to buzz the shoreline back to base. Again the clouds were thick down to the runway, but I managed to land safely.

At last I was racking up some missions, and this despite a monsoon that never seemed to know when to quit. The next morning at breakfast, before briefing for mission number thirty-two, I heard, far in the distance, the BAROOM! of a bomber near Foggia crashing on takeoff. Although it seemed to happen every week or so, I couldn't get used to the conclusion that ten men were suddenly obliterated, along with the plane. Again I paused to give thanks that I was in fighters, not bombers. Clearing the runway of any wreckage that might have remained meant a delay of a half hour or so, and we delayed our takeoff accordingly. When I did finally take to the air, I found a new pilot, Lang, on my wing. Nash was leading the flight, again through heavy overcast, and by the time we emerged in a clearing, Lang was nowhere to be seen. So I notified Nash and turned tail to find the laggard and we headed for home through even nastier weather, with rain, sleet, and snow and the avenging furies of stiff gusts of wind thrown in—making our safe landing all that more hazardous.

Later, as the bombers returned, one of them made an emergency landing at our field, using his braking chute to set down on our short runway. The pilot appealed to us to fix his ship and put up the crew overnight. We would, but he had to pass a test first. "Of the fighters that escort you, the P-38, P-47, or P-51, which in your objective opinion is the best fighter?" Of course he gave the correct answer, and thereupon found us to be the most congenial hosts. That evening we made the mistake of inviting them to watch our basketball game against the 31st, for again this outfit wiped the floor with us, to the tune of 53 to 6!

Friday the 22nd was a busy day. It started with me at the controls of a Link Trainer, "flying the beam" on instruments, and pulling down the top grade of 1AA. After reading "Serviceman," a paper sent to me by Myrt, I loaded up a jeep with some of the guys and drove to headquarters to see *The Mask of Demetrios.* The night was still young as we emerged, and I knew we had a Christmas bash in the works later. So, with a shave and a haircut earlier in the day, and dolled up in my best pinks, I figured the gals at Club Negative in San

Severo would find me irresistible. With that, I borrowed a jeep from Hepner, our communications officer, and picked up Billy Starmer for the ride of his life. It was record time in a frosty ride of thirty-five miles over narrow, winding, and hilly roads, arriving in forty-five minutes. Unfortunately, with but eight Red Cross gals and nurses, they had more booze than broads. I figured that my dandy appearance, combined with a generous dose of sweet-smelling lotion I'd gotten from home, would entrance them into at least one dance. I even took to the piano during intermission to assure them my talents were unlimited, if not admirable. But, sad to say, I had all I could do to wangle just one short hop around the floor, for hardly had I snuggled up so she could get a whiff of my aromatics than I felt a tap on my shoulder, turned around and looked a light colonel in the face. I resisted letting go until he gave me a dig in the ribs, as much as to say, "Get lost, Lootenant!" Worse, as I left her I looked to see her actually relieved that she'd found choicer pickings.

It was no use, so I headed for the door, Starmer in tow, but nowhere could we find Hepner's jeep. Had another officer, no doubt that light colonel, taken it? Had some Itie made off with it? Had the brakes given way and let it roll down the hill? We searched for a half hour, but in vain. At last, desperate now, I called the local MP station. "Yes, Lieutenant Curtis, we have your jeep here, if you'll come over and claim it." So we bummed a ride over, there to find a lieutenant—a second lieutenant—smugly seated with his feet up on his desk. "Lieutenant Curtis, don't you know that you never, ever leave your keys in an unattended vehicle?" I was tempted to rack him back for not standing and saluting a superior officer, but thought better of it. So, with my apology, he handed me back the keys and I was off for the 52nd, but at a slower pace than usual.

While we were laying plans for Christmas parties, living the good life in Italy, our "dogfaces," to use Mauldin's term, were fighting for their lives in the Ardennes forest in France. For the Germans had launched a surprise counterattack there, scene of some of the heaviest fighting in World War I. On the 17th they'd broken into Belgium and Luxembourg, and by the 20th they'd managed to isolate American units at Bastogne, in what became known as the Battle of the Bulge. Three days later Patton's 3rd Army struck at the southern flank of the Belgian sector, and the next day the Allied ground troops, under an umbrella of Allied air cover, began to retake the ground they'd lost. It was a Christmas eve that must have reminded some of Washington's crossing the Delaware back in the War for Independence.[6]

While this fierce fighting was taking place in France and the Low Countries northwest of us, we at the 52nd, along with our Limey and South African friends, were planning a gala Christmas party for the native children. Rain or no rain, we former Rovers and Scouts were going to welcome Santa and his reindeer. Just how his troop was going to handle the rain and mud was up to him. We would have all we could do to handle the screams of delight as almost two hundred children crowded into a big room at headquarters. But first I had to round up enough guys to help fill paper bags with assorted candies. We started, but I took note that nobody from the 5th had shown, so I dispatched a jeep to find them. And there they were, their weapons carrier stuck deep in the mud. With no time to pull it out, we left it marooned in the bog and rescued them with a couple trips by jeep. And none too soon. For in short order kids were descending on us by the score, some with their parents. *"Grazie"* was the order of the day, with big smiles and outstretched hands for candy, doughnuts, and hot chocolate, which, as I ladled it out, spilled on my newly cleaned and pressed forest greens.

Since nobody else would do it, I served as emcee, strapped on my red accordion, and, with Hart at the little portable organ, the kids were soon belting out "Jingle Bells" and the like in their best Italian/American/English. The Brits and South Africans seemed to be enjoying it as much as the parents. Even the two colonels, Malcolm and Chapman, were getting into the act. I was so impressed that I introduced the top brass to the kids, but they didn't seem overly impressed. No matter. It was a great time. As I turned in that night, I slept better than I had in weeks.

COMPLETING THIRTY-FIVE MISSIONS TO THE NEW YEAR

Monday was a Christmas holiday back home, but in war there are no holidays, at least in this war. In the first Christmas of World War I, the troops on both sides of the Western Front gathered in "no man's land" between the trenches. There they exchanged chocolates and sang Christmas carols, and even engaged in soccer games with improvised balls. No such threats to discipline and fighting spirit in this war—so said the big brass, safely ensconced in the rear.

So on Monday I completed my thirty-third mission, escorting bombers to Brux. No sooner did our wheels leave the runway than we were in the clouds, still shedding heavy rain. Rendezvousing with the B-24s, we approached Brux, only to find it socked in as well, so chose our secondary target, Wels. There was flak but no Jerries. Then, with Stinch leading the flight, we spotted a Liberator below, trailing smoke, so dropped down to provide escort over the Alps and down to the Yugoslav coast. Suddenly Stinch spotted what he thought were bogeys on the deck, so we dropped our wing tanks and dove down to challenge them, only to discover they were friends. As we regrouped, we saw a big splash ahead of us in the Adriatic. Thinking another crippled B-24 had gone into the drink, we investigated. There wasn't so much as an oil slick, so we headed for home. There the weather had worsened, if that were possible, forcing us to go around three times before we could land. That evening, after another sumptuous turkey dinner, we listened to the radio, bringing us the latest war news. The German counteroffensive had succeeded in reaching Celles, just fifty miles from Brussels. But the hard-driving Patton was leading his tanks in ramming through a rescue corridor, reaching the besieged Allies the next day, the 26th. That was the day I exchanged my high boots for a low pair and joined Chappy in spreading a coat of tar on the chapel roof, determined that another Sunday wouldn't find those braving the elements to get there for worship services having to dodge the raindrops.

With mail call came two more letters from Myrt, glad to have graduated as a nurse's aide. With her mother an RN, it seemed the natural thing to do in wartime. Also in the mail was a letter from Red Crowder, my old friend from Brady, now flying P-47s in strafing and dive-bombing missions in the Burma theater. He and Tom Crull, though graduating with 44C in March, were only now entering combat, and here I was, with two thirds of my tour completed, graduating a month later. All I could do was to chalk it up to continuing good luck.

With evening came a noble try to forge a choir from a half-dozen of us, with Hart at the organ and me with my squeeze box. Satisfied that we'd crucified the hymns, we turned to something livelier, with one of the guys breaking out a pair of drumsticks. Before long the chapel was rocking with an impromptu jam session, surely a fitting christening for this new chapel.

My thirty-fourth mission proved to be a memorable barn-burner. Each of our three squadrons was to provide a flight. These twelve, plus a couple spares, were to accompany a single P-38 reconnaissance plane up over the Alps to Munich, where Intelligence had learned there might still be a factory turning out the new ME-262 German jets. Our squadron took the rear, with the other two squadrons on either side.

The brass was taking no chances, so they provided some fourteen planes to make sure they got back some good pictures.

As we crossed the snow-covered Alps below we made out the city in the distance. Suddenly we looked up to see a twin-engine ME-262, trailing a thick, short contrail, barreling along at least 70 mph faster than we were. Though it was several hundred feet above us, Barney Chaskin and I set our Mustangs on their tails, our noses pointing straight up in hopes of putting the bandit in our sights. Our potshots did no good, but we did get some film footage to show we'd at least tangled with it. Apparently the jet's pilot figured, even with his superior speed and cannon power, that the odds were not in his favor, and didn't attack.

Then we noted that the boys from the 5th, sensing the jet was a lost cause, dropped to the deck to single out targets for strafing. And it cost them. Back at debriefing we learned that Adams, targeting a locomotive, was hit by ground fire and ran directly into his target. Varnum, also hit, managed to climb high enough to bail out, probably ending up a POW.

We returned to base, figuring we'd had enough excitement for one day. But it was not to be. For as we sat down to supper we seemed to smell smoke coming from the direction of the heating stove where its pipe met the ceiling. We'd seen the stove scorch the ceiling before, and thought no more of it, until the smoke became thicker by the minute. Then an enterprising pilot took his chair by the stove and stood on it for an inspection. Pulling aside part of the plywood ceiling, he let out a yell: "Hey, you guys, the roof's on fire!" That was all we needed to forgo our supper and leap into action. We ripped off big pieces of plywood the length of the roof. Some clear-thinking pilot grabbed the phone and called the fire department and, sure enough, within minutes we heard the clang and siren of fire trucks in the distance. The trouble was, they were getting no closer, and for good reason. At last one of them pulled through the mud and to us twenty minutes late, arriving in time to see our bucket brigade had done the trick. The upshot: it took a week to clear the air of the black, rancid smoke, and another week to repair the roof and replace the ceiling.

The next day, December 28, I completed my thirty-fifth mission, enough to entitle me to a third Oak Leaf Cluster to my Air Medal. Again it was to escort B-24s to Brux. The brass was as determined as we were to put those oil refineries out of business and starve Hitler's war machine of gasoline. Flying element leader on Nash's wing, my heart skipped not once but three times as we executed split-Ss and dove down on supposed bogeys, only to find, each time, that they were friends.

Back to base and mail call, I found a sheaf of papers from the War Department. I was to file a claim for reimbursement for travel and per diem for my trip—eight months earlier—would you believe it?—from Texas to North Carolina. I could only conclude that it wasn't just the "mills of the gods" that ground slowly.

On the 30th I learned from Chappy a story that was as sad as it was true. He had just returned from Bari, where he'd conducted a funeral for an enlisted man from the 2nd Squadron. How did he die? It seemed that two of the enlisted men got in a bar fight in their club, the big guy, a blonde, making short work of the smaller guy, a Mexican-American. He returned to his tent, bent on revenge. Later that night, when all were sleeping, he grabbed his carbine and made for the tent of the culprit who'd thrashed him. Opening the tent flap carefully, he spied a blond head protruding from a sleeping bag. Here was obviously the big blond who'd done him in. He fired. That was it. Or was it? Come to find out, this was a different blonde, just intent on getting some shut-eye. In addition, the gunman wounded another guy who jumped up at the sound of the shot and tried to subdue him. The gunshots roused the camp, the MPs arrived, but the shooter had vanished. Within the hour several posses had been organized, and he was finally hunted down in Campo Marino.

So while Chappy was conducting the funeral of the unfortunate victim, a court-martial was finding the shooter guilty of murder and sentencing him as only the Army knew how. Rather than execute him on the spot, it immediately transferred him to the front lines and assigned two sharpshooters to watch his back. If the Germans didn't cut him down from ahead, the Army made sure if he tried retreating or escaping, he'd get it. Either way, there was little chance he'd ever see the States again.

December 29, 1944

My darling Myrt,

We have at least 1 decorated Christmas tree here in Italy this year. It is perched high on a mountain 7 miles from the front line and all wired up with plenty of lights and a big sign, "MERRY CHRISTMAS." Neither time, weather, nor transportation have permitted our basketball team a suitable place for practice.

As for transportation, you should have seen the jeep I drove! Above 25 mph and it shimmied like the dickens, just shaking us all over the place. The brakes were about shot and 1 cylinder kept cutting in and out. Meanwhile the steering was balky until I reached a certain point in turning—then she'd wheel sharply and almost turn us over. To complicate matters, it was pouring and our windshield wipers were on the fritz. Then, to top it off, the oncoming truck headlights were blinding us every few minutes. I'd take a good, rough strafing "do" to a repeat of that, anytime!

With winter settled in, there was snow as well as rain, mist, and biting wind. The elements would help us see the old year out. On New Year's Eve we again were treated to a great turkey spread, followed by the guys lined up three deep before the bar as the Itie bartenders broke out the best hootch our Allied currency could buy. Content with Coke and conversation, I learned that Morris and Starmer, having made flight leader, were now in line for their captaincies. I wondered if I'd ever be able to add a second silver bar to mine. Fortunately, I'd been scheduled enough to have finished more than two thirds of my tour. Now, instead of our squadron having seventeen pilots for twenty-seven planes, as it had when we arrived in June, it now boasted six flights of nine each. It would be a close call to be able to get in fifteen more missions before this European war was over.

Actually, far from being over with year's end, it looked like the Germans would never give up—as Hitler had been admonishing them. Especially was the war far from over in Italy. As I lay my head on my makeshift pillow, well after midnight, I could thank my lucky stars that I'd lived so long. Now what would a new year—1945—bring?

8

THE PROMISE OF A
NEW YEAR

"Lieutenant, you've got hepatitis and jaundice. You're going
to have to spend three months in a hospital in Bari."

—MAJOR DILLON, Flight Surgeon, 52nd Fighter Group

THE COST OF ANOTHER TRIP
TO ROME

Rain and cold. Cold and rain. Would it ever let up? Too
many pilots now. Hard enough to fit us all in the mess hall/
dining room at once, much less schedule us to fly missions
even every other day, weather permitting. Would I ever complete my tour of duty? I had but fifteen more missions to fly,
but the odds of my completing them seemed to be diminish-
ing with every passing day of 1945.

Would there ever be relief from the deadening monotony
of rain falling on my tent, on the club roof, and on my head
as I sat, stranded in yet another puddle or pond in a jeep? A
week passed and the stultifying boredom was eating at all
of us.

January 7, 1945

My darling Dick,
Words are inadequate to express the thrill that went racing
through me when I learned of your silver bars. It makes me
so happy to know your efforts are being recognized. After

I got your letter I read it over five times, then cleaned off the gold plating on the pin you gave me—by means of a strong solution—and now it's silver and shines like a bell!

So it's the 33rd mission on Christmas, huh? At that rate you ought to be home by next summer, right? Gee, I hope so. Whenever it is, I'm saving my vacation until you come home.

On January 9 a crew of us hopped aboard a weapons carrier for a trip to Termoli, where the RAF had its fighter airdrome, home to Hurricanes and Spitfires. There, in a barn converted to their officers' club, we'd been meeting to plan for our Christmas party. Just how ignorant I was of the South Africans came home to me as they told us of houses much like our own, of cities and suburbs like those in America. What was I thinking, they must have wondered, when I told them I'd pictured them living in bamboo huts and dressing in loincloths for the daily elephant hunt? On the other hand, they seemed surprised that there were neither gangsters nor cowboys in my family, that I didn't have a cool million salted away, or that I couldn't lay claim to a mansion, servants, or a Rolls-Royce.

What we did share in common became evident as we talked of the war, of our common enemy, of our love of flying, of our background in scouting and, of course, of our common language, despite minor differences in dialect and idiomatic expressions. Another difference stood out on our final night, when we enjoyed a sumptuous banquet, served by the South Africans. Contrary to Americans eating in their cars, eating on the run, stuffing our faces as though we were trying to beat the time clock, this was a long and leisurely affair, consisting of no less than nine courses. Many of the dishes were strange to the taste buds of Americans, especially when it came to dessert. The chocolate crunchies were delicious, until they revealed that these were nothing but ants rolled in chocolate.

Still, they were a cut above the pickled fish eyes and roasted dog. Yet each course was served separately and with great fanfare as waiters—Negroes all—in great sweeping arcs, carefully placed each morsel on our plates. The banquet finally concluded, it was time for Lieutenant Logue, a South African, to lead us in a rousing songfest. There were hymns, with exaggerated pauses between the verses—making abundant sense if we were concerned about the words. There were old American standbys, such as "Old McDonald." And there were marching songs from each of our countries.

It was a great evening, we Americans agreed, as we stepped from the club to return to the 52nd. We looked in vain for our weapons carrier, so—recalling all too vividly my recent experience in the lost and found—I phoned the local MP office. Sure enough, they'd confiscated the truck. Hensfield, the driver, had left it unattended and unlocked, and was court-martialed. Chappy, having requisitioned the weapons carrier, drew an official reprimand, to go on his permanent record. Having drawn neither of these for my screwing up with the jeep, I once again paid tribute to Dame Fortune.

With the rainy days straggling by, no missions scheduled, and time weighting us down, I appealed to the top brass at headquarters to release several of us for a trip to Rome. Why not? So the boys from the 5th Squadron commandeered the best transportation the motor pool could come up with. It was nothing less than a command car, the kind I'd chanced to see Gen. Mark Clark riding in on a recent trip to Foggia. We had no stars on our epaulettes and the car, fittingly, looked as though it had met head on with one of Patton's tanks. Looking more closely, we concluded that old "Blood 'n' Guts" would have dispatched this car with a few shots from his pearl-handled revolver, as he'd reportedly done with his jeep.

Taking turns driving for some twelve hours, we hove into a snow-covered camp, chilled to the bone, tired, yet relishing the thought of a week in the Eternal City. We were not disappointed. At the luxurious officers' club in the former Excelsior Hotel, there were interminable games of Ping-Pong, splendid meals, hot baths, and American movies. Venturing out, we took in piano recitals and even an evening at the opera. There I came to understand why the Italians preferred singing to fighting. Again and again Rossini's *Barber of Seville* was interrupted by men in the sold-out audience leaping to their feet with "Bravos!" and "Encores!" at the top of their lungs. This was what sent their blood racing. Had they that much enthusiasm for fighting, we'd still be struggling to find even a toehold on Italy's boot.

It was a fantastic week, we all agreed, as we took leave of Rome in the dilapidated command car, to thread our precarious way up and down narrow, winding, snow-covered roads. We were still relishing retelling the luxuries we'd been enjoying when we came across a pathetic sight, so much so that we felt a bit guilty at our good fortune. For there, among the pedestrians, bicycles, horses, burros, and wagons—all burdened down with enormous loads—was a little old woman, barefoot, bent over under the weight of a load almost as tall as she was. Like the rest, she was undoubtedly headed for the nearest market, where she could sell or barter for the necessities to keep body and soul together for a few more days. And here we were, bitching about the pathetic condition of our command car, even when it continued to run without so much as a cough or whimper.

That car, I confess, stood up better than the jeep I borrowed from Hepner so Billy Starmer and I could make it to the dance at the Club Negative in San Severo a few days later. Bundled up in our warmest, we were flying as the wind whipped our frosty breath from us. It was pitch dark, and with what little lights we were permitted we could barely make out the road thirty feet ahead. I had the accelerator to the floor, hitting the top speed of 60 mph, when suddenly the road disappeared before our eyes. With no warning, it had taken a 90-degree turn to the left—and I didn't. Straight ahead I barreled, hitting a rise and railroad tracks, as I became airborne. We landed with a bounce that turned us sideways, almost capsizing the vessel as it rattled and shook like a dog shedding water. As I ground to a stop in the middle of a field, I found my knees shaking almost as much as the jeep after it hit pay dirt. I literally crawled the rest of the way to return Hepner's jeep, somewhat worse for the wear. Sad to say, however, Starmer would take no more rides with me.

January 12, 1945

My darling Myrt,

I have been giving a great deal of thought to the possibility of getting married when I go home on a rotation furlough— I love you, sweetheart, more than anything else in the world—I would have gotten married before I left the states if it had been at all possible. The leave will last about 3 weeks actually at home, during which we could get married and spend our honeymoon in whatever place your heart desires.

I expect to go home as a Captain—drawing a yearly salary of $5,185—that is if I were married, with one dependent, I would draw an extra allotment of $100 monthly. I would transfer this allotment to you, except for $30 a month for living expenses (overseas—as I will, of course, be sent right out again).

I am just selfish enough to want you all for myself before I go out again—and if I never did get back, I am just selfish enough to have the woman best fitted for the job of bringing up a child the way I would want him brought up.

As January gave way to February, it seemed that long periods of boredom were interrupted by one thing or another to break the monotony. With the 8th of February came another tour of duty in the tower for forgetting yet another appointment with the Link Trainer. Just the day before, three of our Mustangs had pranged on the runway when trying to land in a fierce crosswind. Many eyes were on me, therefore, as I tried to bring in the returning planes safely. As usual, each flight of four approached in tight, finger formation, buzzed the runway, and peeled up to the right to form a single line as it came in to land.

Suddenly I spotted a plane stall out about fifteen feet above the runway and drop like a rock, bounce, then—its engine catching—head straight for us in the tower. Crowded in with me were some dozen others, all of us mesmerized by the thought of our fate. There was no way even one of us could have descended the twenty-five steps to the ground in time. On the radio I was bleating, "Go around again. Go around again." Inside was Sobszak, a pilot from the 4th. Seeing he was going to hit us, he dug his left wing into the runway, turned two cartwheels, dug the nose into the ground, and flipped over on his back, just twenty feet short of the tower, there to disappear in his canopy under the mud. Within a minute or two the crash truck was there, while the thirteen of us tumbled from the tower shaking. "Sob" emerged with nothing more than a minor cut above his right eye, not even enough to earn him a Purple Heart. On the other hand, we thirteen caught in the tower paused to think how close we'd come to having Purple Hearts sent to our families. And this was the second time Sob had pranged within a week. Would he, like Stevenson, be grounded permanently?

January 28, 1945

My sweetheart Myrt,

Will you buy for our future reminiscences an "Air News" magazine for January—there on the front cover you will see "Four P51Ds in Flight." These 4 belong not only to our Group but to our Squadron. Willy Parent is in M—Buck Gassman is in X—George Nash (my flight leader) is in

D—and Jim Callahan (now MIA) is in H. An A20 took it of the 4 while they were flying on a special formation flight for a decoration ceremony here several months ago.

I've got no idea as to when I'll be getting home—aside from the fact I'll prob'ly be home before the end of the year.

February 7, 1945

Chuck opened up a can of pre-cooked chicken that we put on the stove to warm. This, together with some salted nuts, fruit cake, and fruitjuice, made a delectable evening snack!

Am a bit sick—not from the food—but from the loss of a buddy on a strafing mission today. We played Ping-Pong a lot and I borrowed $10 from him to buy some paintings an Itie brought around. I hope my letter will not get pessimistic. If it does, please forgive me.

I was bemoaning the loss of McKinsey, another pilot from the 4th, when I realized my discomfort was arising from more than sorrow for him. I was not only down in the dumps, but possessed of something strange indeed for me—a loss of appetite. What I needed, I concluded after five days of this melancholy, was some exercise. So I borrowed three shotguns from the skeet range, and in the company of Rudy Schweizer and Nails Ludwig, I went duck hunting along the coast.

As we waded through swamp after swamp, we saw no ducks, but what we did suddenly see was unnerving. For high above us was a Mustang disintegrating in midair. From its runaway engine issued a loud wail, rising and falling in volume and pitch as the fuselage plunged to earth with a dull thud, followed by wings fluttering down like falling leaves. Later we learned that the pilot, like Jack Chidester six months earlier, had passed the red line on his airspeed indicator and, in trying to pull out of a dive, put so much strain on the wings that they buckled and peeled off. Now he'd dug his own grave, twelve feet under, in a dismal coup de grâce for a pilot whose luck had run out.[1]

RECUPERATING IN A BARI HOSPITAL

Momentarily I'd forgotten my condition. But soon I realized I was feeling worse, so I sought out Major Dillon at headquarters, in the absence of Doc Curran, our own squadron flight surgeon. The good major took one look at my yellow eyes, my sallow complexion and, learning I was listless and had forfeited my appetite, he pronounced what I almost interpreted as a death sentence. "Lieutenant, you've got hepatitis and jaundice. You're going to have to spend three months in a hospital in Bari." I asked how I got it, and learned it was from polluted water or food. I could only conclude I was paying dearly for my recent trip to Rome.

Back to the 4th I rode, each bump in the road registering a sharp pain in my gut. Then, with my B4 bag under one arm and my accordion under the other, I climbed into a waiting ambulance, joining three others. Over to the 332nd we made our gut-wrenching way, there to wait for a C-47 transport. As I stood by the runway and watched the red-tailed Mustangs disappear in the distance on yet another mission, I added envy to my misery. A three months' "vacation" was certain to put an end to my dreams of completing my tour of duty. I'd not return to the flight line till the middle of May, when surely the war in Europe would have rung down. From *Stars and Stripes* I learned that the Allies had regained the offensive in the Battle of the Bulge. And on February 7 FDR had met with Churchill and Stalin at Yalta in the Crimea. Already they were laying plans for the occupation of Germany and attending to the plight of the liberated millions.[2]

January 24, 1945

My darling Dick,

As to your proposal to get married when you return, let's have it this way, dear—even if we definitely decided here and now to get married on your rotation furlough, we could hardly make any more plans as we know not when you'll be home, so let's leave the deciding to then too.

I'm determined that as long as my family needs me I'm going to be here to do what I can for them. I realize I've given you no definite answer to your question. I can't, dear—I honestly don't know. You know my plans for a wedding—that kind of a wedding takes time.

You seem to have thought it all over very carefully and arrived at a decision. Bear with me in my indecision, darling. I promise you that when you come home and we are faced with deciding either to get married then or to wait until you're home for good—no matter what the circumstances, I'll do my best to see things just the way you do—without hesitation.

I'm proud of you, Dick, and I shall be proud to be your wife.

As sorry a plight as I was wrestling with, it could have been worse, I thought, as I heard the sputtering and coughing of a plane in trouble. For there was a Mustang, just having cleared the runway, now settling down, and out of runway. Just beyond lay on orchard. In between two of the trees the pilot managed to guide his plane, ending up on its nose. The Negro pilot emerged without a scratch. Here was luck, I concluded, but not without skill.

When the C-47 landed, we climbed aboard and strapped ourselves into the blanket-lined bucket seats lining either side of the chilly, spacious interior. I was happy to see two attractive nurses ready to help us if we needed it. We didn't, but when we got to Foggia and picked up several of the wounded from the bomber crews there, the nurses got busy. An enlisted man appeared to be mercifully drugged, his one ear purplish-black from frostbite, while the other side of his face, partly covered with compresses, was also discolored and swollen. Subzero temperatures six miles up claimed many such victims, particularly the gunners in their cramped positions, with only a piece of Plexiglas between them and the elements.

Our sagging spirits got a dramatic boost when a charming young nurse picked her way through us and chirped that she was married to a P-47 pilot. Furthermore, we should try to make the best of it since we'd be aboard for another couple hours before hitting Bari. Taking that as a hint, and determined to drown out the constant roar of the two big engines, I took out my bright red squeeze box from its case, figuring the color, if not the music, might help cheer us up. As I went from one favorite to another, I hoped the others would join in. Only silence. So I broke into song myself, with my best bass croak. At last a couple of the guys joined me. Still others seemed to be measuring with their eyes the distance between them, me, and the door. So I took that hint too and we returned to the dull roar of the transport.

I had better luck with my attempts at harmonizing when we reached the 26th General Hospital, and more particularly, the hepatitis wing, indicative of the many GIs who'd also downed tainted food or water. My diet now would consist of Swiss steak, morning, noon, and evening, together with lots of water and concentrated amounts of sugar and vitamins. The weather was warm, as were the smiles and voices of the lovely nurses, especially when they applied back rubs. It was uncanny that when "plain Jane," an older nurse, offered a rubdown, nary a hand went up. But when a young looker appeared with the offer, every hand shot up. It was evident the ministrations of the nurses were boosting our morale, even as the steady diet of Swiss steak was boosting our livers. Mid-mornings and mid-afternoons we could count on nurses bringing in sandwiches and orange juice. Evenings after the lights were out, the twelve of us in our wing could be counted on engaging in bull sessions—and the topic we began and ended the sessions with was invariably, as I wrote to Myrt, "wimmen." But in between, the patients, most of them members of bomber crews, revealed conditions that made me more glad than ever that I was flying fighters.

February 15, 1945

Myrt, sweetheart,

Perhaps the most spectacular of the mishaps among the B-24 guys happened on takeoff—with a full bomb load and gas load in soupy weather. This meant they had to go on instruments from the time their wheels left the runway. But no sooner were they in the soup but first, one, then the second engine failed, so the big bomber had no place to go than to settle down beyond the runway. A couple of the bombs blew up, killing 4 of the crew outright and blowing big gaping holes in the sides of the bomber. Out through those holes the other 6 dashed, running like mad while the rest of the bombs went off. That finished the plane as well as one of the 6 on the run. Miraculously, the other 5 got out without a scratch!

This was just one incident that was multiplied many times over as the guys related, each of them, accounts just as hair-raising. One fellow upstairs in another wing, we discovered, had bailed out at three hundred feet, leaving not enough time for his chute to open. He landed in a muddy field and suffered only a fractured ankle and collarbone. Another fellow was cleaning his small Itie pistol—a Beretta—when it accidentally fired. The bullet pierced his wristwatch, then traveled up his arm, stopping just short of his elbow—but carrying the remains of his watch up through his arm. The docs just left everything, including the bullet, in his arm so he went back on duty, taking regular doses of penicillin to counteract any complications.

February 18, 1945

My darling Myrt,

We had a new patient admitted to our hepatitis ward yesterday. He'd been here 98 days already. A 1st Lt. ground officer, he'd been out in his jeep on an errand at night and got stuck in a quarry. He hiked a mile and a half for help, coming to an Itie farmhouse. He knocked and was suddenly jumped by 3 Ities, 2 of whom held him down while the 3rd clubbed him on the head. He squirmed loose and ran, only to be downed by a bullet in his right thigh. Again he picked himself up and tried to make a break for it. They fired again, this time hitting him in the left leg. Where the first bullet missed the bone, the second shattered the bone. Then the 3 hoodlums *really* went to work on him, kicking and beating him. He fought back as well as he could, lashing out with his right leg. They finally left him for dead, but he managed to crawl for help and now he's in our hospital, bearing a bitter grudge against *all* Ities. . . .

Every other day we could count on a visit from the doc, the light colonel in charge of our wing.

"How do you feel, son," emphasizes that he's not only your elder but your superior in rank.

"Oh, swell," you lie, and wince as your liver, raw, ragged, and ruff, reproves you for your deception. You know he's onto you, and he'll find out for sure.

"Lie flat, now. Take a deep breath. Hold it. O.K. Exhale."

WHAM! He's jabbed his hand halfway through your solar plexus, and it seems he's missed so tries again—and again—each time asking, "Hurt?" or "How's that?" And each time you lie.

At last he gives you a mighty fist, rocking your 200-odd bones from stem to stern—first on the right side, then on the left. "Did you notice the difference?" If by this time you haven't given up the ghost, you can count on a return visit in a couple more days.

As the days passed I found more of the guys were joining in when I fetched my accordion. One day a ward boy brought me a fresh change of linen and towels. As I unfolded them I found a new pencil, three cigarettes, thirty-two lira, and two candy bars.

"Say," I put it to the ward boy, "you've given me somebody else's stuff."

"No, sir, it's yours."

"But I never saw this stuff before."

"If you'll read the note, sir, I think it'll explain it."

There, in a short note, was a big thank-you from the nurses for trying to cheer up my fellow patients. I didn't know how much I'd lifted the spirits of the guys, but I'd definitely lifted my own, especially when the nurses added a list of songs they also wanted to hear.

After a week of the runs, I began to feel a bit stronger, so left my bed for the short walk to another wing where I'd heard they had a barbershop. After ten steps my head was woozy. Five more steps and that head hit the floor, facedown. The next thing I heard was the voice of a flight surgeon bending over me. "Amazing! He got thirty feet before collapsing. The last record was eleven feet, and he'd been here three weeks!"

February 22, 1945

My darling wife-to-be,

I think Doc would have a fit seeing me in the gym playing basketball, and playing horseshoes outside this afternoon. I'm supposed to have shower and latrine privileges, plus freedom of the ward. Thus I'm overstepping just a mite. Oh, well, I'm feeling better now than I have in ages! One other guy went into town and got soused while almost cured of "hep" and is now in a private room with no visitors but with a severe relapse.

Another week and the guy next to me left, to be replaced by William "Bucky" Walters, from Littleton, Illinois, Pete Fulks's hometown. One day a familiar voice interrupted our game of gin rummy, and I looked up to recognize Chaplain Pope, the kind soul who, back at Aloe Field in Texas, had lent me his '37 Ford for a date with a cute lass from the Lone Star State. There he was, now, sporting a mustache and grinning from ear to ear. Somehow he'd learned of my stay there. By this time both Bucky and I were feeling well enough to walk to Pope's jeep, and soon we were trundling over town to the nearest substitute for ice cream. Things were looking up, I figured, as we walked the bright, sunlit streets.

February 22, 1945

My darling Myrt,

I'm the only "pea shooter" (fighter pilot) in my ward, and these bomber boys—mostly B-24s—not only appreciate us but just about all would give their right arm to be flying a 51.

Some of our guys carry grudges against all Ities and carry their guns—pistols—into town. A couple GIs were lured into a trap in town nearby and grabbed—one was castrated, the other killed—if something isn't done over here right quick about feeding these people, crimes are gonna become more widespread.

February 27, 1945

Myrt, my sweetheart,

Have been given the job of censoring some of the enlisted men's mail. It's remarkable how illiterate and poorly written are some of the letters, while others betray a college education. Some of the love letters really lay it on thick, too. It seems ridiculous when you read someone else's love letters. Probably ours would seem just as crazy.

One fellow finally left for home after being cooped up here for over 2 months. Although getting back to the States would be wonderful, to go there on a stretcher is no way to go!

March 1, 1945

Myrt, my dearest,

Got a letter from the mother of my flight leader, Bob Frye, KIA in a Yugoslavia strafing deal last September, when I was flying in his flight. She asked for more details—and I tried to oblige by sending her an account as meticulous in detail as possible—kinda ticklish letter?—hard to say what you want, the way it should be said, without hurting her. With all the neat weather lately—and all the missions my outfit's racking up—and here I rot in a hospital!

March 2, 1945

My dearest Dick,

Twice I've written you telling of buddies of yours who have been reported missing in action—Richy Gordon and Jack Arbour. Now both are POWs. Jack is safe and well according to a telegram his mother received from the Red Cross, even though he's been missing since December 21st over Germany.

I remember when those newly married couples got on the train when we went to New York, you said it was a heck of a way to start a honeymoon—going on a train. I think so too, and I hope that wherever we go we can drive.

Released at last, after twenty-three days cooped up, I was ready and eager for some action. The flight back to the 332nd was nothing like the flight to Bari. The pilot, obviously a frustrated transport pilot who'd have given anything to be flying fighters, gave us an exhilarating ride on the deck, buzzing everything he found worthwhile. Though slower by half the speed of the Mustang, I found it intensely satisfying after hibernating so long. It was, however, something less than satisfying to have Dillon read the note I handed him from the flight surgeon at the hospital. I was being released, it stipulated, only on the condition that I was to get plenty of rest and maintain a tame schedule. What really got to me was the condition that I was not to fly for a week, and not to fly combat for at least two weeks.

BACK TO THE FLIGHT LINE

I returned to the 4th Squadron on Friday, March 9, to discover that in my absence they'd flown eighteen missions. Had I flown just eleven of them, I'd have completed my tour of duty, and would probably be returning to the States by this time. I simply couldn't wait to settle back in the cockpit of *Myrt's Dickie-Bird,* so that afternoon, unbeknownst to any of the docs who'd been on my case, I took to the air, relishing my aerobatic regimen as I darted in and about the bright clouds drifting across, filtering the bright sunshine.

All well and good to get back in the air, but what I hungered and thirsted for was more combat. So on Monday the 12th, I got my chance. To wait two weeks would have constituted cruel and inhuman punishment. As it turned out, it was but a milk run for five hours, to complete my fortieth mission. I returned to find that Monster Ward and Rudy Schweizer had blown in from France, two days after their mission had returned.

They had quite a story to tell. It seemed that Rudy's oxygen supply had sprung a leak, meaning he couldn't possibly have cleared the Alps on his return trip from Germany. So Ward, always the compassionate fellow, had kept him company. Why, they testified to the brass, Rudy had felt woozy at just "sixteen angels." In actuality, the highest of the Alps in their vicinity was only twelve angels. Now the brass might have been inclined to stretch the height to sixteen had these derring-do pilots been thoughtful enough to return with some fine French wine. But no, they were thinking only of themselves as they luxuriated in a quaint but hospitable French village while the oxygen system was fixed at a nearby airfield. So they caught hell from the brass. As much as I liked both of them, I found some measure of satisfaction in knowing others were also screwing up. Yet that satisfaction was nothing like the unalloyed joy I experienced as I opened a large envelope at mail call, to find a magnificent colored photo of Myrt.

March 2, 1945

My dearest Dick,

Just called home (I call every day at 12:15) and Dot tells me I have a letter from you. Happy Days!! Until yesterday, it was 10 days since I'd heard from you. This letter makes the whole world bright and sunny!

Remember when you called me that Sunday you got home from Texas and I yelled D-I-C-K! so loud it's a wonder it didn't break your eardrums?!

I hate like the dickens to tell you this, honey, but Jack Arbour has been reported M.I.A. Mrs. Arbour is taking it in her stride.

A week later, March 19, was anything but a banner day for the 52nd. I wasn't scheduled to fly, but joining the gang at the debriefing, I learned the mission had been a bust. It was a strafing job at an airfield near Munich. That done, the guys were supposed to seek out targets of opportunity, always a dangerous business with German ack-ack gunners and others manning machine guns ready and waiting.

The 2nd Squadron lost three pilots, including their CO, Maj. Jim Curl. Back in North Africa he'd been awarded the Silver Star for leading his squadron of P-40s in jumping a flock of slow, cumbersome Junkers Ju 52s, trying to evacuate Germans from Tunisia. It was like shooting fish in a barrel, as he put it, and it became known as the "Palm Sunday Massacre." Now this veteran pilot, awarded the second-highest medal for valor in combat, had bought it.

Another pilot, Maj. "Pinky" Brewer, a replacement, was returning to land after some transition time, and made the mistake of embracing the "Purple Heart Pattern." This involved pulling up too sharply after buzzing the runway, stalling out and spinning in. He managed to straighten out the plane before it slammed into a field just north of the runway—the very field I'd hit nine months earlier. In my case it had only buckled a wheel. But in Brewer's case he lost both wheels, part of his wings, his tail assembly, his prop, and part of his fuselage. He was lucky, for the part of the fuselage that remained intact included the cockpit.

Hearing the crash, many of us raced to the wreckage, expecting to find no sign of life. We were astonished to find Pinky releasing his shoulder harness, throwing back his canopy, and quickly stepping out on a wing. He jumped to the ground, and none too soon, for the plane immediately caught fire from the spilled gasoline. There he was, with scarcely a scratch, to greet the fire trucks storming up. Was he such a lousy pilot that he'd pranged Ward's plane? This was, in fact, the fourth ship that had been assigned to Pinky. The first three had likewise bit the dust. Again it appeared that rank had its privileges, for had he been less than a major, he'd have been grounded long ago. But now it seemed he was a life member of the "Born Lucky Club," which I'd joined eighteen months earlier.

Almost every day brought incidents that reinforced that this was indeed a deadly business, whether flying combat or just getting prepared for it. And when three of our 52nd pilots failed to return, it was a somber group who met at headquarters that night to review the combat film.

Yet in between the tough times, there were times of high jinks, and few more hilarious than the tale spun around the "cracker barrel" heating stove at the club of the 4th Squadron. Hugh Ottley and Ed Paleczeski, returning from their week of R&R in Rome, gathered us around the stove and wove a story fantastic yet true, they swore. There in Rome they'd learned, with some envy, that the finest of Rome's hotels had been set aside for the exclusive use of officers of field grade—meaning majors and above.

After a few snorts at the bar of their own hotel, these two enterprising pilots got to wondering just what privileges were being bestowed on the high brass. So they approached the clerk at this poshest of hotels and explained that they wanted to see a certain "Major Pal . . ." They couldn't quite manage that last name, so the helpful clerk quickly thumbed through his list of occupants and suggested, "Major Palfrezski?"

"Yes, that's him!" With that, they made a beeline for the stairs leading to the ballroom-restaurant, to be seated by the headwaiter as they waited for their imaginary friend. They ordered drinks and sat back to enjoy the floor show, a master of ceremonies appearing to announce a grand prize for the winner of a sporting game. The object, he announced, was to catch and hold to the count of ten the pig he held in his arms, adorned with ribbons and greased from stem to stern. With that, he released the porker, which soon was darting hither and yon, seeking refuge beneath a table, then a chair.

Now here was the kind of challenge that Hugh, emboldened by his booze, simply couldn't resist. So off he went in hot pursuit, lunging at the critter and careening across the floor. The grunts of the porker had turned to high-pitched squeals as she dashed from one hiding place to another, brushing the feet and ankles of onlookers as they roared their approval. Determined not to be outdone by this refugee from barnyard mud, Hugh made a spectacular dive, colliding with a table and sending food and drinks into the laps of the brass and their dates.

By this time a number of these inebriated spectators had become participants in the chase, entreating as they ran, "Here, Porky! Here, Porky!" Suddenly, sensing she was outnumbered and being cornered, the pig made a desperate dash right between Hugh's legs and he clamped them together like a vise. He reached down, lifted Porky up and, instead of counting to ten, put a half nelson around the animal and bolted for the stairs descending to the lobby, Ed right behind him. By this time they were drooling at the prospect of a great pig roast back at the 4th, surely the envy of the rest of the 52nd. But there, in hot pursuit behind Ed, was the emcee, shouting at the top of his lungs, "My peeg! My peeg! He's getting away with my peeg!"

Racing across the lobby, Hugh headed for the exit, but quickly realized it was a revolving door. Now to rush through such a door empty-handed takes some coordination even for the sober. But fortified with several drinks, and holding a snorting, squealing, slippery pig, Hugh saw it was useless, dumped the porker and disappeared into the night, Ed hard on his heels. They were satisfied they'd seen enough of the perks of the high brass.

March 5, 1945

Darling Myrt,

In Dana's letter to me he told of his gradual loss of memory during the past year. When home on furlough he asked Midge where she'd gotten the necklace she was wearing. Surprised, she reminded him that he'd given it to her a couple summers ago. He seems to have difficulty connecting names of even his close friends with their faces. And by this time he must be well on his way overseas.

A few days later the 4th became the recipients of a newfangled recording machine, care of the Signal Corps. We were to use this to identify and, if possible, to eliminate any speech mannerisms, including exotic dialects, that could interfere with accurate communication over the plane radios that loomed bulky behind the seats of us pilots. Just how seriously we took this was seen when, after several weeks saw dust begin to gather on it, I spirited it away to my tent for a couple days of experiment. Speaking, whistling, taking turns with the harmonica and the accordion, I was fascinated by the playback. Then I cornered three other guys and we fashioned a barbershop quartet to set the contraption back even further on its heels. So, it turned out, the recorder was put to use, even if not its intended use.

It was possible, even plausible, that others of our Allied troops were engaged in similar high jinks to relieve the boredom and the frantic combat as they drove the Germans farther and farther back into their own country. By March 1 the Allies had thrown back the Germans on all fronts. Three weeks later pontoon bridges were being laid across the Rhine by British and American engineers as the Allies continued in hot pursuit of the fleeing Germans. Dismayed by the prospect of defeat, Hitler replaced the leader of his forces on the western front, Gerd von Rundstedt, with the man who'd done so much to halt the Allied advance in Italy, Field Marshal

Kesselring. By the 26th, however, the entire western front had moved east of the Rhine.[3]

Berlin was now the target, as Germany contracted under the twin onslaughts from east and west. This meant fewer and fewer targets for the 15th Air Force, until they could be numbered on our fingers. One of these was Ruhland, some seventy miles southeast of Berlin. This was our target on March 23, when I served as a spare on my forty-first mission.

With Sobszak flying my wing, and no early returns, we continued on to the target area, escorting a group of B-17s that had become separated from the main force, and thus needed protection. Copying the crisscrossing technique of the major group of fighters, above and below the bombers, we hoped to protect the bombers from fighter attacks, yet spotted none. But as we neared the target, we pulled aside as the flak from below filled the sky with black puffs of smoke and deadly shrapnel. For every explosion above there was at least one bright orange flash from far below in the marshaling yards. I watched with almost hypnotic fascination as one orange burst after another wreaked havoc on Hitler's dwindling means of transport.

I couldn't help but compare this Führer with Samson of old, pulling down the temple of the Philistines dedicated to their god Dagon. In this case, however, Hitler was pulling down the entire German nation around him. By the time the Flying Fortresses turned around and headed for home, the many single fires had merged in one giant funeral pyre. Here was yet another signal that, for Hitler and his nation, the end was near.

Were we but heaven's avenging angels, bringing this nation to the judgment seat? The thought had crossed my mind in my ten months in wartorn Italy. More than once shudders coursed my back as I saw the dead and the dying, and especially the crippled children of the land, begging food before it was dumped as garbage. Always, it seemed, it was the children who paid the steepest price. Their future, if they managed to survive, never seemed bright. We would rid the world of Hitler and his henchmen, but at a frightful cost. Still, no matter how noble we thought our cause, or analyzed our motives, in the final analysis war for the individual was invariably reduced to that bare-bones equation: kill or be killed. Nothing could be more personal, nor more final, than one's own death.

These morbid thoughts were increasingly preoccupying me as I headed for home, leaving behind another funeral pyre dedicated to Mars, god of war. In this case we were lucky. I saw no enemy fighters attacking our bombers, sending a dozen or more spinning to earth as "flamers." Neither did I see any flak crippling bombers or fighters. I saw no chutes of men who, having bailed, tugged furiously at their shroud lines to avoid a melee of planes, friends and foes, as they clashed about them. Almost certainly they would be taken prisoner if they managed to avoid the planes, the bullets, the exploding flak, and the enemy on the ground shooting at them deliberately as they floated to earth.

As our six bombers completed their bomb runs and headed for home, I looked around for my wingman, in vain. "Hey, Sob, you got me in sight?" I was worried.

"Yes," came the reply.

"Well, let's head for home." With that, I eased my stick forward to descend to fifteen angels, where I could remove the oxygen mask pinching the bridge of my nose. Again I looked around for the familiar yellow tail, and again I called. He answered he'd lost me but was joining the main force. This was somewhat discomforting, knowing I was seven hundred miles from home, and all but two hundred over enemy territory. I was just the kind of loner now that a few Jerries would consider duck soup. So the next five hundred miles I wove back and forth across the sky, trying to cover my own tail, lest a bogey sneak up and drill me. Finally I crossed the Po

Valley and breathed easier. When at last I stepped from the cockpit, I was relieved to be home, for lone stragglers had a way of disappearing from our missions.

Earlier I had written Myrt that Chappy had invited us to display photos of our gals on an overhead projector for all the gang to observe. And mine, as far as I was concerned, took the blue ribbon!

If my forty-first mission had some harrowing moments, my forty-second was the milk run of all milk runs. It didn't start that way, for briefing informed us that this was to be the largest escort mission of the war in Europe. We were to rendezvous with many hundreds of bombers over the northern Adriatic and escort them far up into Germany. It was a 1,500-mile trip for the bombers, but more like 1,700 miles for the fighters as we crossed the skies above them. It would be well over five hours and, strapped into that tight cockpit, sure to be a genuine butt-burner. The bombers were more vulnerable than we were, but at least the men could enjoy the comfort of being able to relieve themselves when their bladders complained.

Heading north over the Adriatic, I suddenly spied a big oil slick below, so I called the group leader's attention to it.

His answer: "Caviar red number three, drop down and inspect it for survivors."

It looked as though a bomber had gone down into the drink. I descended and circled, just above the waves, for two hours, but caught sight of no familiar life jackets, no rafts, no survivors. Then a PBY Catalina appeared to take up the vigil, undoubtedly the result of the group leader calling the homing station. So I returned to base, thankful that I wasn't aboard that bomber.

9

VE DAY APPROACHES

"Curtis, you know you're a damn fool! You just blew any chance of getting the captaincy we put in for you. What in hell were you thinking about, doing a victory roll off the roof of General Headquarters?!"

—Capt. Paul Steinle, Operations Officer, 4th Squadron

ANOTHER CLASH WITH JETS

It was a "stroke of fortune," Churchill wrote, that on March 7 the 9th Armored Division of the 1st U.S. Army found a key railroad bridge at Remagen, Germany, still usable, even though heavily damaged. Within hours four divisions had crossed and established a bridgehead several miles into Germany. This sounded the death knell for Hitler, breaching the boundary that he had promised the German people would never be breached in all the thousand years of his "glorious Reich." For one whose profound belief in "good fortune" had been his lodestar in what was already a long life, Churchill was to test this fortune again as he met with Eisenhower on March 25 at the front. Enemy shells landed in front of them and behind them, some no more than a hundred yards away. Yet the two escaped unscathed.[1]

On the home front, Myrt had written of schools closing in Worcester for an indefinite period for lack of fuel to heat the buildings. And, in a winter with more snow than in a decade, there would be no more plowing. She also wrote of Dad wanting each and every one of us in the family to invest in his new stamp business so he could quit at Norton's and undertake this new business full-time.

Dame Fortune must have been playing favorites. For here I was, still intact in Italy, with less than ten missions to fly to complete my tour of duty and return to claim my bride at the altar. And this despite my being the youngest, the greenest, and the most foolhardy pilot in the squadron, if not the group. One day after Churchill had put himself at risk on the German border, I put Dame Fortune again to the test. Already I'd tangled with the Luftwaffe's new twin-engine jet, the ME-262. On this day I'd be reacquainted as six of our P-51s escorted two P-38s on a reconnaissance mission up over the Alps to Munich, where they were building the ME-262s. Hitler's jets were his last best hope for turning the war around, and we were determined to put an end to those aircraft plants.

From start to finish it proved to be a memorable day. Paul Steinle had replaced Swede Larson as our squadron operations officer while I was recuperating from hepatitis in Bari. Paul nudged me awake at 0600 hours. I was drowsy no more once I'd dashed cold water on my face, shaved, and made for the club for breakfast. By that time I realized that it was again a bummer for flying. Nimbostratus clouds, heavy with water, hugged the ground, restricting visibility to one hundred yards at best. Preparation for takeoff by this time had become routine. Climbing into the big GI truck to briefing, we listened closely, then picked up our chutes. That I was one of six picked gave me a boost. I kidded Sergeant Kline about his dying to get back to Texas for a furlough. Then I rummaged through my locker, improvised as was so much of our housing and furniture from wing tank crates. I pulled out my Mae West, my oxygen mask, and my helmet with goggles and mike attached. Finally I made sure I had my maps, including a big *National Geographic* map of Europe I always slipped into the pocket on my knee in my flying suit. Then, with pistols, knives, and money kit all in place, I slung my chute over my shoulder and lumbered over to *N*. Along the way I greeted Willie Groselma, our squadron engineering sergeant. The day before, I'd watched the armorers loading big strings of .50-caliber machine gun bullets in the wings. As usual, Bob had seen to everything. Already my crew chief had warmed up the engine, tested the mags, and cleaned the canopy over the cockpit.

"Mornin', Bob," I greeted him, "how's my favorite crew chief and *Bird* this morning?"

"OK, thanks, sir, she's all ready to go."

As if it would have been any other way. He'd awakened an hour or more before I had, just to make sure his plane and his pilot would be safe, going and returning. Here again, I figured, Dame Fortune was smiling at me. For many of the crew chiefs, it turned out, were responsible for the early returns that plagued our outfit and put our spares to use. Never did I experience an early return due to Bob's neglect. I was glad to have earned his respect in return.

"Got a little 'rec' hop with 38s over Munich," I confided to him as he checked my chute and shoulder harness once I'd climbed into the cockpit. Although we pilots had been warned never to divulge in advance the nature of our mission, I figured if I couldn't trust my crew chief, who could I trust? So I'd gotten used to dropping some idea of our mission to consolidate the trust I was placing in him. And he seemed to appreciate that. Hopping on the end of my right wing, he directed me to the edge of the runway, where he jumped off and gave me the thumbs-up.

It took but a minute or so for each pair of us to become airborne. Then our flight of four, plus two spares, headed north. Capt. Jake Klerk, a West Pointer from Bernardsville, New Jersey, was our flight leader. I flew number three element leader off his right wing, with Snuffy Moore on my right wing.

Now Snuffy, like so many I'd met in training and again in the 52nd, was a "Reb" from the Deep South, and proud of it. He prided himself on his Rebel flag, his Rebel drawl, and—above all—his Rebel cry, a full-throated yell that he'd perfected to an art. On the other hand, here in *N* was a "damned Yankee," who prided himself on descending from the Titus line in southern Vermont. For there, Dad's mother had revealed, her father's brother, Herbert Titus, had commanded the New Hampshire–Vermont regiment during the War Between the States, retiring as a general. That war had concluded eighty years earlier and now Snuffy and I, Reb and Yank, were facing a common enemy. Despite lingering bitterness on the part of many in the South, we knew that our survival depended on close cooperation. So, despite occasional digs, tongue in cheek, we Yanks had no trouble bonding with the Rebs.

The importance of this mission was seen in the two spares attached to our flight, where the two usually accompanied the whole squadron of sixteen or more planes. The brass was taking no chances that the Lightnings, unarmed and with their armor plate removed to accommodate the high technology necessary for taking good photos, might not return with their precious footage. We had to know just what buildings were continuing to turn out the deadly jets, so our bombers could pinpoint them. In addition to the camera equipment, the 38s were carrying extra fuel in their wing tanks, even as we were.

We were off and heading for San Severo at two angels when we spotted the two Lightnings off to one side.

"Hello, Grassland Nineteen, this is Drumbeat white leader," Jake called, "we're joining you."

"Roger, Drumbeat white leader," came the response, "am setting out on course."

With that brief exchange, the 38s began climbing about

three hundred feet per minute as we joined them, easing forward on the throttle for a couple more inches of mercury manifold pressure. Dingy layers of rain clouds stretched ominously before us as we uncaged our gyros and passed through the clouds on instruments. We hugged each other so we'd neither lose each other nor collide, emerging occasionally in a splash of bright sunlight.

Ever climbing, we proceeded without incident on our northern journey over the Adriatic. To the left we were flanked by the Appenines of Italy and to the right by the mountains of Yugoslavia. These latter were especially treacherous in the late afternoons when the winds would pick up and howl down through the passes to the sea. There they easily capsized unwary fishermen—or unwary pilots flying too close to the waves.

Our target was Munich, the city where Himmler had been chief of police before being tapped by Hitler to head up the dreaded SS. So it was no coincidence that there in the little village of Dachau, on the outskirts of Munich, Hitler had established the first of more than two hundred concentration camps during the war. Of course, as we made our way, we were unaware of this, intent only on capturing footage of aircraft factories.

Finally, above the clouds, we saw ahead of us towering cumulus, topped off here and there with the dreaded hammerheads, suicide for a pilot venturing too close to the vertical drafts that could tear the wings off any plane, bomber or fighter. So we detoured to the east and found a hole after descending several thousand feet on instruments, emerging close to the craggy peaks jutting up from below. A thick mist of heavy cloud cover cut our visibility to half a mile as we drew within sight of our target. Through occasional breaks in the overcast we could make out the huge city, its factories still turning out war matériel, and its marshaling yards still transporting it by rail.

Suddenly we were jabbed alert by two dark forms almost on a collision course with us. "Jets!" Jake shouted as he cut left to head them off. I could make out the ME-262s with their twin nacelles, swinging in a huge arc as they climbed above us and prepared to come in on our tails. Breaking sharply to the left, I shoved the throttle to the firewall, hoping to intercept one of them. But they were so much faster than our Mustangs, there was no way I could get close enough for some clear shots. But I let loose a deflection burst, hoping for a lucky hit. I was lucky, but not that lucky. Then one of them became a disappearing spot on the horizon ahead of us, weaving back and forth in great arcs in an attempt to lure us away from the 38s so his partner could have them to himself. Farther and farther the jet lured us, staying just out of shooting range. The pilot would give his engine a burst, then coast for a while, before hitting it again, conserving his fuel even as he was making us burn up ours. Before long we were thoroughly exasperated and cussed him over the radio for not coming out and "fighting like a man!"

Finally, afraid that we'd run out of gas with our throttles full forward, we reversed course to see how the 38s were doing. Fortunately our two spares, Gaisser and Cochran, had stuck with the "recs." Suddenly the second jet came out of the clouds and at us like a bolt from the blue—except it was above us by two hundred yards or so. Hauling back on my stick, I put *N* on its tail, pointed directly ahead of the jet and squeezed the trigger. Was it possible just one of my bullets would collide with that jet? I was in range, but hardly in a position to get in a good shot. Rapidly I lost airspeed and was about to stall and go into a spin, when I did a quick wingover. It was then I noticed that my wing tanks were still attached, so I quickly pulled the release, dropping them. Meanwhile Snuffy was doing his best to keep up with me and protect my tail.

In a flash the first jet was at us again and we broke into it, following it for five minutes more before at last giving it up as hopeless. Each time one of the jets tried diverting us from the 38s, the other attacked them, to be diverted by the two spares turning into it. When we finally reversed course a second time to try to find the 38s, they were nowhere to be seen. By this time I was ahead of Jake and Pete, his wingman. Apparently *N* was faster than theirs, perhaps due to my hitting the "tit," the emergency boost handle that gave me an extra 5–10 mph burst of speed for just such an occasion as this.

Suddenly I made out the first jet bearing down swiftly on their tails. "Break left, Drumbeat! Break left!" I shouted into my mike. They broke left, and none too soon for the jet in its shallow dive. Again we gave chase, firing an occasional burst in hopes that we'd register a lucky hit. No such luck. Weary by now, and worried that, with our wing tanks gone, we'd have all we could do to make it back to base, we turned homeward reluctantly. After all, we'd been at it for perhaps twenty minutes with the ME-262s, at top speed, and our fuel was going fast. By this time Snuffy had lost me and teamed up with Jake, while Pete, his wingman, was now on my wing. A few more minutes passed, and still no sign of the 38s or the spares, so we descended through the overcast toward Ancona, south of the Po Valley and our northernmost emergency landing base.

"Hello, Big Fence . . . Hello, Big Fence." I was tuned in to Channel A now. "This is Drumbeat one three. Will you give me a homing to Ticonderoga, please? One . . . two . . . three . . . four . . . five . . . four . . . three . . . two . . . one . . . Over to you, Big Fence."

By counting in this manner I was able to get two of the homing stations, separated by a distance, to triangulate, so where their lines intersected they could give me a fix and direct me to Ancona. Back came the directions: "Hello, Drumbeat one three, this is Big Fence. Steer one seven nine . . . one seven nine . . . over."

With the needle on my gas gauge dropping fast, I was grateful for the help. "Hello, Big Fence, this is Drumbeat one three. Understand steer one seven nine . . . one seven nine. Thank you."

Every few minutes I repeated my call to the homing station to make sure that I remained on course to Ancona. High in the overcast, with gusty crosswinds able to blow me off course, I was increasingly nervous as my gas gauge was flirting with "Empty." At last Pete and I broke through the rain-drenched clouds to find the cold waters of the northern Adriatic beneath us. There, off to my right, I could make out through the mist the big rock that marked Ancona. I put in another call to Big Fence to let them know I was "happy," meaning I had the emergency base in view. We landed to find that Jake and Snuffy had already landed and been refueled. So once we were gassed up we were off for home.

As I pulled off the runway and onto the taxi strip, I was pleased to see Bob standing there, his face lit up with a broad smile and his thumbs both pointing up. He hopped on the end of the wing and guided me to my parking space, where I gave him a brief rundown of the excitement of tangling with ME-262s again. Then, debriefing at Intelligence, I gave them a blow-by-blow description of this memorable mission. I then learned from our squadron armorer that I'd used up two hundred rounds of ammo from each of my six guns. I could only wish that my tracers had shown at least one of them hitting home on Hitler's best.

While I was wishing what might have been, I heard the sound of two more Mustangs buzzing the runway, and looked up to see again our two spares, Gaisser and Cochran, peeling up and back to land. I was eager to hear their story. They reported that they'd stayed with the 38s as they climbed for the safety of the cloud cover. One of them, however, climbed too steeply, stalled, fell off in a spin, and headed for the Austrian Alps below. All the way down the two Mustangs stayed with the errant Lightning, thinking the pilot would certainly pull out as the snow-covered mountains rushed at them. He didn't, apparently gripped in a panic from the jets rushing at him. Up from the snow-covered mountain there came a plume of black smoke, marking yet another grave of a 15th Air Force pilot. Apparently the other 38 pilot made his way back without incident, but also without the precious film he'd been sent to shoot.

Back at the 4th, they were all ears as we divulged our story of yet another clash with the infamous ME-262s. In truth, I confessed, had they been the least aggressive, with their vastly superior speed and firepower, they could easily have shot the eight of us out of the sky. So I was grateful to be back.[2]

March 25, 1945

Dearest Dick,

Gee, honey, I didn't know anything about Dana's condition. Your Mom told me yesterday he's been in a hospital in California for the past two weeks. Why, she didn't say. She also asked me about our plans when you get home and I told her we'd like to get married. She said you'd mentioned it in your letters to them and that both your Dad and she felt the sooner the better. I'm glad they feel that way, dear, and that they seem to approve so wholeheartedly. In regard to my "indecisiveness," as you put it, I'm sure that when you come home things are going to work out just swell!! We both are waiting for the same day—dreaming the same dreams—planning the same plans—both with the idea of making each other happy. I love you very much and because I love you I want for you only those things that will make you happy—you know that.

The last week in March found me one evening in a very impressive and meditative service—an Anglican service conducted by an Irish chaplain friend who was instrumental in our starting a Scout troop there in Italy. As impressive as was the service, his service of offering Scouting to these boys was even more impressive. Some sixteen boys between the ages of eleven and thirteen were learning the rudiments of Scouting under adverse conditions of poverty, politics, and religion. Six of the boys were Roman Catholics. Yet it was a local Lutheran minister, who had years earlier been an Italian Scout, who took on the task of continuing what we had started. The kids eagerly memorized the information from a printed introduction to Italian Scouting.

We had tried to offer a varied program on Tuesday afternoons. At one of them we had a British football or soccer game, which went well until the kids got in an argument about some point of rules or scoring. Finally one of the teams stalked off the field and quit, not to show up the next Tuesday.

But perhaps the most comical—and pathetic—situation occurred when Corporal Oyer, Chappy's assistant, ran the inspection gauntlet up and down the row of kids. "Let's keep those shoes shined," he barked out as he inspected their footwear. The two kids who boasted what loosely could be called shoes looked at the battered remnants of what had been shoes, while the others stood in shower clogs, or burlap, or rags, and wondered what the good corporal was talking about. "And make sure to bathe at least once a week—and dig behind those ears." And that was an order, given to kids who bathed only when they went swimming at the seashore in the summer, who lived in a town where the only water was toted on the back of a mule more than a mile from the main water spigot.

CELEBRATING VE DAY IN STYLE

The foul weather was such a major factor in either scratching projected missions or complicating them that I decided to learn more about forecasting. I remembered as a kid how I'd pressed my nose against the window glass to watch, transfixed, as another blizzard blew into New England. So one morning I arose to join George "Infallible" Pope, our meteorologist, in his office at headquarters. There, lining the walls, was a series of big maps, along with imposing documents, while a rattling machine nearby was spitting out yellow ticker tape every few minutes.

From all this "ice," as he put it, Pope put together a report for the day's briefing if a mission was scheduled, using what he called an "octoscope"—what we later called an overhead projector. I joined the pilots assembled that day to listen more carefully to him.

"Air Force is calling for upper winds of 72 mph, coming from the west. They predict you'll encounter an overcast from the deck, all the way from base to target." So, I asked myself, what else was new? Pope continued. "Base will have a nine-tenths [of a mile] visibility when you return. That is Air Force's prediction."

"Infallible" was by no means done. "Now I'll give you my prediction. You'll have variable upper winds from 30 mph to 80 mph . . . more or less. The cloud situation may vary some from cumulus to stratus, or vice versa. Of course this condition is subject to change without notice. Your target may—or may not—be in the clear, depending on whether or not there are clouds intervening between you and the target. Likewise the base when you return. Naturally you understand that these conditions are very fluid. It may turn out to be just the opposite of what I've given you. So, to play it safe, use your own judgment. And remember, you can always count on the homing station to get you back."

At any rate, this was the impression he gave me. Since the Air Force report was as often wrong as it was right, "Infallible" was taking no chances. With that kind of caution, he could be assured his moniker would stick. Little wonder, then, that within a week or so, he was wearing captain's "tracks." Had precision been the name of the game, he'd have been court-martialed back to a private and dumped in the infantry—along with his superiors at general headquarters!

By the last week in March the monsoon rains had quit. Italy's boot had been upended and the water poured out, leaving a surface of mud that had turned to a hard crust. To celebrate, we put up a volleyball net and measured off the court next to the squadron club. It was March 28 when a dozen or more of us were hard at it, dressed in Uncle Sam's finest GI-issued, olive-drab undershorts. As riveted as we were to the game, our attention was suddenly diverted skyward to a couple 38s engaged in a rugged rat race, less than one thousand feet above our heads. Then we watched as one of the pilots, to gain more speed and maneuverability, released his wing tanks. We held our breath as we followed the two tanks plummeting on a course close to us. The first fell harmlessly into a thicket perhaps the length of a football field from us. But the second, still holding 100-octane gasoline, landed squarely on a tent in the bivouac area of the 332nd Fighter Group just south of us. There the tank struck a heating stove and exploded in a huge burst of flame. The next thing we knew, a man burst from the tent, running as I've never seen a man run, clothed from head to foot in flaming gasoline. In a desperate attempt to avoid the flames, he managed only to feed them with oxygen, and in a hundred feet or so he collapsed in a field, setting it afire. Other men ran to help him as a fire truck pulled up. But it was no use.

I later learned that this was a pilot who, like me, had racked up over forty missions and was looking forward to returning to the States and his family. Now all they'd get was the terse announcement my folks had gotten from the War Department that their son, too, had been killed in action.

Seeing what he'd done, the Lightning pilot immediately landed at the 332nd and apologized again and again for his stupidity. Later the pilot's brass made a trek to the 332nd to add their profound apology. I never did learn what happened to that pilot. All I knew was that one pilot, a member of what would later be called "The Tuskegee Airmen," had been immolated in one of many such accidents in the 15th. Asleep in his bed at the time, he was burned alive, much as Bob Frye had been back in September on our strafing mission to Yugoslavia. Here are memories so seared in my mind that, after almost sixty years, they remain vivid, grim, and painful.

March 28, 1945

Dearest Dick,

It's been ten months since last I saw you—it seems like ages—yet your letters make you seem a lot closer than I ever dreamed possible. When I see other girls whose husbands or sweethearts have been gone two and three years and those whose mail comes through perhaps once in a month or two months—if they're lucky—I count myself fortunate. So the brownies were O.K., were they? I'm off to the kitchen to whip up another batch. I'm enclosing a clipping telling of Jack Merrill, a co-pilot on a B24 who was declared M.I.A. and is now reported to be a P.O.W.

With the coming of Easter and a sunrise service, more men than usual gathered at one of our parking strips to watch the sun rise above the Adriatic and with it the hope that soon the war would be over in Europe and we'd be headed home. We sang to the accompaniment of Ward at the little portable organ. We prayed and gave thanks, if for nothing else than just that we were still alive and able to sing and pray. It was solemn. And it was quiet as we made out a giant red ball rising out of the sea to the east. Chappy spoke briefly but unusually eloquently of the cost to the 52nd in helping to ring down the curtain on the war Hitler had started. For that curtain, it appeared, was about to fall—at the most perhaps in a few more weeks.

By the end of March it appeared that the twin pincer movements against the shrinking Germany were succeeding far beyond expectations, even as the war in Italy continued to be bogged down. On March 28 Eisenhower told Stalin that he intended to isolate the Ruhr Valley, home of Germany's principal war industry. Ike would then join the Russians in dividing the enemy's remaining forces. Stalin agreed, but added that he was discounting Berlin as having "lost its former strategic importance." Therefore, he added, he would allocate only "secondary forces" there. Now Stalin may not have been wise, nor even smart, but he was clever. On April 1, Churchill telegraphed FDR, contradicting Stalin and emphasizing, "Berlin remains of high strategic importance. Nothing will exert a psychological effect of despair upon all German forces of resistance equal to that of the fall of Berlin." Churchill added, ominously, that if the Russians captured it, along with Vienna, they would conclude that they'd done the lion's share in victory. And to the victor go the spoils. Therefore, Churchill concluded that "we should march as far east into Germany as possible, and that should Berlin be in our grasp we should certainly take it."

By this time Roosevelt's health was so precarious that Gen. George Marshall and the Joint Chiefs were in command. And they were relying on Ike, now commanding general of Allied forces approaching from the west. On April 1 he assured Churchill that the remainder of the war was all a matter of timing. Therefore the ports to the north as well as other targets should be taken before attacking Berlin. It may well be that Ike knew that those still loyal to Hitler would put up a fierce defense of the capital city, costing the invaders dearly. Therefore, perhaps it would be best for the Russians to take the brunt of the final battle.

Churchill, however, having had to deal with Stalin in several summit meetings, was wary. He telegraphed Ike that regardless of Stalin's claim that Berlin deserved only secondary forces, the Allies should be sure to "shake hands with the Russians as far to the east as possible." His reasoning: "As war waged by coalition draws to an end, its political aspects have a mounting importance." He added that Americans were not as concerned about dividing up the spoils of war as they were about simply returning home. Yet, he added, these political issues play "a dominating part in the destiny of Europe and may well [deny] us all the lasting peace for which we've fought so long and hard."

With the passing of FDR on April 12, so passed an unprecedented opportunity for the Americans and British to take Berlin and Vienna. It was left to the Russians to take these two prizes and insist on their share—and more—of the spoils.

April 8, 1945

My Darling Dick,

You've probably heard from your folks that Dean Gordon was killed there in Italy—a member of the ski patrol in the mountains there. I hate to mention things of this nature to you—but I know you're anxious to know about these fellows whom you knew so well. It's getting late and I'm sleepy, so "Good Night. Sweetheart," (one of my favorites).

If the war in Europe appeared to be winding down in March, its end seemed certain by April. This was the month that the 52nd made its long-expected move northward about three hundred miles to Modena, just northwest of Bologna. It would shorten our few remaining missions to Germany by some six hundred miles. Yet that turned out to make little difference, for the remainder of our missions were but milk runs, with no bogeys and little flak.

It was to this base that McIntyre, Straut, and I returned after a delightful week of R&R at Cannes, on the French Riviera. I didn't know how it compared with Nice, the vacation spot for the enlisted men there on the southern coast of France, but it was everything I'd hoped for. Though I'd earned a reputation among some in my squadron as a stick-in-the-mud, if not a Goody Two-shoes, I found it impossible not to ogle the French lasses sunbathing on the warm sands, stripped as they were to the waist. The dances each evening were well attended by these same French girls, whether at our hotel or at others. But of course this was tame stuff to the likes of Mac and Straut, who enjoyed kidding me that I was missing out on all the real fun. When we rented a sailboat to cruise the waters offshore, they lost no time regaling me with their nightly frolics in the sack with these same belles.

Apparently the three of us, when we registered, made the mistake of emptying our pockets of candy for the kids crowding the entrance to our hotel. For from that day on we could count on reveille being sounded, not by a bugler, but by the screams and shouts of a chorus of kids assembled in the street below our window, who would not be silent until we'd sent more candy through the air to watch them scramble in delight. This invariably happened before 0600 hours, making it impossible to return to the sack for a few more hours of precious sleep until we'd satisfied the ragamuffins below.

I made one other mistake while resting and relaxing at Cannes. That was to meander out on the tennis court behind the hotel, looking for some competition. Seeing none, I began practicing my serves, when I heard a voice from behind me. Would I like to hit a few? I turned around to see a wizened, white-haired old man, sitting on the bench. Would I condescend to hit a few with this man, obviously way beyond his prime? Oh, well, nothing else to do, so I condescended. I'd take it easy and humor the old codger.

Before a half hour had passed I was out of breath and dripping sweat. Meanwhile, there he stood, seemingly rooted to the spot where he'd been returning my best shots, and sending them invariably just out of my reach. Worse, he'd not broken a sweat as he stood there, smiling ear to ear. I couldn't believe what was happening. Surely he needed a breather, I suggested.

"Oh, are you tired?"

"Not just tired. I'm exhausted!" was my response. Between gasps, I asked his age.

"Seventy-five. How old are you?"

"Twenty-one," I had to confess. Then I asked how long he'd been playing.

"Sixty-five years. Oh, by the way, I was French singles champion for several of those years."

That brought to mind Wilbur Marisa, the shrimp who'd pinned me on the wrestling mat back on the *Frederick Lykes,* almost a year earlier. Was I still grossly underestimating my competition? It appeared I hadn't learned much in that year.

The week was over before we knew it, and we were back at the 52nd, moved to its new location. One afternoon we three decided to pay a visit to a couple other pilots we'd met at Cannes. After an hour or so in a jeep, we found them the picture of hospitality. First it was Ping-Pong. Then we sat down at their officers' club to an unusually fine supper, which Mac and Straut washed down with copious spirits. Then Mac took to their piano and for an hour banged out boogie-woogie the way I wish I could. Continuing to imbibe from a glass on the piano, and encouraged by this new audience, Mac demonstrated an uncanny coordination for somebody so soused.

It was time to return to the 52nd and, as we started for the jeep, Mac allowed that he was looking forward to getting behind the wheel, Straut having driven us there. But, being the only sober guy among the three, I wasn't about to end my career as a pilot smashed up in a jeep. So I ran ahead and jumped in behind the wheel, Mac in hot pursuit. When he found I'd co-opted the steering wheel, he was not a happy man.

"Curtis, you son of a bitch, I told you *I'm* driving back!"

I'd made up my mind. "Like hell you are. I'm not about to get wrapped around a tree!"

So Mac decided to pull rank, he and Straut both having recently gotten their captaincies. "Move over, *Loo*tenant, and that's an order!"

Having evaded, as a lowly cadet, an order by a *general* that I be court-martialed, I wasn't about to obey this drunk captain. "You're not pulling rank on me. You're too damn drunk to drive!"

With that, Mac lashed at me with both fists through the open window, drawing first blood. There I was, stuck behind the wheel, unable to defend myself, until I gave the door a shove and knocked Mac backward, reeling. "McIntyre, you bastard, I'm going to *kill* you!" With that, I laid into him, knocking him to the ground. I was just about to jump on him and finish him off when Straut, with a couple of our hosts, intervened, probably saving me from the threat of another court-martial.

And who drove home? I did, but with Mac sitting directly behind me, blasting me every foot of the way. The next day I asked him how he got his split lip and blackened eye. He had no idea.

During the last few months I'd learned from Myrt of offers she'd gotten to go to work for others. Her first boss, Jack Hawkins, wanted her to work for him in New York. Clem Easton, her second boss, wanted her to join him in Springfield. Dad wanted her to help him in his fledgling postage stamp business. But, most of all, I wanted her on a full-time job as Mrs. R.K.C. And that, I gathered from her letters, was what she wanted, above everything.

April 15, 1945

Dearest Dick,

I hardly knew which of the two photos you sent to keep and which to give your folks, but I do love to see you smile, dear, just as you did the first moment I saw you the day you came home. Now, with your picture standing on my cedar chest, I can see you smiling all the time, and almost hear you saying, "It won't be long before I'll be home."

Yesterday was officially declared a National Day of Mourning in the loss of our President. The news of his death was indeed a shock to the nation and to the entire world. All offices and stores in Worcester were closed and people gathered to lift their voices for guidance as a new Chief Executive takes office.

Myrt had lost a president, but I had lost both a president and my commander in chief. The overhanging, nagging question was whether Harry Truman could fill FDR's shoes. As April was winding down, I figured it was time to bring Myrt up-to-date on the gas situation in the States—as I understood it.

April 15, 1945

Myrt, my sweetheart,

The latest news on the gas situation is one gallon for each day of furlough. So that should come to 21 gallons. How far will that take us on our long-awaited honeymoon in a '41 Ford, darling? Some guys have presented duplicate copies of their orders to wangle extra gas. And where on our honeymoon? I don't think we'll find trouble in discovering *what* to do, but a pleasant environment can do wonders! I just love to reminisce as I think of the events just a year ago. I remember kissing you good night—oh so sweetly you looked! Then how sorry I was to have to leave and sleep in another room. But one of these great days coming, it won't be that way, darling. Unfortunately, many of these guys can't wait till marriage or to return to their wives to indulge—and many find deep regret. For that, if nothing else, can not only spoil a guy's life, but also those of his family—and those to come. This reason is probably as great as any why I want to marry you before going overseas on another tour. The sooner we're married, the better!

Had I convinced her? I wasn't sure. But one thing I knew; she was as anxious to see me again as I was to see her. Another letter from her only confirmed this.

April 27, 1945

My dearest Dick,

As I write this we have the radio on awaiting news concerning the German situation. False rumors of Germany's unconditional surrender last night caused a few riots, etc., but now folks seem to have resigned themselves to the fact that these reports were not official. It's so grand to know that the fighting over there is about to be brought to a close and that peace is on the lips of all. To realize that soon you'll be home and I'll see you again—it's really most wonderful!!! I almost have to pinch myself to see if I'm dreaming. Words can't express how much I'm looking forward to it.

By May 7, I had fifty-one missions under my belt, the extra one in honor of Lady Luck, who'd never left my shoulder. And also in honor of the plane I'd been flying. More than once I'd heard of pilots pranging on their last mission, so I figured I'd do them one better and assure myself that luck was my middle name. My concern now was to get in my four hours each month so I could continue to draw my flight pay.

So that morning I strapped myself into *Myrt's Dickie-Bird,* determined to get in my time—and have some fun.

First I took aim at the 4th's bivouac area and, from five thousand feet, dove down, skimming the tent tops at over 450 mph, pulling up just in time to avoid the hill overlooking our area, but catching a few leaves in my air scoop in the process. I figured some of the guys would then join me in some great mock-dogfighting. I waited a few minutes and saw none heading for the flight line, so decided to mosey over to a couple other groups and buzz them.

Suddenly the radio crackled with the familiar voice of our CO. "This is Colonel Malcolm. The war is over in Europe. Germany has surrendered. All planes are to return to base immediately. This is an order." Then he repeated himself, but before he'd finished, I decided my radio must be on the fritz. No such order should interfere with my four hours of thorough enjoyment in celebrating VE Day in style. So I headed south along the coast, buzzing one town after another, and one airfield after another. It appeared this announcement had come from General Headquarters to all groups, for none leaped into their planes to challenge me.

After another hour or so buzzing everything in sight worth buzzing, I found myself approaching Bari, home of General Twining's headquarters of the 15th. There I spotted a large brick building, sporting a huge American flag—undoubtedly Twining's home away from home. What better way to celebrate the victory of the Allies over Germany than in a victory slow-roll off the roof of the commanding general of the 15th Air Force? Already he'd issued the order banning victory slow rolls when we pilots returned having polished off a Jerry. So, climbing to five thousand feet, I dove down, approaching the famous red line on the airspeed indicator, and roared just a few feet off the good general's roof in as fine a slow roll as I'd ever done. I could only assume a veteran pilot such as Twining would fully appreciate such a maneuver at such a time.[3]

But there I was, a couple days later, face to face with Steinle, operations officer for the 4th. It appeared that Twining and his crew, like the sheep farmer back in Texas, had identified the *N* on my yellow tail, and called our group CO and found that I was flying that sucker at that time. To make sure, Steinle and our own brass had reviewed the film I'd been shooting on my gun camera as a souvenir to take back to the States. So he had all the evidence he needed.

Paul came right to the point. "Curtis, you know you're a damn fool! You just blew any chance of getting the captaincy we put in for you. What in hell were you thinking about, doing a victory roll off the roof of General Headquarters?!" With that, he stalked off and I slunk away, amid the curious stares of my erstwhile buddies, agog that I'd been such "a damn fool." Then Steinle turned and gave me a parting shot. "In fact, Curtis, if you hadn't finished your tour of duty, you'd be facing a court-martial!"

May 8, 1945

My Dear Myrt,

I was tickled to learn that my crew chief, Norman "Bob" Bobcean has been put in for a Bronze Star for having 71 missions completed in *Myrt's Dickie-Bird* without so much as a single early return. He sure is happy!

From Chappy, who'd overheard the top brass discussing my case, I discovered that rather than my captaincy being turned down by the 15th Air Force Fighter Command, I needed another month and a half in rank as 1st Lt. to qualify. That meant I'd have to remain in combat till the last week in June, and I would have cinched it. As for my D.F.C., though it hasn't come through yet, our Group Intelligence Officer, who wrote it up for me, seems confident that it'll come through O.K.

By the way, I heard from Dana that he's now training as a mechanic on the flight line rather than using his gunner's wings and practicing for his tour in the Pacific.

I eagerly anticipate returning home to my "lil" sweetheart who, I hope, will be my wife before I leave again. That is, if Japan doesn't throw in the sponge in a surprise surrender. It's possible—but hardly probable in view of their past performance.

Chappy's news about my captaincy put me in a quandary as to what was going on. Was Paul Steinle's browbeating me for my VE Day stunt no more than that? Did it have nothing to do with my rejection for the captaincy? Or had the brass taken a hard look at my file and seen that I'd come to the 52nd without the eighty to one hundred hours of transitional/combat training—not to mention the two hundred hours in a P-51 required for combat in the 8th Air Force, before entering combat? Had they seen that on my seventh mission I'd earned the DFC, and on the ninth mission was left alone among the original twelve to complete my tour of duty? Were they planning to make me an exception too—until I pulled that damn fool stunt? I didn't know and would never know. But one thing I did know. If I had to be deprived of either the promotion or the DFC, I'd far rather have had the DFC.

My tour was over—that is, my first tour. Would the second one turn out as well?

IO

THE LAST LAP

"Curtis, where the hell have you been? Don't you know that
you've been AWOL the last three days? It's a wonder you
don't face a court-martial! If you hadn't finished your tour
of duty, you would be."

—Squadron CO, Air Transport Command, Memphis, Tennessee

WEDDING BELLS ARE RINGING!

It was a magnificent day, that May 25, 1945, when I left
Naples for home. I'd spent almost twelve months in Italy. I
pinched myself to make sure it wasn't all a dream. Now I was
boarding another Liberty ship, returning to my family, my
friends and—above all—to Myrt. For all those months I'd
been counting the hours between her letters, reading them
and rereading them as though my life depended on them.
And it probably did.

The return trip to the States was a study in contrasts with
the trip from the States. There was no convoy, no U-boats to
evade, no wondering if this might be a one-way trip as it had
been for so many of my buddies. But mainly, I was returning
to my fiancée, not leaving her. Day by day I'd been keeping a
diary, making note of the main events and scribbling down
details of the most outstanding ones. In addition, I'd been
writing Myrt, on average, once every three days, providing
even more details of my life separated from her. Now, sitting

at a table astride the center line of the ship to minimize the roll, I tried to type some semblance of continuity to my scratches. The ship's steward, Bob Kurth of Hempstead, Long Island, was good enough to lend me his Underwood upright and paper.

As I described the past, I couldn't help but contemplate the future. The war with Germany and Italy was over. But there lay the third member of the Axis, Japan, and *Stars and Stripes* was predicting that the invasion of those Pacific islands might cost as many as a million Allied lives. I couldn't count on my prospects for returning home any more than when I left for Italy. The Japanese Zero fighters were every bit as good as the ME-109s and the FW 190s of the Germans. And I shuddered to think I could well be leaving Myrt a widow, as Bob had left Margie two years earlier.

Myrt had promised to marry me—when the war was over. Would she settle for half a war being over? Here she was, her father dead a year and a half, leaving her the sole support of two younger sisters and her mother, whose Social Security check was a minuscule benefit. Would Myrt—*could* Myrt—leave them to join me until I shipped to the Japanese theater? She was earning about forty dollars a week working for Mutual Trust Life Insurance Company in Worcester. But that, together with the Social Security, was enough to sustain them, since her father's insurance benefit had paid off the mortgage balance on their house.

But perhaps the central question was how she, as talented as she was smart, as sensitive as she was beautiful, could marry the likes of me. As has been said of greatness, so could it be said of stupidity. Some are born stupid. Some have stupidity thrust upon them, through some accident affecting the brain. Then there are others of us who, through dogged determination, cultivate stupidity day after day, polishing it as though it were a fine diamond. Was it possible that my having Myrt by my side would keep me from putting my big number twelves in my mouth, or keep me from trying to beard the Grim Reaper in his den? Would marriage put a stop to my reckless misadventures, which had endangered others as well as myself? There could be no doubt but that she had her work cut out for her, if she decided to take the plunge.

It was two weeks later, June 8, that I disembarked at Newport News, to the welcoming band's rendition of "Sentimental Journey." From Camp Patrick Henry the train took me to Fort Devens where, on June 11, I picked up a phone in a booth to call my folks. In all the excitement I forgot the beautiful ebony walking stick, topped with an intricately carved ivory skull, that I'd carefully guarded since buying it in North Africa the previous summer. Oh well, I rationalized, it would hardly do for me, if a clergyman, to call on my parishioners with this prize. The next day the train chugged into Union Station in Worcester. As I embraced my folks I felt a surge of emotions. Relief to be home and in one piece, elation at seeing them again—they who'd already lost one son in this war—but also something bordering on embarrassment that I should be hugging my dad. For this was the first time in my short life that he had ever given me a hug. Undoubtedly this was a result of his alienation from his own father years before when, though a brilliant inventor who'd developed an automatic screw machine in the 1890s and been awarded a gold medal at the Paris Exposition, he'd been divorced from Dad's mother to marry Ellen, the New York woman he'd been seeing on the sly, a woman who couldn't tolerate Dad as a boy, rebellious and hungering for attention. So I came to understand Dad's reluctance to touch even his own children.

But, joy of joys, I found no hint of reluctance to embrace on the part of Myrt, as I swept her into my arms. Would she—could she—marry me now, even though the war was still on with Japan? Her answer triggered a run on my heart.

She agreed to, if we could work out the financial arrangements for her family. In fact, one of the reasons I loved her was just this measure of commitment she felt when she had a responsibility. As it was, Dad had more objections than Myrt's mom did, for the $150 each month I'd been sending home to him to invest in war bonds he'd been investing instead in his stamp business. And now it would have to be cut to $100. Myrt agreed to send home to her mother another $100 a month as soon as she landed a job. My pay, a little over $300 a month with a housing allowance, plus what Myrt had left after her commitment to her family, meant that we'd be strapped for the foreseeable future. But, we agreed, we would do it.

Now Myrt had less than a month to plan a big wedding at her Swedish Baptist Church on Belmont Street. To my amazement, she continued working a forty-hour week, planning all the details of the wedding, and seeing me as much as possible. And she took it all with aplomb, with a graciousness that made me ever more grateful that Mom had introduced us, via mail, less than two years before. Among the details was obtaining a marriage license from Specs Midgley's dad, the city clerk who'd written a recommendation for me when I applied to the Air Corps in November 1942.

Before I knew it, it was July 7. And where was I that Saturday morning but down in back of the house, helping Dad with the homemade house trailer that he'd improvised ten years earlier, and in which we'd enjoyed several memorable summer vacations. Then Mom was at the door, calling for me. Myrt was on the phone, calling to check on some last-minute details. No, Dad answered for me, I'd call Myrt back later. I should have rushed to the phone, but habit dies hard and, over the years, I'd grown wary of crossing Dad. He had become imperious in his demands, to the point of expecting unquestioning obedience, creating an atmosphere that we teenagers were bound to find stifling. So repressive had it become that it was yet another reason that the three of us boys enlisted as early as we did. In any case, Myrt was hurt, and even more so when seven o'clock arrived, time for the wedding to start, and my folks were not yet there. To be fair, they had to wait for a chauffeur we'd arranged for, who'd forgotten to pick them up. So they came ten minutes late. At last, in this candlelight service that she'd dreamed of for so many years, the wedding march sounded out, the audience stood, and Myrt, wreathed in a luminous smile, approached me on her uncle Ted's arm as I stood, dazzled by the sight of her in her beautiful wedding gown.

Never was the sun brighter than her smile, despite the disappointments of the day. She was composure personified as she took my arm and we exchanged vows before her minister and mine. I did take note that, when it came to her vow, she omitted "to obey," an improvisation that she insisted on. I suspected that, if nothing else, she must have been hedging her bets with this madcap pilot who'd proven himself a hazard to life and limb of others as well as himself. Next to her engagement ring that I'd bought her at New York's Commodore Hotel I slipped the wedding ring. She reciprocated. We were now married, the ministers said in unison. We kissed, then descended to a magnificent bounty of food, flowers, and other decorations, seen to by Myrt's mom. After relaxing the smile that had greeted some 250 guests as we stood in line with our parents, bridesmaids and groomsmen, we left for our first night together in what would be a glorious honeymoon. I came to realize what Bob meant when he wrote, back in May 1943, that his honeymoon with Margie was the happiest time of his life. And I couldn't help reflect on how tragic it was that their marriage should have been cut so short by his death in June, less than two months after their wedding. Now the question was, would ours be cut short by yet another tour of duty in the Pacific theater?

The next day we were off, using a wedding gift of gas ration coupons for Dad's '41 Ford as we headed for New York City via the Merritt Parkway through Connecticut. The 35 mph federal speed limit was no problem for us. Who was in a hurry? That everybody else seemed to be as we entered the city was as apparent as their immediate conclusion that here were honeymooners. How did they know? Was it so obvious that we couldn't take our eyes off each other? But what they didn't know was that each of us had remained a virgin, something that my buddies in the 52nd would have found laughable. Before we knew it the week was over and we were back in Worcester, savoring what was to be only our first honeymoon. For we were soon bound by train for Atlantic City, where the Ritz-Carlton Hotel on the Boardwalk awaited us and other Air Corps officers. Here was a second honeymoon, a week in which I frequently compared the city to the frigid February of 1943, when I marched the Boardwalk as the icy winds from the Atlantic sent shivers up and down my spine. Now there was a lavish room, sumptuous meals, shopping on the Boardwalk, sunning on the beach, and dancing to a classy orchestra.

My only ordeal was the daily visits to the Army dentist to fill no less than fourteen cavities. But it wasn't this that sent him scurrying to invite other dentists to take a look. For there, he pointed almost with pride, the enamel was off my front teeth. How could this have happened? What had I eaten or imbibed overseas? I explained that I'd swapped my beer and cigarettes for the big #2 cans of fruit juice, which I'd sipped through a hole I'd made in the can. They concluded that it was the acid in the fruit juice that had done its work, undoubtedly eroding the entire lining of my alimentary canal. This was hardly good news. I concluded that had I stuck with the water, or with the beer, I'd undoubtedly have been a lot better off. As it was, it took the week to fill all the cavities, and each with the slow, grinding drills of the day, with no such thing as novocaine to lessen the pain. But there was

Myrt, and the pain quickly subsided as we savored each hour together. All too soon Myrt was taking the train back to Worcester, even as I headed south to Dothan, Alabama, to find suitable housing.

July 31, 1945

My darling husband,
Just got your letter now and was so glad to hear from you. I was so disappointed though, dear, to know that it will be such a long time before we'll be together. I'm so lonesome and I miss you so much. Everyone here at home is asking about you and they are all naturally surprised to find me at home. I haven't been able to find a job here, so time goes very slow. It's not the same being back here now—without you. More than anything I want to be with you and I'm trusting that this will be possible very, very soon. I've been home almost a week now, and it's seemed like an eternity! If you find you can't fly up to get me, I could take the train down—unless, of course, I could find a car that isn't too expensive. The sooner I can come, the better, 'cause it sure is lonesome here. Your loving wife, Myrt.

With her letter she enclosed a recent clipping from the Worcester *Evening Gazette,* along with a picture, taken back at Curtis Field. The news had been sent from the Army Air Forces at Atlantic City.

1st Lt. Richard K. Curtis has been assigned to Napier Field, Dothan, Alabama, as an instructor after reporting to the AAF Redistribution Center at Atlantic City, New Jersey. A veteran of 13 months overseas service where he was a pilot with the 15th Air Force, Curtis wears the Distinguished Flying Cross, the Air Medal with 4 oak leaf clusters, the ETO ribbon with 7 battle stars, and the Presidential Unit Citation with 1 cluster. He engaged in 51 combat missions.

Then came the good part.

Curtis married the former Miss Myrtle Fisher while home on leave July 7th and Mrs. Curtis will join him soon at Napier Field.

Had I been writing this news, I'd have concluded with *HALLELUJAH!!!* At Dothan I found a single room, with kitchen privileges, and Myrt soon joined me. She took the Civil Service exam, passed with flying colors, and was soon at work on the base. Meanwhile, I returned to the AT-6 to get in my four hours of flying time each month.

This time "The Texan" almost did me in. For one day Nails Ludwig, a buddy from the 4th, joined me in some mock dog-fighting. I was chasing him and, figuring to take a shortcut to head him off, I resorted to something I'd vowed not to do months before. I dashed through a big cumulus cloud, emerging on the other side in a dive straight down on Ludwig's plane. He looked up in astonishment, horror written on his face. It looked like a certain collision and the end of both of us. Would I end my flying career as Tom Kuykendall's brother had back in Italy, colliding with another plane? Ludwig and I undertook violent evasive action and barely missed each other, but only by inches. So close was it that we were both shaking uncontrollably after we landed. I apologized for another round of my stupidity. An hour later we were still shaking as I rued what could easily have been a fatal mistake, cutting brutally short my marriage to Myrt.

Having actually concluded fifty-one combat missions overseas, and returning with not so much as a scratch, was I now to become a suicide statistic? I'd frequently heard of pilots returning to the States, clobbering themselves with foolish stunts like this. When I related my close call to Myrt, she blanched. Was I out of my mind? I vowed, this time to her, that I'd not put myself or another pilot at risk again. This war, it seemed, couldn't end too soon for her. She couldn't wait to have me back in civvies. Yet this was, at best, a thin hope. Meanwhile, I was hearing of the devastation Japanese kamikaze pilots were wreaking as they crashed onto the decks of our aircraft carriers and battleships. If they were that determined to win this war, what hope was there for the likes of us who continued to prize our lives?

VJ DAY AND ITS AFTERMATH

My next tour of duty was very much on our minds as I contemplated the future at Napier Field. I'd paid $650 for a 1940 Dodge with money Margie lent me, and Myrt and I were soon luxuriating in our newfound married life. Even as she typed hour after hour in her new job, I confess to tennis games and card games with some of the guys from the 4th, including Ludwig and McIntyre. Myrt and I loved the swimming pool, the big milk shakes and hamburgers at the officers' club, and the dancing under the stars in the cool of the evenings. Yet we knew it was just a matter of time before all this would be cut short and I'd be under orders to head to the Pacific.

Then it happened. It was another hot, sticky day in the Deep South. I was planning on another game of tennis as I stripped to the waist under a glaring sun. Suddenly the speaker system on the field was crackling with news that I couldn't believe. Japan had surrendered! How could it be? I was mesmerized as I learned that not one but two atomic bombs had been dropped by a B-29 bomber, first on Hiroshima on August 6, then on Nagasaki on the 9th. I'd never heard of atomic bombs before. They must be powerful beyond imagination, I concluded, when I learned that more than 100,000 had been killed, and many times that wounded—with just two bombs! Not simply blocks, but entire cities had been obliterated.

Trees, buildings, anything that stood in the path of the incredible firestorms was turned to ashes and rubble.

The Germans had suffered city after city consumed, such as Dresden, in firestorms created by massive incendiary bombing, when individual fires in a city merged into one giant firestorm. The Japanese had suffered a similar fate when, on March 9, some 334 B-29s came roaring in over the rooftops of buildings made of wood and paper and dropped their incendiaries, consuming a quarter of the city of Tokyo. By August more than 330,000 civilians had been killed and 40 percent of sixty-six cities had been destroyed.

Now, however, it was different. Not that the Japanese had not been warned. Many thousands of leaflets had been dropped from Allied planes, warning the enemy of further "intensive air bombardment." Therefore, they should evacuate their cities. They did not. And now those two bombs had introduced the Land of the Rising Sun to temperatures approximating those within the sun. Armageddon had arrived with a single bomber, the *Enola Gay.*

It wasn't till later, of course, that we learned these details. Nor did any of us have the slightest idea of the Manhattan Project, executed in a supersecret place in the desert of New Mexico, under the military direction of Gen. Leslie Groves and the civilian direction of Dr. Robert Oppenheimer. In the backlash of the bombing of two of Japan's largest cities, there arose another firestorm—of criticism—aimed primarily at President Harry Truman, the commander in chief who'd made this fateful decision. Overnight the costs of war had multiplied exponentially. Wars would never be the same again.[1]

But for all the skeptics, for all the critics, for all the naysayers in the years to come, there were millions of us GIs more thankful for Truman's decision than we could express. The buck, as he famously said, had stopped right there in the Oval Office of the White House. Beyond us GIs and our families, Truman had others, such as Churchill, who could only applaud the decision. For Japan, he pointed out, had no less than nine thousand kamikaze planes and twice that number of pilots to deter any invasion fleet. Already the Allies had been witness to the toll taken by just a few of these suicide pilots. Scores of our warships, including the aircraft carrier *Hornet,* had gone to the bottom, and hundreds more had been damaged in the last few weeks of the war. At Okinawa alone these "flying missiles" had sunk 42 Allied ships and damaged 216 others. These constituted the greatest losses ever suffered by our navy in a single battle.[2]

Rather than questions or criticism, the men and women at Napier Field erupted in a paroxysm of joy, mixed with profound relief. The hysteria was such that the speaker system was soon crackling with the terse message, "The field is closed. No one is to leave the field. I repeat, no one is to leave the field." In a way it sounded like the announcement of VE Day three months earlier. Except that I had no P-51 to fly to celebrate the occasion over another general headquarters. As it was, Myrt and I watched as sheer bedlam ruled. A caravan of cars, jeeps, and big GI trucks, all overflowing with ecstatic GIs and girls, paraded around an airfield electrified by the news. Horns were blaring, booze was flowing, throats were turning hoarse with the shouts. Had the field not been closed, Dothan itself would have been rocking.

Myrt and I could scarcely believe the good news. Yet the next day an attitude of uncertainty took over. What next? Would we all be released to return home? If not all, who? We discovered there would be no mass exodus. Within days I found I'd been reassigned to the headquarters of the 554th Group of the Air Transport Command at Memphis, Tennessee.

Packing "all my worldly goods" I'd endowed on Myrt, plus hers—minus the wedding gifts we'd left with Myrt's mother— into our Dodge, we were off to our new station. Again we found a sleeping room with kitchen privileges, this time in the home of a Red Cross administrator. Myrt again went to work for the Army in a giant warehouse. Meanwhile, I learned that my job was to warehouse some of the thousands of planes Uncle Sam had accumulated stateside. I was to pick them up at various fields across the country and fly them to their "graveyard" on the outskirts of Tucson, Arizona. There in the desert, the brass apparently figured, the planes would be exposed to less humidity and bad weather, and there was plenty of parking space. They'd keep there as well as anywhere, just in case the nation needed them again—something none of us thought possible at the time.

I flew fighters, I flew bombers—as copilot—and I flew training planes. But I was not prepared for the one plane that almost did me in. "If you don't have a will drawn up, I suggest you do so." The speaker was our squadron CO. He then described our next "graveyard mission," and implied that we might well be buried, along with the plane. For it was a miniature, single-seat job with its wings clipped to give it the extra speed needed for takeoff and landing, and boosting the stalling speed to over 100 mph. The job of this plane was to pull the streamers that were used for target practice by our fighter pilots and bomber gunners in training. I recalled these souped-up "hummingbirds" pulling the target streamers for our AT-6s in the skies over Texas. And I recalled wondering at the time what would happen if our aim was so bad we plugged holes in the tow plane instead of the streamer.

As for obeying the CO in filling out a will, I readily complied, though Myrt seemed a bit more nervous than usual at my leaving. But as for obeying the rule of flying above one thousand feet, and flying straight and level, I found it impossible to obey. The takeoff required a good deal more runway than required for such a small plane, but I was soon airborne and headed for Tucson. Now I'd made a pledge to Myrt to stick to the straight and narrow. And I tried. But as the hours passed and the motor hummed and the sun beat down, I found myself dozing. I'd occasionally found myself in a similar predicament driving a car. And sometimes in the Mustang, returning after a long mission, I'd have all I could do to stay awake, even when flying in very tight formation. So, ever the reasonable man, I figured I must stay awake. And what better way to do that than to try some of my aerobatic regimen? So, climbing to five thousand feet, I put it through its paces: snap rolls, slow rolls, barrel rolls, loops, Immelmans, ending up in split-Ss and spins. The little bugger worked like a charm! By this time I was over the plains of Oklahoma and, tired of the same routine, I decided to drop down to treetop level and do some buzzing, presumably to "shoot a station," as Kuykendall had taught me—just in case I was getting lost. Zipping from one town to another, I lost track of time, but was beginning to find this a bore when suddenly, as I was entering a town, skimming the treetops, my engine coughed, sputtered, then died. My eyes darted to the instrument panel, to see that my one gas tank had run dry. Immediately I switched to the other—then waited—and waited. The plane was just beginning to cut leaves from the treetops when I heard the wonderful sound of the engine catching. The ten or fifteen seconds required for the transfer of gas lines seemed like an eternity. Meanwhile my breath was coming in spurts, sweat oozed down my back, and my hair stood on end. I was pulling back farther and farther on the stick, remembering that I couldn't fall below 100 mph or I'd stall, and that would be curtains. With the merciful sound of the engine catching, I couldn't have been more relieved. I had just about let my bride lay claim to "all my wordly goods" on my freshly drawn will.

Dripping with sweat even as my tongue clung to the roof of my mouth, I immediately climbed to one thousand feet and flew straight and level the rest of the way. Far from falling asleep, I found my knees still shaking when I emerged from the tiny cockpit at Tucson. How, I asked myself again and again, could I have done such a crazy thing? And when I returned to Memphis I found these sentiments expressed by my new bride, now exasperated as I recounted my latest close call. She paled, then she drew a bead on me with her blazing eyes, and—her voice choking with emotion—declared in no uncertain terms, "That's it! You're getting out of this Air Corps while you're still in one piece! I have no intention of executing your will!"

And that was that. I feebly protested that I had to fly just one more mission, simply to pick up the dry cleaning I'd left in Jackson, Mississippi, where I'd stopped to eat and refuel. But Myrt had made up her mind. "Forget it. You go to your CO and tell him you want to be released. I don't intend to become another widow like Margie. At least Bob was fighting overseas when he was killed. I've had it!"

There was a finality to her voice that turned me into an obedient wimp. It was useless to argue with her all-too-forceful logic. Of course I did just as she said, and was told by the CO that after the new year my orders would be cut for mustering out. Yet, as it turned out, he and I had other matters to see to even before the end of the year. For Christmas was approaching, and when he ordered many of us to stay on the base over the holiday, I took strong exception to the order. After all, I'd missed going home twice for the occasion, and wasn't about to miss a third. If any should stay on base, I reasoned, it should be those who'd remained there stateside during the war. On the face of it, it seemed grossly unfair. So, I assured Myrt, with a finality of my own, we'd celebrate with her family and mine. I put her on the train, promising to follow in a few days.

However, I made the mistake of not buying my ticket in advance, for the train was packed to capacity, with even the aisles crowded with those standing. The conductor was sympathetic as he saw me standing between the cars. "Sorry, soldier, but you'll have to get off at the next stop. We're already overcrowded. You can see there's no standing room in the cars, and if you stay out here you'll freeze to death." I sputtered. I protested. I even thought of pulling rank on him, but one look at his uniform showed he outranked me. Well, maybe he'd forget me and leave me in the miserable cold and smoke from the overburdened locomotive. No such luck. At the next stop he saw me off, even as I mumbled something about the fat chance I had of getting home nine hundred miles away in time to celebrate the holiday.

I had no pride. But I still had my thumb for hitchhiking. Yet as I stood there in the snow and numbing cold, the cars and trucks passed me without so much as a pause, their windows frosted over. As the temperature continued to drop, so did my hopes. Would nobody take pity on this lonely, lowly GI, his thumb pointed heavenward? At last a car stopped. I hustled toward it, dragging my duffel bag, and saw it was a little Ford coupe, maybe of 1930 vintage. As the door opened I looked in to see three big enlisted men on the only seat. How on earth could they accommodate a fourth?

"If you want to climb up above and behind us in the back window space, you're welcome to ride with us—providing you're willing to take your turn driving." I recalled a favorite saying of Dad's. "If wishes were horses, beggars would ride." I confess I thought it remarkable that these enlisted men would actually stop and pick up this beggar when, in all probability, they—like me in training—had experienced some racking back by lowly lieutenants. Even more remarkable, they were willing to shift around so each of us would take his turn on the frosty window ledge. I hastily agreed to their terms, even volunteering to chip in for gas. As two of them hopped out I hopped in, squeezing my body up next to the cold back window. There I drew my heavy coat tightly about me. This greatcoat, together with my body heat and a tiny, buzzing heater, managed to keep out the shivers. But the most remarkable aspect of the experience was their destination: Hartford, Connecticut, less than a hundred miles from Worcester!

Every sixty miles or so we'd change places, stretch our legs, and continue our version of musical chairs. We made sure each stop was at a roadhouse or gas station, where we could also thaw out, seek relief, grab a bite and, if necessary, refuel. The drive was not only frosty but long and risky, as we navigated the narrow, winding mountain roads, covered with ice and snow. They reminded me of nothing more than those I'd traversed in the mountains of Italy in an open jeep or weapons carrier, except here it was colder. I came to appreciate Henry Ford's little coupe, even older than the '33 Ford sedan I'd inherited from Bob when he entered the service almost four years earlier. Laden down with four big guys, the coupe never missed a beat, and before long we'd crossed into New York, then Connecticut.

Pulling into the bus station at Hartford, we exchanged hearty holiday greetings as I thanked them again for their kindness. Then I was on a bus for Worcester, arriving to find the dusk of Christmas eve settling over the land. It brought to mind the song sung each evening before the six o'clock news on WTAG: "Just a song at twilight / When the lights are low / And the whispering shadows / Softly come and go." That was the signal that all conversation around the supper table—and all horseplay—would cease. For Dad was determined to hear every detail of the news, as war threatened, then broke out.

Once again I took Myrt in my arms and we headed for an old-fashioned Swedish smorgasbord at the home of one of her relatives. When it came to the coffee and the lutefisk, I took a pass, but found the coffee bread absolutely scrumptious. Christmas morning Myrt and I spent with my folks, opening gifts before a bright fire on the hearth. It brought to mind the many times we kids crept downstairs in the early morning to catch a glimpse of Santa Claus and his gifts, only to find the tree and gifts all covered with a big white sheet. And it reminded me of 1929, when Dad took off the fireplace mantel a set of earphones and clamped them on my head so I could listen to music emerging from a background of static, from a radio station Dad said was many miles away. Now the radio had been joined by a myriad of other fantastic inventions that helped us wind down the war.

Betty was there but Dana couldn't make it. After dinner, knowing our 1940 Dodge had given up the ghost, I offered to buy Dad's 1941 Ford, the self-same car I'd risked my neck in trying to travel twenty miles in five minutes for a date in Leominster, almost five years earlier. How times had changed in those four short years! Dad agreed, needing the extra money to make up for $50 a month less in my allotment. Soon Myrt and I were headed for Memphis in a nonstop marathon. Was it possible they'd never missed me? Following the same treacherous roads that had brought me back to New England, I found the forty-eight-hour drive exhausting. Myrt, without a driver's license, was unable to help. Along the way I stopped for a hitchhiker, another GI—and he helped with the driving as we hove into Memphis. More than once I'd slid off the road in my hurry, ending up—luckily enough—in snowdrifts. But there was nothing soft about the reception I received from my squadron CO. Bedraggled and utterly exhausted, I tried standing at attention before the major, and made an effort to salute and explain my absence.

He cut me short. "Curtis, where the hell have you been? Don't you know that you've been AWOL the last three days! It's a wonder you don't face a court-martial. If you hadn't finished your tour of duty, you would be." Why was it, I asked myself, that at almost every station I was assigned, I soon found myself courting a court-martial? As I soon learned, the major had found my home phone number in my records, had called, and was assured I was on my return trip.

"At least," he added, "you could have picked up the phone and let us know where you were. For this stunt I'm going to dock you three days' pay." I winced, and so did Myrt, knowing we were on a tight budget. Oh, well, we agreed, we could eat beans for a month. After all, we were still living largely on love.

With the new year came my orders to proceed to Westover Field, near Springfield, Massachusetts, for mustering out. As we started out from Memphis the end of January, I couldn't help but note it was exactly three years to the day since I'd reported for duty at Fort Devens. We decided we'd take the long way around and stop in Chicago en route. For there, we agreed, I would enroll in the college division of Northern Baptist Seminary. When I first learned of the GI Bill's provision for a year of higher education for each year spent in the military, I could scarcely believe my ears. Not only would the government pay my tuition, but fees and supplies and a living allowance of $110 a month. If I could go on to graduate, I'd be setting a new record for the Curtis family. The closest thing to a college education for Dad—even after his three sisters had graduated from college in Chicago—was a correspondence course so he could be certified as an electrician. At sixteen he'd thumbed his nose at the posh Vermont Academy after two short years and run off to join the Army. Once he was discharged and married, he'd realized he needed to learn a good trade to support a family. Mom had taken a couple years of general education at Gordon College in Boston, where her mother had attended back in the 1890s. Bob had spent two years at Clark University in Worcester, working his way through, before joining the Air Corps.[3] So, having gotten a taste of higher education at Butler three years earlier, I now had my chance. Myrt and I agreed that, with the rush of men being discharged and so many seeking work, this was the way to go.

Before long I was standing before the registrar and his sister at Northern, known on campus—as we discovered—as "Brother and Sister Fouts." It was rumored that he had so many books in his own personal library that there were stacks even in his bedroom and—some claimed—beneath his bed. He must be one smart man, I figured, as I stood before them. They greeted me with wisps of smiles and handed me some reading material, including the catalog of courses for the Th.B. degree, a bachelor of theology course that would take five years to complete—three years of college and two years of seminary. As I perused the catalog, I chanced to mutter, "Gee, I didn't realize . . ." Only to be cut off, as the major had cut me off in my sorry explanation back in Memphis a month earlier. This time it was Sister Fouts.

"Did you say 'G-double-E,'" she inquired, wincing.

"What do you mean?" Here was language I didn't understand.

"G-double-E. G-double-E!" Was I such a dunderhead?

Now, carefully, she labored over each and every consonant. "Did I not hear you say 'G-double-E'?" It was obvious her patience was wearing thin with this one who had the temerity to try to enroll in this institution of higher learning.

She had me. "I guess I did," I finally confessed, wondering if I was about to be booked for at least a misdemeanor.

She wasn't anything if not explicit. "Don't you realize that 'G-double-E' is a minced oath?"

Now I'd heard of oaths, and had taken a few in my short life. But a "minced" oath? Yet she seemed weary as she sought to explain to this novice. "Don't you realize that 'G-double-E' is short for Jesus? Don't you realize that you've broken the second commandment of the Decalogue?"

I was getting mired deeper and deeper in the quicksand of theological parlance, for "Decalogue" rang no bells in my memory chest. Here I was, not even registered to train to be a clergyman, and I was already taking potshots at the Ten Commandments! The thought occurred to me that had I still possessed my ebony walking stick with the carved ivory skull and brought it with me to register, she and her good brother might well have fainted.

Having indicted me, she was not about to let the matter rest. In a flash she whipped out a small paper tract and thrust it into my faltering hand. "Minced Oaths" was bound to set me on the straight and narrow, away from the broad road to perdition. Then the thought of Mom, almost three years earlier, handing a similar religious tract to Myrt on the bus in Worcester—initiating the letter writing that had led to our marriage—made me more sympathetic with Sister Fouts. She and Mom were obviously partners in reformation, out to straighten the crooks in us, the unwashed. The thought of it all was a shock to me. Was this what I had committed myself to? Would there conceivably be enough room for this upstart, this renegade?

I would soon find out, for then and there I registered for what promised to be a long haul. But with Myrt on one side, Sister Fouts on the other, and Mom keeping tabs above me by mail, would I soon find myself steering a conventional path that, until now, would have been a nightmare? Was this maverick about to be corralled? Was this incorrigible scofflaw about to be reined in as few who knew me thought possible?

Soon we were on our way across Canada to Niagara Falls, famous as a destination for honeymooners. As far as Myrt and I were concerned, we were still on our honeymoon, even six months later. The sight of the rising mist from the falls settling and freezing on everything in the morning sun blinded us at first. It was a winter wonderland, reinforced with the constant roar of the river tumbling hundreds of feet down to the rocks below.

As we neared Westover Field, we chanced to pass through the little village of Lee, in western Massachusetts. A light snow was falling, covering the drifts already pushed aside by the town snowplow. The road was packed with snow and ice, and I'd slowed to an astonishing 25 mph or so.

Suddenly a big truck loomed to my right, bearing down hard on us. On instinct, I pulled hard to the left, even as I'd done many times in violent evasive maneuvers in the air. The truck sideswiped our car, the door flew open, and Myrt tumbled out onto the road. I panicked and flew around the car to find her sitting in the middle of the road in a daze. It was sheer luck that she had not taken off the fur coat I'd bought her from Sears for Christmas. As I helped her to her feet I thanked my lucky stars that she'd not suffered a severe spinal injury. By this time a crowd was forming around us. A policeman arrived, took in the scene, and marched the truck driver of this furniture van off to jail for running a stop sign. I surveyed the car, stove in from the front to the rear wheel by a foot in the middle, and realized how close we'd come to stark tragedy. Then I heard a kindly voice. A man from a house nearby was offering a place for us to stay overnight, even as a tow truck arrived to haul away the car.

Arising the next morning, we enjoyed a fine breakfast. I was about to thank our host for his splendid hospitality when he thrust a piece of paper in my hand. It was a bill for $11, the going rate for overnight lodging and breakfast at his tourist home. Only then did I realize that he was Johnny-on-the-spot at the accident to drum up business. Atop that surprise was the news that, though our car was beaten, it was driveable. Yet I couldn't drive it away until I forked over $10 for the tow and overnight storage. I outright balked at paying the $11—that is, until a month later, when a state policeman showed up at the door with the ultimatum, "Pay up or face the consequences!" So though our brief sojourn through the charming town of Lee didn't kill or maim either of us, it did set us back $21, plus damage to Myrt's new fur coat—the insurance paying for the car repair.

To make it to Westover Field from Lee, we tied the door

shut on Myrt's side and, thankful that she'd suffered no more injury than a few black-and-blue welts, we set out. It was February 9, 1946, just five days after Myrt's twenty-first birthday, that I was awarded terminal leave until April 6, with pay. Flush with a few hundred dollars, I found the sting wearing off the accident.

In my discharge papers I paid particular attention to the space devoted to awards and medals. I was especially grateful for the Distinguished Flying Cross, capping the rest of the ribbons I could wear. It was just about a month before this that I'd been pleasantly surprised to get a small package from the War Department. Inside was the DFC, accompanied by a citation spelling out the "valor," as they put it— over and above the call of duty—on a mission I'd flown back in August 1944. This award, as the dictionary put it, was "for heroism or extraordinary achievement."[4] There was no ceremony. No official presentation. Just a small package wrapped in brown paper.

It was just as well. For I was no better a pilot than the rest of the outfit, and worse than some. I was more reckless, yes. I was more irresponsible, yes. I'd put others at unnecessary risk whenever I was in charge of an element or, as in the case of the death of our flight leader, in charge of the flight, yes. And I'd succeeded in breaking about every rule in the book, starting in my earliest flight training and continuing until, at last, Myrt put her foot down, yes.

So here I was, as dumb as any cadet to enter the Army Air Corps. Not only was Myrt relieved that I was at last getting out; so was the Air Corps. Were there any worse screwups? I could only conclude that, yes, it was possible that luck could trump stupidity, that Lady Luck watched over—with special care—the weak, the ignorant, and the stupid. Stupid, yes, but grateful. The overhanging question remained. Could any college, university, or seminary, could any church, denomination, or religion, succeed in throwing a lasso around this incorrigible maverick?

As I write this some sixty years later, I am more grateful than these poor words can express. For Myrt has stood by me, "for better or worse," as she has given me three children, Steve, Dave, and Laurie, and—in turn—four grandchildren, Emily, Brian, Virginia, and Gregory. And we're especially proud of each of them.

Glossary

Angels—a measure of altitude in thousands of feet

AT (as in AT-6)—advanced trainer

AT (as in AT-36)—attack, a converted P-51, used as a dive bomber

augured in—plane crash on earth

AWOL—absent without leave

B (as in B-17)—bomber

BT (as in BT-13)—basic trainer

bandit—enemy plane

bogey—enemy plane

CAP—Civilian Air Patrol

check the mags—a check of the magnetos, preliminary to take-off, to determine that the plane has sufficient power to become airborne

clobbered—hit by enemy fire

CO—commanding officer

CQ—Charge of quarters; a GI assigned to guard prescribed living quarters

CRAF—Canadian Royal Air Force

dead reckoning—flying by orienting the plane to a visible horizon

DFC—Distinguished Flying Cross

flying blind—flying by instruments, using an artificial horizon

friend—an Allied pilot

g—the pressure of the atmosphere, 14.3 pounds per square inch (at sea level), increasing in pulling out of a dive, and decreasing at the top of a loop

GI—government issue, a reference to anyone in the U.S. military service, corresponding to a "Yank" in World War I

gyro—gyroscope, the means by which balance is maintained on the instrument panel

Immelman—a loop, with recovery at the top of the maneuver

Itie—an Italian

Jerry—a German pilot

KIA—killed in action

KP—kitchen police, an assignment to work in the kitchen or mess hall

Liberty ship—a small freighter, often used to transport personnel

Limey—a Briton serving in the military

Link Trainer—a simulated cockpit, used to train pilots to fly on instruments

MIA—missing in action

military time—telling time by eliminating A.M. and P.M.—thus 3:00 P.M. becomes 1500 hours

MP—military police

o'clock—locating a plane, usually an enemy plane, by its position on a clock; thus, a radio message, "Bogey at two o'clock high" signifies the pilot should look up somewhat and to the right to locate the enemy plane

open post—freedom to leave the precincts of a military base

P (as in P-51)—pursuit

PBY—a large twin-engine plane, equipped with floats for landing on water, usually used for search and rescue

police the grounds—an assignment to clean up a specific piece of land, usually around living quarters

POW—prisoner of war

prang—to crash a plane; similar to *augur in*

PT (as in PT-19)—primary trainer

PX—post exchange; the store on a military base

RAF—Royal Air Force; the air force of Great Britain

R&R—rest and relaxation

spin—a maneuver similar to a maple tree seed falling to earth

top speed—the maximum speed of a plane flying straight and level

tour of duty—the required number of combat missions to qualify an airman to return home on furlough

triangulation—the means by which two homing stations, in separate locations, can pinpoint the location of a plane at the intersection of the two lines receiving a given signal

ENDNOTES

1. BY THE NUMBERS

1. Churchill's singular description of the Battle of Britain is highlighted by three memorable but separate quotations. The first is Hitler's gauging of the requirements for an invasion, as told to Admiral Raeder on July 31, 1940: "If after eight days of intensive air war the Luftwaffe has not achieved considerable destruction of the enemy's Air Force, harbours, and naval forces, the operation will have to be put off till May, 1941." The second is Churchill's encomium as prime minister, delivered to the House of Commons on May 13, 1940. Confessing that all he could offer the nation was "blood, toil, tears and sweat," when he replaced Chamberlain, he now paid tribute to the fighter pilots of the RAF on August 20, 1940: "Never in the field of human conflict was so much owed by so many to so few." Richard B. Stolley, ed., *History's Greatest Conflict in Pictures* (Boston: Little, Brown and Co., 2001), 77, 80; Winston S. Churchill, *Their Finest Hour,* vol. 2 of the six-volume set, *The Second World War* (Boston: Houghton Mifflin Co., 1949). A shorter version of "The Battle of Britain" is found in the condensation of Churchill's series, a two-volume set published in conjunction with *Life* magazine, *The Second World War* (New York: Time, Inc., 1959), 114–39. So impressed was President John F. Kennedy with Churchill's moving oratory that he praised him for "mobiliz[ing] the English language and send[ing] it into battle . . . to illuminate the courage of his countrymen." Richard K. Curtis, *Hubris and the Presidency: The Abuse of Power by Johnson and Nixon* (Danbury, Conn.: Rutledge Books, 2000), 112.

2. Stolley, 484–87; Churchill (*Life*), 141–43; Stephen L. McFarland and Wesley Phillips Newton, *To Command the Sky: The Battle for Air Superiority over Germany, 1942–1944* (Washington, D.C.: Smithsonian Institution Press, 1991), 31–38. For an expansion of our lack of preparation, see also Volume I of *The Army Air Forces in World War II,* by Wesley F. Craven and James L. Cate, eds. (Chicago: University of Chicago Press, 1949).

3. Churchill (*Life*), 126, 222, 243. If it takes two to make love, it also takes two to make war. The events leading to Pearl Harbor seem to have occurred with World War I, and President Wilson's threat that if the Senate did not approve his Fourteen Points, or at least what was left of it, we would incur, in a generation, a war much more devastating than the one just closing. With our failure to join the League of Nations, it was virtually toothless to prevent the Axis from rearming and starting the Second World War. Churchill, with the surrender of France, pleaded with FDR to get the United States involved again, as we had done in the First World War. But Roosevelt knew his chances of reelection for a third term in 1940 would be jeopardized by any U.S. entry into the war. So he promised in his campaign speeches that he would keep us out of war, even as he was leaning on the Japanese by using our Navy to help blockade precious oil and prevent other commodities from entering Japan, thus provoking the Japanese attack on Pearl Harbor. It appears that Roosevelt knew of the impending attack and did nothing to prepare this strategic Navy port for war. When this author was teaching at the University of Missouri at Kansas City, and happened to mention this thesis, the wife of an Army officer, in training at the Fort Leavenworth Command School, and a student in the class, came up after class and corroborated this account, saying that her husband had just such an account in a textbook he was using.

4. Ruth Mitchell, *My Brother Bill: The Life of General "Billy" Mitchell* (New York: Harcourt Brace, 1953).

5. Churchill (*Life*), 106, 126, 193–96; Stolley, 50ff.

6. Stolley, 50–53, 193–94.

7. Fort Devens was immortalized by Bill Mauldin in a classic cartoon portraying "an old-time Cavalryman shooting his jeep, which had a broken axle." At that time Mauldin was stationed at Devens. Bill Mauldin, *Up Front* (New York: Henry Holt and Co., 1945), 113.

8. Indianapolis was, and remains today, the hub of Indiana. It prides itself on being the "Crossroads of America" and the "Amateur Sports Capitol of the Nation."

9. Richard K. Curtis, *They Called Him Mister Moody* (Garden City, N.Y.: Doubleday and Co., 1962), 43.

10. Churchill (*Life*), 128; Stolley, 80–81.

11. This account, taken from *The Boston Globe,* was mailed to my parents by its author.

2. THE WILD BLUE BECKONS

1. Francis S. Miller, *History of World War II.* Armed Services Memorial Edition (Philadelphia: Universal Book and Bible House, 1945), 574–606.

2. Ibid., 667–76; Churchill (*Life*), 348–49; Stolley, 230–31.

3. Churchill (*Life*), 348; Miller, 678–85.

4. Miller, 686–90; Churchill (*Life*), 354–57; Stolley, 232–33.

5. Miller, 691–97; Churchill (*Life*), 357–60.

6. Miller, 649–66; Churchill (*Life*), 382–84.

7. McFarland and Newton, 69.

3. GOLD BARS AND SILVER WINGS

1. Miller, 698–703; Churchill (*Life*), 355, 357, 384; Stolley, 232–33.

2. Mauldin, 64, 69.

3. Ernie Pyle, *Brave Men* (New York: Henry Holt and Co., 1944), 118. John Steinbeck paid tribute to Pyle's journalism by explaining the difference between the two wars. The first consisted of "maps and logistics of campaigns, of ballistics, armies, divisions and regiments." The second consisted of "homesick, weary, funny, violent, common men who wash their socks in their helmets, complain about the food, whistle at the Arab girls, or any girls for that matter, and lug themselves through as dirty a business as the world has ever seen and do it with humor and dignity and courage. . . ." The first war belonged to General Marshall; the second to Pyle. See also *The 100 Best True Stories of World War II* (New York: William Wise and Co., 1945), 550.

4. Stolley, 254–55; Churchill (*Life*), 359–92.

5. Pyle, *Brave Men,* 159–62. Pyle also notes that these A-36s flew so close together that they looked like a stream of water.

6. Richard Thruelson and Elliott Arnold, *Mediterranean Sweep: Air Stories from Ei Alamein to Rome* (New York: Duell, Sloan, and Pearce, 1944), 264–65.

7. Churchill (*Life*), 385–88; Miller, 703–9.

4. FROM AN AT-6 TO A P-51

1. Stolley, 258.

2. Thruelson and Arnold, 135–41; Churchill (*Life*), 354–56.

3. Robert D. Loomis, *Great American Fighter Pilots of World War II* (New York: Random House, 1961), 120–23.

4. The 15th Air Force was formed at the start of 1944 as a break-off of the 8th Air Force, with but four fighter groups, all at half strength. It was not until May, the month in which I arrived in Italy, that the 15th was, ostensibly, at full strength. Yet by this time, as I have shown in my introduction to the 52nd Fighter Group, our 4th Squadron had but seventeen pilots for twenty-seven planes. This was the result of Hitler's concentrating his Luftwaffe on preventing the Allies from disrupting his supply of oil from Ploesti and his supply of planes from his aircraft factories. Yet, short of pilots and those bone-weary, the 15th, in cooperation with the 8th on their shuttle runs, in twenty-four raids managed to disrupt 60 percent of Ploesti's oil supply, sharply curtailing Hitler's war machine. In addition, the 15th, and particularly the 52nd and the 332nd Fighter Groups, executed the lion's share of preparation for the invasion of southern France. It was, in fact, the July 5 mission, in which we escorted 228 B-17s and 319 B-24s as they took out the marshaling yards and submarine pens at Toulon, that we lost Jack Chidester from the 4th Squadron. Wesley F. Craven and James L. Cate, eds., *The Army Air Forces in World War II*, vol. 3: *Argument to VE Day, January, 1944 to May, 1945* (Chicago: University of Chicago Press, 1949), 336, 421; McFarland and Newton, 147–48, 183; James R. Whelan, *Hunters in the Sky: Fighter Aces of World War II* (Washington, D.C.: Regnery Gateway, 1991), 157.

5. Mauldin, 42.

6. "Fury of the Mustang," Warbird Series video, *Warplanes of World War II,* The History Channel, December 14, 2000.

7. Mauldin, 185–86.

8. Yet the persistent claim of the 332nd after the war that they'd never lost a bomber they were escorting is, on the face of it, difficult in the extreme to believe. As noted above, the 332nd joined with other groups, including the 52nd, in escorting these bombers. To say in these joint missions that the 15th lost no bombers is well nigh an impossible claim. In addition, does this also apply to bombers lost to flak? For it was flak that claimed most of the bombers lost.

9. The four-finger formation was introduced by the Luftwaffe when they participated in the Spanish Civil War in 1935. Adolf Galland, commander of the Luftwaffe's fighter arm, flew three hundred missions in Spain, giving the Germans a decided advantage at the start of World War II. According to Galland, "This open, four-finger flight formation gave every pilot the possibility to see the air space, [giving] tactical superiority vis-à-vis the French and English, which we used to our advantage. If a wingman was vulnerable, the last man in the flight was most vulnerable. But the loyalty of the wingman to his leader was a two-way street. The leader had always to be on the lookout for his wingman. Better he pass up a possible kill to protect his wingman than to register a kill and lose his wingman." Whelan, 14–15; General Chuck Yeager and Leo Janos, *Yeager* (New York: Bantam Books, 1985), 34, 87.

10. Yeager and Janos, 67; Loomis, 179.

5. COMBAT AT LAST!

1. Pyle, *Brave Men,* 157.

2. Mauldin, 69.

3. Despite how very deadly the strafing missions were for the vulnerable P-51s, Generals Kepner and Arnold were ecstatic over the damage inflicted on the enemy. Kepner was especially excited by our P-51s attacking enemy trains, the kind of mission for which I was later awarded the Distinguished Flying Cross on my seventh mission. McFarland and Newton, 230–34, 242; Whelan, 83, 158; Thomas Childers, *Wings of the Morning: The Story of the Last American Bomber Shot Down over Germany in World War II* (New York: Addison-Wesley, 1995), 87–88.

6. THE RAINY SEASON ENGULFS US

1. There is little question but that the Allies underestimated the enormous capacity of German industry, aided by the forced labor of concentration camp victims as well as POWs, its peak occurring in July 1944. On the other hand, Germany, as well as Italy and Japan, vastly underestimated the virtually limitless capacity of the United States to enlist women as well as men in war production. This tendency to hype one's own capabilities and to minimize the enemy's constitutes one of the most serious mistakes nations can make. Craven and Cate, 792; Winston S. Churchill, *The Second World War,* vol. 6: *Triumph and Tragedy* (Boston: Houghton Mifflin Co., 1953), 89–119.

2. Stolley, 182–83, 550–51; Ian Kershaw, *Hitler, 1936–1945: Nemesis* (New York: W. W. Norton, 2001), reviewed in *The New Republic,* March 12, 2001.

3. John A. Wheeler, *At Home in the Universe* (Woodbury, N.Y.: American Institute of Physics, 1994), 141.

4. Fighter pilots from various countries have tried to identify those characteristics that make for successful combat. Perhaps the one over which we had the least control was youth. "Hap" Arnold, at the outset of the war, was critical of high command for failing to realize the importance of pursuit pilots. Perhaps one reason for this, he suggested, was that "pursuit aviation, being a relatively young man's game, does not offer the lifetime career to an Army officer which bombardment affords." McFarland and Newton, 36. George McGovern, a bomber pilot in a B-24, flying out of Italy, noted that even bomber pilots' average age was twenty-one or twenty-two. Stephen E. Ambrose, *The Wild Blue: The Men and Boys Who Flew the B24s over Germany* (New York: Simon & Schuster, 2001), 185. Another characteristic of a successful fighter pilot over which we had precious little control was sheer luck. "The secret of my success," wrote Chuck Yeager, another P-51 pilot, "is that I always managed to live to fly another day." Yeager and Janos, back jacket. Even flying the relatively slow P-39 "Airacobra," Yeager expressed what so many felt: "You feel so lucky, so blessed to be a fighter pilot." On the other hand, Yeager also knew what bad luck could be. Three times he was turned down, as a flight officer, for his appeal to be a second lieutenant, a commissioned officer, and this because he'd already been court-martialed. Obie O'Brien, a pal of Yeager, put it this way: "We had more balls than brains and figured being outnumbered ten to one were acceptable odds. If you were good and lucky enough to be in the right place at the right time, you'd score victories." Ibid., 70, 75; see also McFarland and Newton, 78. Raymond Toliver, former historian of the American Fighter Aces Association, after citing "skill, dash, courage, and judgment" as being required "to an exceptional degree," also conceded "such uncontrollable factors as luck and opportunity." Whelan, xii. The role of "blind chance" was as critical for fighter pilots as for bomber pilots. And Ambrose's pointing out "dumb luck" as often the case was, if anything, true of me. Ambrose, 111–12, 114.

5. Loomis, 182. Though the 15th Air Force bombers attacked the jet factories at Friederichshafen repeatedly in July 1944, destroying 950 jet aircraft, there were still many flying. And though their pilots were warned not to tangle with Allied fighters, they were free to take out our bombers, especially if they were wounded stragglers. One crippled bomber, flying over the Adriatic, was suddenly set upon by two ME-262s. Consternation turned to

jubilation when from high overhead three P-51s suddenly dove down on the jets. At that the jet pilots turned tail and ran, making for the deck in northern Yugoslavia. Lt. Glenn Rendahl, the bomber pilot, paid tribute to the Mustang pilots: "Without the intervention of our escorts and their willingness to risk their lives for those of us whom they had never met, we would have been most fortunate to end up in the Adriatic Sea below us. Or we might have stretched it to Trieste, which was then German-occupied. Most likely, some of the crew would be lost either way." Ambrose, 211–12. More often, the ME-262 pilots "offered little opposition but hopped almost comically from one airfield to another or to the empty 'Autobahnen' behind German lines." Craven and Cate, 783. Hans Knoke, a veteran German pilot, after flying the ME-262, exclaimed, "One thousand of these are to be in operation by the end of the year [1944]. God help the Tommy and the Yank then!" Alas, for him, it was not to be. And the few that did appear in the skies were presumably to be used, according to Hitler's order of May 28, only as high-speed bombers. McFarland and Newton, 223, 236.

6. Somerset Maugham, *The Summing Up* (New York: Doubleday/Mentor, 1946), 173.

7. Pyle, *Brave Men,* 170.

8. Nash may have had several reasons in mind for not going after the fifteen ME-109s, but these seemed as difficult to fathom as were the possible reasons for the German fighters not attacking us. By this time the Germans were suffering from a shortage of both fuel and trained pilots. And the first affected the second, for Goering was forced to cut short the training of his apprentice pilots for lack of fuel for trainers. Perhaps these fifteen pilots were untrained cadets. More probably, they were under strict orders not to tangle with the Mustangs. For the word had come down from Goering that if a fighter pilot spotted a P-38, he was to attack it anywhere, anytime. If he spotted a P-47, he was to attack it below twenty thousand feet. But if it turned out to be a P-51, he was to break away and head for home in order to live to fight another day. Presidential Unit Citations such as the 52nd received in August were recognition that our commander in chief had taken notice of our work. Of seven of these awarded to the seven fighter groups based in England, one went to a P-38 group, one to a P-47 group, and five to P-51 groups. It was not only the Mustang's maneuverability and firepower that placed it apart from the ME-109 and the FW 190; it was also its superior speed. At twenty-five thousand feet, it was, according to the German pilots, 50 mph faster than the ME-109 and 70 mph faster than the FW 190. McFarland and Newton, 54–57, 248–49.

7. COUNTDOWN TO 1945

1. George McGovern, later a U.S. senator and Democratic candidate for president, was scheduled to fly his first mission as pilot of a B-24, out of Foggia, on November 11, 1944, when this mission was aborted. Ambrose, 153–56.

2. Unlike Fulks, Yeager, after being shot down by an FW 190 over France and escaping to Switzerland before returning to England, was determined not to return home. With only eight missions to his credit, he told his CO he'd be letting the rest of his buddies down if he took off for the States. Scheduled to fly to New York on June 25, 1944, this flight officer, still not a commissioned officer, appealed to his group CO to let him stay. The CO couldn't do that, so Yeager went up the chain of command until he met with Eisenhower himself on June 12. Since it was a War Department regulation, put in place to protect downed pilots who, if later captured, might give away precious information about resistance groups that had helped them escape, Ike could do nothing. But he could call Washington and see if they would give him the authority to make an exception. It would take a few days for Ike to get permission and let Yeager stay. But meanwhile Yeager took to the air for more dogfighting practice with new recruits, when he was ordered to provide cover for two B-17 crewmen floating on the North Sea in their dinghy, until they could be rescued. Then Yeager spotted a Junkers Ju 88 coming from the east, doubtless—Yeager figured—to strafe the escaped crewmen. Yeager turned into it and pursued it across the Channel, finally shooting it down even as German flak was trying to nail Yeager. Back at his base, Yeager was hardly prepared for the operations officer, who took Yeager's gun film and gave it to another pilot to claim a kill for himself. Grounded, Yeager was summoned before the same major, who now handed him his exemption from returning home, direct from Ike. Fulks didn't have any more missions to his credit than did Yeager, but Pete didn't mind returning to Littleton, Illinois. Yeager and Janos, 56–60.

3. Although the 52nd was supposed to have a full complement of planes and pilots the previous May, we were far from the pilot goal at that time. For a full complement of pilots would have been fifty-four, or two pilots for each plane, preventing a pilot from having to fly two days in a row. Craven and Cate, 336. One German pilot, exhausted from flying one mission after another, found the "lack of sleep the hardest part of all." For this schedule meant "you were always very tired, and wanted to sleep every chance you got." Whelan, 48.

4. Incredibly, 35,946 American airmen died in accidents during the war, not including ground crew, which included seven for each pilot. Ambrose, 79, 100.

5. Bomber pilots as well as fighter pilots—like the twelve of us assigned to the 52nd in June—paid dearly for their lack of training. One B-24 pilot, looking back four decades, found it "incredible that we would be flying combat missions with so little training or experience." It is no surprise, then, that this accelerated training took its toll on the losses suffered by the 15th Air Force in the less than eighteen months it was in operation. Among bombers alone, of the 3,544 B-24s, it lost 1,756, and of the 1,407 B-17s, it lost 624—a loss rate of almost 50 percent. Ambrose 126, 170. Just nine days after this pileup at Viz, Lt. George McGovern managed to land his crippled

B-24 at the same island and received the DFC for his effort. Ambrose, 192–96.

6. Stolley, 300–301; Churchill, *Triumph and Tragedy,* 521–22, 540–43; Miller, 776ff.

8. THE PROMISE OF A NEW YEAR

1. While this particular accident was probably due in part to the pilot's lack of training, as well as to his lack of attention to his airspeed indicator, it became increasingly evident that sheer chance, or luck, played a critical role in the survival of many, including myself. George McGovern, for example, considered it sheer luck that he had been assigned his particular copilot. And when it came to his B-24 being hit by flak or by enemy fighters, he saw it as a matter of blind chance—a roll of the dice. Ambrose, 98, 111–12.

2. Churchill, *Triumph and Tragedy,* 523–26.

3. Stolley, 314–17; Churchill, *Triumph and Tragedy,* 527–30.

9. VE DAY APPROACHES

1. Churchill, *Triumph and Tragedy,* 527ff.

2. Yeager describes his nailing of an ME-262, in which the jet, approaching its own runway at about 200 mph, was fair game for Yeager's guns. The German pilot had no idea Yeager had been high above him, observing his every move. Though the German didn't see him, the control tower did. "Ground gunners began blasting at the lunatic American swooping right at them . . . I pulled up 300 feet off the ground with flak crackling all around me. Climbing straight up, I looked back and saw the jet crash-landing short of the runway, shearing off a wing in a cloud of dust and smoke." For this, Yeager was awarded the DFC. Yeager, "always up to something," as he put it, had been court-martialed as a corporal "for shooting a horse with a thirty-caliber machine gun." Later, in flight training, Yeager bounced cadets at another base as they were entering their flight pattern for landing and came close to another court-martial. It seemed that one of the pilots he bounced followed him back to his own base, emerged, and Yeager found himself face-to-face with the bird-colonel in charge of the base Yeager had invaded. As he put it, "He accused me of busting through the traffic pattern, endangering the lives of his cadets, and disrupting his training program." Yeager and Janos, 18, 23, 27.

3. This is the same Twining who was fond of quoting "a top World War II ace" as having divided pilots into two broad categories: those who go out to kill and those who, secretly, desperately, know they are going to get killed—the hunters and the hunted. Whelan, vii. It appears that George McGovern chose to celebrate VE Day in a similar fashion. One of four pilots scheduled to be the first to fly home after VE Day, each took a Liberator up and promptly got down on the deck for some high-powered hedge-hopping, just missing a power line. Their main target: the headquarters of their 456th

Bomb Group. So close did they fly to the roof that the prop wash tore the flag from the building. The CO, furious, decided that the four, rather than being the first to leave Italy, would be the last. "But," as McGovern recounted it, "by the time the orders were cut, it was too late." Whether this had anything to do with McGovern's not getting his captaincy is not revealed. He, too, had just completed his tour of duty, in this case thirty-five missions. Ambrose, 58. Fighter pilots typically regarded bomber pilots as staid, conventional "bus drivers." Perhaps Yeager's closest pal, Bud Anderson, the leading ace of Yeager's outfit—with seventeen kills—was on target when he described fighter pilots as "young, wild, and crazy." It seemed to him, as he later reflected on it, that it was "a miracle that any of us survived." Yeager, 21, 54, 74–77.

10. THE LAST LAP

1. Truman's decision to drop these two atomic bombs was roundly criticized, yet he had no hesitations before doing it, and no regrets after doing it. Neither did Churchill, who later wrote, "There was unanimous, automatic, unquestioned agreement." Stolley, 333; Churchill, *Triumph and Tragedy,* 639.

2. Churchill (*Life*), 336–37, 472, 560, 569, 574.

3. Just how desperate Bob was to enroll in college is seen in the fact that, for the two years he was at Clark University, his arms were up to his elbows in oil in a machine shop where he cleaned parts. As a result of this miserable job, he contracted an infection which was diagnosed as "blood poisoning," and for which the only remedy was Dad's old Indian mixture of herbs, called "Ikura Salve."

4. *Webster's Seventh New Collegiate Dictionary* (Springfield, Mass.: G. & C. Merriam Co., 1969), 243.

BIBLIOGRAPHY

Ambrose, Stephen E. *The Wild Blue: The Men and Boys Who Flew the B24s over Germany.* New York: Simon & Schuster, 2001.

Blum, John M., et al. *The National Experience: A History of the United States,* 6th ed. New York: Harcourt, Brace, Jovanovich, 1985.

Childers, Thomas. *Wings of the Morning: The Story of the Last American Bomber Shot Down over Germany in World War II.* New York: Addison-Wesley Publishing Co., 1995.

Churchill, Winston S. *The Second World War,* vol. 6: *Triumph and Tragedy.* Boston: Houghton Mifflin Co., 1953.

Churchill, Winston S., and the Editors of *Life. The Second World War.* New York: Time, Inc., 1959.

Craven, Wesley F., and James L. Cate, eds. *The Army Air Forces in World War II,* vol. 3: *Argument to VE Day: January, 1944 to May, 1945.* Chicago: University of Chicago Press, 1949.

Curtis, Richard K. *They Called Him Mister Moody.* Garden City, N.Y.: Doubleday, 1962.

———. *Hubris and the Presidency: The Abuse of Power by Johnson and Nixon.* Danbury, Conn.: Rutledge Books, Inc., 2000.

Hitler, Adolph. *Mein Kampf.* New York: Houghton Mifflin Co., 1939.

Johnstone, Sandy. *Enemy in the Sky: My 1940 Diary.* San Rafael, Calif.: Presidio Press, 1979.

Kershaw, Ian. *Hitler, 1936–1945: Nemesis.* New York: W. W. Norton Co., 2001. Reviewed in *The New Republic,* March 12, 2001, by Omer Bartov.

Lawson, Ted W. *Thirty Seconds over Tokyo.* New York: Random House, 1943.

Loomis, Robert D. *Great American Fighter Pilots of World War II.* New York: Random House, 1961.

Maugham, Somerset. *The Summing Up.* New York: The New American Library of World Literature, 1946.

Mauldin, Bill. *Up Front.* New York: Henry Holt and Co., 1945.

McFarland, Stephen L., and Wesley Phillips Newton. *To Command the Sky: The Battle for Air Superiority over Germany, 1942–1944.* Washington, D.C.: Smithsonian Institution Press, 1991.

Miller, Francis T. *History of World War II*. Armed Services Memorial Edition. Philadelphia: Universal Book and Bible House, 1945.

Mitchell, Ruth. *My Brother Bill: The Life of General "Billy" Mitchell*. New York: Harcourt, Brace, 1953.

Pyle, Ernie. *Here Is Your War*. New York: Henry Holt and Co., 1943.

———. *Brave Men*. New York: Henry Holt and Co., 1944.

Stolley, Richard B., ed. *Life: World War II; History's Greatest Conflict in Pictures*. Boston: Little, Brown and Co., 2001.

The History Channel. "Fury of the Mustang," video. *Warbird* series. December 14, 2000.

Thruelson, Richard, and Elliott Arnold. *Mediterranean Sweep: Air Stories from El Alamein to Rome*. New York: Duell, Sloan, and Pearce, 1944.

Time-Life Records. *The Swing Era, 1940–1941: How It Was to Be Young Then*. New York: Time-Life, 1970.

Wheeler, John A. *At Home in the Universe*. Woodbury, N.Y.: AID Press, 1994.

Whelan, James R. *Hunters in the Sky: Fighter Aces of World War II*. Washington, D.C.: Regnery Gateway, 1991.

Wise Co., ed. *The 100 Best True Stories of World War II*. New York: William H. Wise, 1945.

Yeager, General Chuck, and Leo Janos. *Yeager*. New York: Bantam Books, 1985.

INDEX